W9-AJD-377

The Politics of Deafness

Owen Wrigley

Gallaudet University Press / Washington, D.C.

Gallaudet University Press
Washington, DC 20002

Book design by Dennis Anderson

Library of Congress Cataloging-in-Publication Data

Wrigley, Owen
    The politics of deafness/Owen Wrigley.
        p. cm.
    Includes bibliographical references (p.) and index.
    ISBN 1-56368-064-5 (alk. paper)
        1. Deafness—Political aspects. 2. Deafness—Social aspects.
    3. Deaf—Social conditions.   I. Title.
    NV2395.W75   1996
    305.9'08162—dc20   96-5266
                                                          CIP

The Politics of Deafness

Contents

Preface

I am who I am, doing what I came here to do.
—Audre Lorde

We refuse to be what you want us to be. We are what we are, and that's the way it's going to be.
—Bob Marley

I y'am what I y'am.
—Popeye the Sailor Man

As a project in late modern, if not postmodern, explorations of identity formation, I suspect first-person representations of ethnographic authority. However, the personal backdrop of how I, a Hearing American, came to be living and working among a group of Deaf Thais is pertinent to the writing that follows. My concern is that should this aspect of my presence be hidden or submerged, it would be no less present. Instead, I must attempt to recognize both the biases of my position and the privileges of my gaze.

I arrived in Thailand in 1981 to take up the position of regional representative and country director of a foundation that implemented a range of social and educational development projects in Thailand and several neighboring countries. This program had been without a director for nearly six months and was in severe disarray. Two modest-sized grant programs funded by USAID[1] were the primary concern of the foundation headquarters. In addition,

1. The United States Agency for International Development, a quasi-independent agency of the U.S. State Department.

there were also several smaller grant projects funded by various do-nors. Among these was a very small grant to a group of deaf adults. As the year 1981 was also the United Nations Year of the Disabled Person, USAID had found it politically expedient to give token grant support for a "disability" project.

The beginnings of this project are described more fully else-where;[2] by the time of my arrival, the program was in serious trouble. The Thai authorities, both the Ministry of Education and the Royal Foundation for the Deaf, were demanding that the project be canceled (and the budget given to them), and the foreign donor, USAID, was eager to cancel the grant with "no hard feelings," just to be free from the complaints that its formal Thai counterparts were raising over such a minor project. From the standpoint of my foun-dation, the grant provided no overhead funds and zero support for administrative salaries. The main office of the foundation had no in-terest in the project and was eager to follow the USAID advice. The project was seen as a "charity" effort by both the grant donor and the foundation, occasioned only by the coincidence of the UN Year of the Disabled Person: they felt they had given at the office.

Perhaps if the project had been less intriguing, or perhaps if I were less stubborn by nature, I would have taken the "friendly advice" of the USAID administrator to cancel the grant. I was already respon-sible for designing and negotiating a grant for a new million-dollar national rural youth program, and two larger existing grant pro-grams had their own share of problems. Nevertheless, I did not agree to cancel the grant. My earlier academic interests, including my earlier thesis for a master's in regional and community planning (on regional planning in Telengana, India), focused on the repre-sentation of linguistic minorities in the administrative processes of dominant groups. My initial impression of the circumstances of the deaf group involved resonated strongly with those interests. This grant project was not about disabled people: it was about language rights and acceptable identities. It was an impression I came to hold even more strongly over the coming years.

2. See Suvannus 1990.

For some years, I resisted the idea of writing on this subject. This resistance was overcome only after my colleague, Charles Reilly, began his own doctoral work. Reilly came to Thailand as an Oberlin Shansi volunteer working with deaf children at the main school for the deaf in Thailand and remained to work with projects in the adult Deaf Thai community. He joined the staff of IHAP,[3] and, somewhere in this process, also became a housemate, a friend, and a colleague. We have worked together closely for nearly fifteen years, and I gladly acknowledge the friendship and professional partnership we have developed. He and our Deaf Thai friends were my introduction to this very different experience of the world. Reilly's decision to focus his doctoral work on issues specifically relating to the self-education of deaf children[4] allowed me to focus on the more politicized terrain of identity formation.

Certainly my life has been deeply affected by the Deaf Thai friends I have made after entering the Deaf Thai community. I was not a passive voyeur of that community but actively aided in the collective efforts to build a representative organization. I remained in Thailand nearly a decade longer than I had planned because of a joint commitment with my Deaf Thai colleagues to our work. The all-Deaf Board of Directors of the National Association of the Deaf in Thailand (NADT) presented me with an honorary life membership in 1985.

Much of my actual work within this community, particularly from 1982 through 1991, revolved around the language, both its particulars and how it is perceived and positioned socially. The purpose of this study is not an exercise in sign language linguistics—that basic ground is presented in *The Thai Sign Language Dictionary*[5]—but a more careful look at the ongoing ways in which discourse about Deaf culture is undermined and, at each level of attempted resistance, reinscripted by Hearing notions.

The two volumes of *The Thai Sign Language Dictionary* were

3. The International Human Assistance Programs, Inc., formerly the American-Korean Foundation; IHAP was established in 1952 and ceased operations in 1990.
4. Reilly 1995. Field research in 1991 was supported by a Fulbright award.
5. Suwanarat, Reilly, Wrigley, et al. 1986 and Suwanarat, Wrigley, et al. 1990.

published in 1986 and 1990, respectively, the result of a team effort involving many committed individuals. In undertaking the research to produce and publish those works, I came to know a substantial part of this community in some considerable depth. The partisan nature of my perspective was born in the process of this collaborative work. While I cannot and do not claim to speak on behalf of my Deaf Thai colleagues, I hope that my representations are loyal to the spirit of exchange and mutual appreciation that we sought and many times achieved.

Yet the dictionary research should not simply be noted in passing as creating a reference work: it was also a political activity, an understanding of which informs much of this work. Of particular importance was the decision to organize the research and the presentation of the final materials around a priority of perspectives that was "Deaf" rather than "Hearing." What does this mean? The work is still a book, printed on paper and containing the traditional parts of a published text. In this sense, it is certainly no different. The same could be said of many of the research and linguistic collection methods, including the modern reliance on computers to generate research databases. The contested terrain, however, is both how the sign representations are visually positioned and on what principles the vocabulary is ordered.

The work contains both written English and written Thai, with English privileged on the title and credit pages, Thai privileged in the main body of the dictionary and the index. The sign illustrations are on the outside of each page, whether left or right. There are generally three illustrations fields per page. Thus, as a reader flips through the pages, the sign illustrations are located in the easiest field of view. This design was primarily aimed at creating a readerly convenience for an audience unused to reading and unfamiliar with the habit of flipping through large books: it was oriented to the first language of that primary audience. The political interpretations regarding the significance of how the languages were placed on the page, with that positioning potentially perceived by readers as rank, were perhaps of most interest to our production team; few others may notice them.

→| |← ⊤ ⊥ ⌐ ⌐ ⌐ ⌐ ⌐ ⌐ |⌐| ⌐ ⌐ ⌐ | ⌐ → |

สร้อยคอ

ท่ามือในหน้านี้ใช้นิ้วหัวแม่มือและนิ้วชี้ด้วย ตอนเริ่มต้น
ของท่ามือดูเหมือนดังว่านิ้วทุกนิ้วกำลังใช้อยู่ แต่นิ้วที่
อ่อนกว่าสามนิ้วกางออกเสมอ ดังนั้นจึงมีเพียงนิ้วหัวแม่มือ
และนิ้วชี้ที่สัมผัสกับร่างกาย

necklace

The signs on this page also use the thumb and
index finger. The beginnings of the signs look
as if all fingers are in use, but the weaker three
fingers are often extended so only thumb and
index touch the body.

289.1

ชาวเขา

นี่เป็นท่ามือในอีกหลายท่ามือสำหรับชนชาวเขา ท่ามือ
บอกถึงการสวมใส่สร้อยคอหลาย ๆ อัน เป็นแบบ
ประเพณีนิยม รูปท่ามือ "ล" ได้วางหลายครั้งที่หน้าอก
และแต่ละครั้งจะค่อย ๆ ต่ำลง ในท่ามือนี้มือไม่ปิด

hilltribe(s)

This is one of several signs for hilltribes people.
It indicates several necklaces worn in traditional
style. The "L" handshape is placed several times
on the chest each time slightly lower. In this
sign the hand does not close.

289.2

ชาวเขาเผ่าม้ง

ชาวไทยเรียกพวกม้งว่า "แม้ว" จากภาษาจีน "เมียว"
ที่ใช้เรียกคนป่าเถื่อน ซึ่งพวกม้งไม่ชอบให้เรียกอย่างยิ่ง
ส่วนที่สองของท่ามือคำประสมหมายถึงเครื่องประดับ
เพชรพลอยที่สตรีชาวม้งใช้ตกแต่ง

Hmong hilltribe people

Thai people call the Hmong "Meo," from the
Chinese word "miao" for barbarian, which is
strongly disliked by the Hmong. The second
part of the compound refers to the ornate
jewelry worn by the Hmong women.

289.3

Width of rectangle; distance   ความกว้างของสี่เหลี่ยมผืนผ้า; ระยะห่างระหว่างนิ้วหัวแม่มือกับนิ้วชี้
thumb to index finger

Figure 1. Sample image from *The Thai Sign Language Dictionary* (Suwanarat, Wrigley,
et al. 1990, p. 289).

The more contested and deeply political ground was the ordering of the vocabulary. In simple terms, there is a choice: Is the
book "alphabetized" by the A, B, Cs of the spoken languages, regardless of which spoken language? Or is the book ordered by
the internal rules of the sign language itself? An interesting question, and very political. The answer can be given easily, but there
is no clear consensus on methods of realizing that answer. If framed
from the external referent of the spoken language—that is, by that
language's A, B, Cs—the work is, at best, a glossary. Indeed, the
majority of so-called sign language dictionaries are really only
glossaries.

A dictionary, however, is necessarily not so simple. Again in brief,
as these are peripheral issues here, there is no general agreement on
the precise principles of ordering sign vocabulary, although the Thai
Sign Language work is the largest to have undertaken to apply such
principles. Cross-references, one each for written Thai and English,
are in the back of the books for those seeking access via the spoken
languages. The first volume was organized by a grammatical ordering principle, which focused on verb types. The final volume, consisting of more than 3,500 images in a work of 1,500 pages, was
alphabetized by root radicals in a descending order of frequency of
use.[6] Further details are given in the technical notes in the respective
volumes. The point here is that both volumes are political documents, both in what is presented and in how it is presented.

Very few works have presented sign languages in any format other
than glossary-like approaches to assist the beginning outsider-
learners to learn the language from a perspective privileging their
view. Hearing learners may look for words they know in the order
of their own language. Part of the contentious politics of this revolves around Hearing school policies that refuse to allow deaf children to learn written and spoken language as other students do:
based on their first language. Thus, presenting a sign-based ordering
principle highlights two political fields: first, sign is a full linguistic

6. The ordering principles used in both these volumes represent the pioneering
research work of Dr. Lloyd Anderson.

entity, a language in its own right; and second, if Hearing people find it useful to learn one language from the cognitive foundations of their mother tongue, then Deaf people might well benefit from the same approach. This is vehemently contested by some who have administrative power over deaf children. The discursive economies that support those objections are part of my inquiries; to engage those objections more directly was part of my personal motivation for making those inquiries.

In the past two decades, that sign language is the means by which those who are deaf may communicate has begun to approach the status of common knowledge. Far less commonly known, however, is just how fragile the formal status of sign language is—as a language, let alone as a native language that might be claimed as a birthright. The formal recognition of the linguistic status of sign languages is actually of very recent date.

It is significant to remember that UNESCO, which was the first United Nations body to address the topic, *only in 1984* asserted the following: "Language of deaf children is developmental. Furthermore, sign language should be recognized as a legitimate linguistic system and should be afforded the same status as other linguistic systems." The UNESCO report begins with a statement of principles: "Intellectual capacities of deaf persons are equal to those of the hearing. Earlier misunderstandings in this respect were mainly due to the lack of an early system of effective communication and to methods which concentrated only on lost abilities."[7]

The World Health Organization (WHO) only in 1986 began to note in its documents that "the use of the term 'dumb,' an archaic form of 'mute,' is both inaccurate and misleading. As the lack of speech is a secondary result of deafness, [this term] should not be applied to describe the primary condition."[8]

The World Federation of the Deaf (WFD), at its Tenth World Congress in Helsinki, *in July 1987*, adopted its first ever Resolution

---

7. UNESCO, "Final Report," Consultation on Alternative Approaches for the Education of the Deaf, Paris, 18–22 June 1984.

8. WHO, 1986.

on Sign Language, overturning years of oralist leadership.[9] The resolution was readopted at the Eleventh World Congress, held in Tokyo
in 1991.

And the Global Meeting of Experts convened by the UN
Secretary-General at the midpoint of the Decade of the Disabled in
1987 presented among its principal recommendations the statement, accepted by the General Assembly *in December 1987*, that
"deaf and gravely hearing-impaired people [are] to be recognized as
a linguistic minority, with the specific right to have their native and
indigenous sign languages accepted as their first and official language and as the medium of communications and instruction, and
to have sign language interpreter services."[10]

The dates are italicized to emphasize just how recently such dec-
larations were made. It is also worth noting that the last two were
due directly to official Thai delegations, as the WFD Resolution and
the UN Global Meeting of Experts recommendation were written
by Manfa Suwanarat and me. Officials within the particular suboffice
of the United Nations responsible were initially surprised by the
enormous demand for copies of the documents that contained those
statements. The reason remains simple: institutions the world over
pursue policies that directly contradict these principles.

There is a crucial appropriation that does take place, one that
must be acknowledged, when "speaking" about "the deaf" or any
notions of deafness. I am not an "expert" on the deaf. I have no and
make no claims of "native" or "near native" status. I was born hearing and with no Deaf relatives. The fluency of my signing skills are
in the Thai Sign Language (TSL), not in the American Sign Language (ASL), and I first learned sign long after I was an adult. Thus,
anything that I say is not "of" the deaf, privileged neither from a

9. World Federation of the Deaf, "Resolution on Sign Language," Tenth World
Congress, Helsinki, 20–29 July 1987. See also "Recommendations of the Scientific
and Cross-Scientific Commissions."

10. United Nations, "Final Report," Global Meeting of Experts to Review the
Implementation of the World Program of Action Concerning Disabled Persons at
the Mid-Point of the UN Decade of Disabled Persons (DDP/GME), Stockholm,
17–22 August 1987.

hermeneutic nor ontological ground. At most, in the language of popular culture, I am a late-adopted child of a specific Deaf culture. This position needs to be restated occasionally.

My disclaimer itself relies on privileging that hermeneutic of the direct experience. In recognizing this, do I become more responsive, or am I freed from the constraints of making and maintaining accepted or even new truth claims? By positing an ethnographic authority—gained by translating and producing the TSL dictionary, by receiving honorary awards and royal recognitions—I claim the privileged gaze of traditional positivist anthropology, even if back-handedly. By leaving it out, "silent" we might say, I avoid but do not evade the need to acknowledge the position of my gaze. My attempt is to make evident certain biases from the vantage points I have had available. Mine is not a neutral voice.

Traditionalists from medical schools will insist that the experience of a heart attack does not make you an expert on heart surgery. But my discussion is not about the experience of being deaf. My concern is more with the discursive positioning of those individuals labeled either by themselves or by authority as "deaf." I am concerned with the collective institutional prescriptions available to this categorical grouping, which casts lives and delimits options, most particularly those relating to access to the content of education (as opposed to the vehicle of education, speech therapy), as well as employment.

There is no simplistic unity to "the Deaf community." This is true whether the discussion is about a Deaf Thai community or "the deaf" in general. The text moves in and out of a stance that calls attention to this problem. While this generalizing frame cannot be entirely avoided, I attempt to heed the particularity of both the individuals and the experiences that constitute this consensual notion. My own perspective is likewise not a single view. It shifts frequently between a programmatic concern for "working with what we have," the concern of someone who daily confronts immediate needs and demands, and a privileged academic perspective that has afforded me both leisure and distance to raise more subtle questions, questions no less important but less constrained by the immediacies of daily experiences.

The programmatic view is informed by my experiences living with and among a diversity of Deaf Thais, as well as by travel over the past fifteen years to a wide range of international Deaf congresses and festivals, at which I have also served as a conference interpreter for both English-to-Thai Sign Language and TSL-into-English. I have been intimately involved both in the cultural politics and in program-oriented responses to the organizational development goals of elected Deaf Thai leaders. This is the voice of programs and administration; it speaks to the logistics of training and organizational support, the political support and bureaucratic clearances for entering each public domain, the mustering of finances to cover rents and salaries, the training of others to accomplish these tasks themselves, and related daily chores. Though it is not the voice privileged in a deliberately reflective academic discussion, it need not be absent or discounted. I hope to take guidance, and humor, from the one that I might better serve the other.

My academic view has been strongly informed by though not limited to the genealogical stance of recent continental political theorists such as Michel Foucault, the textual politics of Neal Milner on rights discourse, Kathy Ferguson on feminist theory, Michael Shapiro on practices of representation, and William Connolly's critiques of late modernity. I use their works deliberately to focus on specific discontinuities in the fabric of Deaf history and identity. This stance seeks to reveal the contestable unity of conventional presentations.

Rather than search for the origins of Deaf culture and the fall from grace of sign language, which is the hagiographic frame of Harlan Lane's dominant study (1984), Foucault would have us recognize that "History teaches how to laugh at the solemnities of the origin." He calls on Nietzsche in reminding us that the "lofty origin is no more than 'a metaphysical extension which arises from the belief that things are most precious and essential at the moment of their birth.'" In the desire to prove a divine birth, we find "a monkey stands at the entrance."[11]

11. "Nietzsche, Genealogy, History," in Foucault 1977, p. 143.

I would suggest that neither perspective, detached or grounded, is alone adequate for charting the political terrain of Deaf identity formation. Each perspective, as well as the moves between them, seeks to disturb the usual presumptions about those who are deaf. Moreover, the inquiry has wider ramifications. There are further appropriations by which the questions raised by the exclusion of those who are deaf highlight other forms of social marginalization.

While I intend to draw attention to these questions, the appropriations must also be foregrounded. I will repeat in more than one place that no promises of liberation, no authentic voice of the excluded, no final surcease of the appropriations of the Deaf experience or the person who is deaf is promised here. Rather than finality, I pursue a purposeful ambiguation; and rather than certainty, I pose further questions about all appropriations. The questions are ones I find both troubling and politically compelling. I hope that they may lead to further questioning of accepted practices of exclusion and oppression—as well as the forgotten presumptions that still engender those practices.

The Politics of Deafness

Introduction

I am convinced that the only people worthy of consideration in this world are the unusual ones. For the common folk are like the leaves of a tree, and live and die unnoticed.

—The Scarecrow of Oz, in L. Frank Baum,
The Wonderful Wizard of Oz

The common leaves referred to by the Scarecrow of Oz[1] are never so passive as the literal leaves of a tree. Human leaves are a dynamic aspect of the trees that produce and are products of the social forest. They further define what is usual and unusual. By so doing, the common also dominate. In the reactions of the common to the unusual, and in the practices by which the common dominate the unusual, ironic insights into the politics of identities are best illustrated. In particular, the uses of the unacceptable, either of body or image, to reproduce and enforce naturalized categories serve to clarify both those identities that are allowable and the interests that are served.

Deafness is less about audiology than it is about epistemology. This work is about belonging to and among those the Scarecrow might call the unusual, and it belongs to a genre concerned with what is currently known as otherness and difference. This genre explores techniques of inclusion and exclusions in identity formation. It is not ethnography in the usual sense.

The classic view of ethnography presumes an explorer who enters into a foreign culture or space and who then returns with authentic

---

1. Growing up in the Land of Ahhs, I too felt the call of the Yellow Brick Road as the way out of Kansas.

stories, stories that authenticate both the authority of the story-teller and the positions of the "original we" (the empire, community, or academy, who are the audience) to validate empirical truths. The economy is one of recognitions of the tales told as evidence of truth, a self-referencing authenticity. To complete that metaphorical frame: this story is more about a return of the explorer with stories to tell of how the "original we" talk about those we presume available to be explored. It is an ethnography of the dominant gaze, particularly as applied to those deaf to its textual order.

The traditional counterthemes of appropriation, domination, exploitation, colonization, and oppression remain useful narrative embellishments by which both structural and ultimately personal relationships with otherness and difference might be better understood—possibly a more honest goal for an ethnography in any event. An ironic or oppositional ethnography seeks to explore the presumptions behind such relationships with knowledge.

Thus this genre is not about centers, but about borders and margins. Here there are neither simple nor unified theories, as those are about creating centers that will in turn need to be evaded. Such theoretical framings require the exclusion of those outside the borders and margins of their newly claimed centers. The hermeneutical anchors in use for frames of meaning in late modernity are most often those rooted in the surveillance of bodies. As the site for naming distinctions, the body is a recurrent theme in studies of otherness and difference. Deafness is about a body surveilled.

Deaf people are mentioned even in early recorded history, including in Babylonian records, the Mosaic Code of Holiness from the sixth century B.C., and both Old and New Testaments of the Bible. The majority of these references, however, either concern the status of legal rights for property inheritance by deaf people, an enduring issue for the noble families, or are appropriations of "the deaf-mute" to demonstrate moral truths. The latter category includes John Bulwer, who in 1648 suggested deaf children were the result of their parents' sinfulness and little better than "Dumbe Animals." A similar perspective and appropriation emerges from the U.S. Federal Census, which, from 1830 to 1900, included "the deaf" in the odd category of "defectives."

Deafness could well be about a sensory "deprivation," life in a world marked by an absence. Yet, a contrasting view might see a world built around the valence of visual rather than aural channels for processing languages—not just semiotic signs, but languages of a visual modality. As we shall see, in a political framing this shift rejects the site of the body and relocates meaning and its production onto the social. This re-valence of a visual modality means not a loss but an entry into a richly textured visual world of languages not dependent upon sound. Rather than a bifurcated world of meaning production, which searches for visual signs while relying on organizations of meaning around arbitrary serial sequences of acoustical phenomena to convey explanatory narratives, a visual world both perceives and produces signification through visual channels of a spatial linguistics. It is a world not necessarily better or worse, just distinct and different.

The "meanings" available to such distinctions and differences are an explicit focus of this work. This is not an ethnography that attempts the artifice of an "authentic voice" for "the deaf," or the artifice of empirical analysis of "objective data." Such unities, either of voice or frame, are contested here. Rather, this work is an ethnography of the appropriations, colonizations, constraints, and constructions by which "we," the dominant Hearing, have come to "know" and "make use of" those who are Deaf.

I will explore a series of perspectives on d/Deaf identity, each of which seeks "to disclose the operation of power in places in which the familiar social, administrative, and political discourses tend to disguise or naturalize it."[2] There is a particular politics here; a dimension of politics, which I will try to enact throughout this text, adheres in my writing. The tactics of this ethnography are primarily those of irony and displacement. My intention is a disruptive one, disruptive of both presumptions and practices that derive from and

2. Shapiro 1992, p. 1.

descend upon deaf bodies. This disruptive intent requires me to shift the frame or perspective from place to place in this work. Each of the chapters that follow both represents and contains such disruptive shifts. These shifts, in part, show that there is no one interpretive frame; instead, there is a politics of interpretation that needs to be made more visible. While certain questions about identities available and acceptable will remain constant, no single interpretation yielding fixed answers is possible. My purpose is to explore inherent ironies invested in Hearing practices that administrate social identities for deaf children, as well as those identities available to deaf adults, and to provide distance from those normalizing frames that have tended to fix both common and professional perspectives about deafness and those who are deaf.

The perception of Whiteness, so long naturalized in Western political theory as to mark the only race that rarely needs to be named, is not unlike the recognition of Hearing as a social category that is not all-inclusive, that is other than simply "normal." Such recognition comes slowly and remains at a high cost to those named as Other-than-Hearing. The names assigned to the Other-than-Hearing include "mute," "deaf-mute," "hearing impaired," a range of other politically correct euphemisms, and the one that is preferred by most of those who identify themselves as such: "Deaf." A further discussion of the distinct significations of such labels follows in chapter 1.

The Politics of Deafness deploys a range of disruptive views of these distinctions and of why such differences may matter. I will not spend great effort on reproducing the homeboy epistemology of "educational rehabilitation" experts on the deaf. Suffice it to say that the traditional view of deaf people and of deafness is of an existence contained within boundaries clearly understood as "less than normal." As outsiders whose language options are determined by Hearing cultures, these people are damaged goods, not normal, to be administrated under various rationalizing concepts from infancy into oblivion. Edward T. Hall (1992) refers to this perspective as a "deficit" model.

Within the domain of such views, prospects for deaf children are reproduced within a subset of education called "special." Rarely, in the case of education, does "special" mean anything in addition to the usual; it is rather a subset or delimited portion thereof. Presumptions are made about an "absorptive capacity" of such marked children, about the possible limitations of their cognitive potentials, rather than questioning if alternate "absorptive channels" might be available to them. Ironically, all instructive and rehabilitative efforts focus, often exclusively, on the "lost" missing channel as the very feature around which all teaching should revolve. This ironic reversal by and within special education reproduces a limited world of learning and social interaction. While this obsession with hearing can be traced to the conflation of speech and language, the immediate result is a direct oppression of deaf children and a denial of the social identities that may be available to them as deaf adults.

The modality of language that is (manifested through) sign language makes visible a range of assumptions (and concomitant ironies) of cultural traditions long normalized. The constant requirement for cohort regeneration of Deaf culture, both unconstrained and unassisted by cross-generational ties, is a difference between Deaf and Hearing cultures. Both the temporal and spatial aspects of a cognitive framework that is "natively" Deaf are also embodied in the linguistic modality by which this culture is carried. Sign languages deploy spatiality in visually based grammar and syntax that are unavailable to sound-based languages. Certain aspects of these cultures cannot be adequately conveyed through this (a written English) textual vehicle, a vehicle bound to the modality and to the ontology of sound.

But what is Deaf culture? And, more to the point, why is this a question of political significance? This question would be simple if, and only if, we were willing to settle for pat narratives about what Deaf people do together, in what distinct ways they go about it, and what the experiences of "silence in a world of sound" must be like. But this view builds from generally accepted notions: a damaged body, the experience of a lack, and a subculture that is, at best, a delimited subset of broader cultures. These assumptions, both dominant and dominating, are critically challenged here—not that such delimited subcultures or damaged denizens are not to be found, but rather that when they are found they are better understood as products of Hearing practices than as evidence of a nature "essential" to the Deaf. Chapter 1 introduces the spectrum of contrasting views that either deny or valorize deafness. The answer to "What is the political significance of Deaf culture?" depends greatly upon the presumptions of those asking the question.

Working with and from a terrain of terms that actively seek to defamiliarize common notions of "normal," chapter 2 opens a genealogical inquiry into the historical emergence of practices now taken for granted, practices we treat as if they were "natural," part of "simply how things are." A genealogy of deafness offers a contrasting perspective to the traditional pieties of Deaf history. It is less about heroic accomplishments and tragic failures than it is about an emergence of a dominant view of what it means to be deaf. The social mechanics of how that meaning is both produced and sustained shift dramatically, yet the functional meaning is left untouched.

Geology, archaeology, and genealogy: each term has been appropriated for its metaphorical value in constructing critical inquiry. One focuses on sedimentation, another on incrementation, the third on mutation. *Mutation* is neither the most pleasing nor politically correct way of encapsulating the concerns of genealogy, yet it best expresses the conflicts of purity and defilement, of origins and virtue, and the qualifications of a body that might convey spirit—conflicts and qualifications that mutations occasionally evade.

William Connolly observes, "Genealogy is a dirty game which can only be experienced to be depreciated. It asks embarrassing and impertinent questions, those which upset tidy arrangements as well as the social decorum of understood protocol. It can be upsetting, and even annoying."[3] This accurately portrays the intent of my critique of the usually pious history of the Deaf.

This impertinent genealogy of identity formation continues from

3. Connolly 1988, p. 151.

the perspective of a postcoloniality in chapter 3. The practices of denial by the Hearing, rarely conscious and even more rarely acknowledged, have produced overt repressions of intellectual, economic, and social opportunities for peoples who are deaf. An underlying impetus to this denial, the demand for accommodation only on Hearing terms, arises partly because the difference deafness represents is so foreign and "unnatural."

Colonialism is usually depicted as a cultural hangover incurred while squandering the bounty gained from heroic voyages of discovery and the attendant exploitation of native populations. As with Western domination of other foreign "discoveries," the relation of Hearing to Deaf cultures has primarily been that of a pastoral colonialism so long naturalized as to have faded into the consensual "normal." Thus the dominance and oppression are more complex than a simple exploitation narrative of natives versus colonialists might suggest. This economy structured by recognitions makes visible, in critically new ways, a more complex relationship with practices of exclusion and inclusion.

The analysis here also addresses tensions little noted in the current literature on deafness and on the popular move to reconstitute Deafness as a global culture. The projected or "lived" universalism being claimed by Deaf activists is an attempt to constitute imaginal memories. Such universalism draws on the experience of many deaf people who, in their deafness, find a commonality that, in this frame, transcends other distinctions of race, ethnicity, or nationality. Yet, as will be shown, new claims of homogeneity produce endogenous colonialisms, as well.

Tensions in the articulation of these claims result, in part, when the historic discourse on deafness becomes entangled with attempts to reframe the discourse while still using traditional and familiar terms. Other tensions arise within and between modernist and ironic portrayals of power. For example, leaders of the various Deaf communities have numerous misgivings about the rhetorical strategies necessary to use the "disabled" channels of and to power. Some Deaf leaders vigorously refuse the identity label "disabled," seeing themselves strictly as a linguistic minority, while others are willing to accept the label's inherent limitations in exchange for shorter-term payoffs in social welfare privileges.

Some of the particular characteristics by which culture is marked, as well as some of the particular tactics by which those so marked evade authority, belong to domains of ethnicity and regionalism. Thus Deaf cultures may mimic the flora and fauna of the dominant Hearing cultures that surround them, but the search for similarity offers little of value and is not pursued here. This search is itself tightly bound or twinned to its mirror. The practices by which modern societies have chosen to mark and manage deafness, however, illuminate the techniques (and the dissemination of those techniques) by which marginality in general is produced and managed. The displacement of logistical anchors, the ironic stances, and the disruptive perspectives are tactics of a politics of de-naturalization, a politics that demands space within and between the normalizing frames of our daily lives.

The recognition of human limitation, both in ethnographic authority and in resources that might directly address exclusion and alleviate basic human needs, informs chapter 4. This chapter draws on nearly ten years of collaborative work with and among a loosely defined "community" of Deaf Thais in both urban and rural Thailand.

Ethnography is not about finding fact, about empirical data that might reveal truth. Nor is it about self-referencing "bodies" of literature, self-generated and nourished through a politics of citation. It is instead about the juxtaposition of viewpoints. Ethnography is a logistics of perceptions by which practices that support or sustain certain sets of interests are arrayed against other sets of interests and their support mechanisms.

Chapter 5 marks a radical shift in perspective, borrowing heavily from the genres of science fiction and cyberpunk to explore the biopolitics of the body in the postmodern. Venturing from deafness and the surveillance of deaf bodies into the cyberpunk world of disembodied dataspheric terrains of consensual networks may seem wildly digressive. Yet this perspective radically demonstrates dramatic changes in the epistemology of the social bond, as well as making visible the ironic exploitations of the Deaf that have taken place under the auspices of modernity. The conflation of language with speech (and vice versa) by the Hearing underpins both mental and material technologies. The connection between Deaf bodies and the parameters of modern communications technologies is both a presumption and an appropriation long forgotten, but it is an intimate link nonetheless.

Deafness is about language and communication. The curious linkages between the enormous investments in certain mental and material technologies, including major systems of the telecommunications industry, provide a critical knife (perhaps a neo-Occam's razor) to dissect limitations in the foundational presumptions of such industries and of the language technologies that support them.

Such an analysis rests in part on the sense of what constitutes a language at all. The gestural codes used by Deaf peoples have been alternately accepted and vigorously repressed. As rapid shifts in intellectual disciplines have accompanied as well as partially driven the emergence of modernity, new theories of language that mirror our view of the universe and that view's new interpretive physics have been required. Languages that do not rely on a serial and sequential presentation of data, as all spoken languages do, question cherished epistemologies. Those coping with an information-rich environment may reinvoke visual and spatial grammars to create graphic displays of information that will borrow heavily from sign language metaphors.

Chapter 5 is also inspired in part by the speed with which the corporate business sector and the global communications industries have adopted the metaphorical framework of the SF cyberpunk genre. Cyberpunk exploded in 1984 following publication of William Gibson's *Neuromancer,* which suddenly made available a metaphorical treasure trove for portraying the sheer volume and complexities of relational fields of data already available—and exponentially expanding.

As we struggle to convincingly evoke relational representations of such vast amounts and varieties of information, we are finding that both our mental and material presumptions of sound as the sole signal modality of cognition and language are limiting us. The serial sequence of phonemes that constitutes—is—spoken language begat serial sequences of mechanically generated and electrical pulses along copper wire. Digital protocols are direct descendants of technologies both mental and material. Both technologies build and depend on that same presumptive conflation of speech and language. Not deafness per se but the visual terrain of grammars and semiotics in a signed modality threatens that previously unquestioned assumption.

The physical and linguistic exclusion of the Deaf that is built into the practices of these mental and material technologies is also intimately linked to the body of the deaf, physically as well as metaphorically. The body of the deaf has been site of surgical explorations; these have been medically legitimated voyages of discovery in search of the missing Word, the physical site of human language.

The curious obsessions of Alexander Graham Bell produced the telephone, the most enduring artifact of this long-standing conflation. Both in the mental and material domain, through those obsessions and the profits of his invention, his legacy has empowered medical experimentation—the colonial explorations of the physical bodies of the deaf—underwriting cochlear and neural implant technologies ever in search of the site of language, the unmediated experience of the word. The console cowboy jacked into the net via a direct neural connection, a cranial jack, to achieve an unmediated experience of dataspace is not fiction. This is merely the next commercial artifact being medically mined from the physical body of the deaf with U.S. Food and Drug Administration approval.

The arguments made and questions raised in this part of the work are disturbing and resistant to simple solutions. They are meant to be. I accept Connolly's challenge to ask embarrassing, impertinent, upsetting, and even annoying questions. I cannot say that I necessarily like all that I describe, but the linkages with the body of the deaf, though often bitter or ironic, are unmistakable.

Finally, chapter 6 explores certain intractable problems that emerge both from the theoretical issues raised and from the practical decisions facing those who would present demands (and must confront their desire) for inclusion in the face of exclusion. One of the recurring difficulties is the question of meaning and language. Meaning may have been cut loose from its moorings, but language is still tied—although only by convention—to acoustics, a way of being that is linear and sequential. But if meaning and its expression are related, as in an expressivist view, then our concern with either spoken or written signs obscures a prior choice of modality. Sign languages, and those who use them, pose troubling questions to most of the dominant schools of language theory. But, as is made visible here, there are indeed circumstances in which language does not belong to talk.

The contentious terrain of "rights talk," itself a ground defined by intractabilities, makes visible the competing claims that animate conflicts over language choice and access for those who are deaf. Claiming a "right to speech" for all deaf children does little to address the problem of how to alter deaf children into hearing adults. As with the social conflict over abortion, there is no neutral territory. The battle over reproductive control is only the most obvious instance of opposing camps each seeking justification for their position through strategic deployment of rights talk. Yet here too, as with questions of reproductive freedom, there are very basic principles at stake. I argue strongly that practices of state control over the body resonate intimately with practices applied to the deaf.

The tension between resistance and complicity is a theme that runs throughout these pages. Each level of participation denotes some complicity, even during the most overt actions of resistance. This work is about making such tensions, as well as peculiar and long unquestioned forms of oppression, both more visible and more accessible. It aims at a wider social discourse on interpretive models and on the identities allowed to those marked "abnormal."

The questions raised here, while still tied to the mundane world of individual and collectively lived lives on the margins of the economic, social, and linguistic world, seek to call attention to deeper exclusions in our ways of knowing language and conveying meaning. Such questioning includes a politics of seeing that has more than one body for semiotics, as well as more than one semiotics of the body. This oppositional history of language choice explores how one linguistic modality has been deeply buried under calcified layers of other histories that not only "silence" but render unseen that which might be most distinctly visible. It offers a postcolonial view of deafness, examining institutions and practices that render speech visible but occlude language.

My goal is to change many of the "normal" questions, as well as questions about "the normal," as I point to new understandings of how earlier questions emerged, why they may no longer be of primary interest or of use, and why many of them help maintain exclusion and marginality. This work is about the political meanings of deafness, about the politics of Deaf identity, and about what it costs to be "unusual."

1

Deafness Is a Big Country . . .

How best to greet readers bringing divergent backgrounds to a text about new terrain, a place in which identities are either forged or forgotten? A work on the politics of Thailand, for example, would begin with a basic overview of the country, even if some readers might be experts on Thailand. Were the topic Thailand, one might begin, "Thailand is a big country." Indeed, chapter 4, "Merit Accounting in a Karmic Economy," is about what a big country Thailand may often be, as it focuses on the politics of deafness in Thailand.

So, in part, this is a work about a foreign place and the people there. But, clearly, deafness is not a country . . . or is it? Deafness is democratic in its occurrence. Membership, or "citizenship," cuts across all boundaries of class, gender, or race. Contrary to how the average individual defines deafness—that is, as an audiological impairment—Deaf people define themselves culturally and linguistically. The global Deaf population is currently about fifteen million—on par with a modest-sized nation. Yet it is a "country" without a "place" of its own. It is a citizenry without a geographical origin.

The difficulty posed by this missing place, or absent anchor, will be recurring throughout the work. Without claim to a specific place, and without the juridical and policing agencies by which we know nations in the late twentieth century, deafness is not a recognized nation. In keeping with the medical model of the body inherited from the nineteenth century, deafness is commonly viewed as merely a "condition." But the claim of a distinct "ethnic" identity that has accompanied the resurgence of Deaf Awareness in the past two decades forces a reassessment of this and other identities excluded from the equations of the "normal."

These exclusions and equations are the focus of this work, which examines ethnographic-like aspects of Deaf cultures. They, like other cultures, are not homogeneous, either in the makeup or experience of the individual or group. But this is not an ethnography of deafness. Rather, it is a study of exclusion and inclusion, of the availability and administration of acceptable identities; it details the construction of perceptions by which particular differences are most effectively excluded and others most effectively included. Deaf people—their experiences and their representations as "the deaf"—represent a peculiar intersection of issues that resonate in terrains seemingly far removed. Just how far, and how close, is the topic of this work.

Hearing Notions of Deafness—Terms of the Terrain

The words *Deaf* and *deaf* are both used in discussions of issues concerning profoundly deaf children and adults, although each has a distinct significance. The use of the term *Deaf*, in uppercase, is now widely used to refer to the cultural category of self-identification. The lowercase term refers to the simple fact of audiological impairment and is distinct from the process of self-identity. This "d/D" distinction was first made in 1972, by sociolinguist James Woodward,[1] but it is now widely understood and used by most writers in the field.

Among those focusing on educational issues, it is widely understood that children who are either hard-of-hearing or become deafened later in life fall into a distinct group. These children and young adults have known an ontological way of being through the experience of and as hearing, which is to say they have directly heard spoken language. I will make little reference to this category and will concentrate on those who have not had and will not ever have this direct experience. The search to recreate or produce that on-

1. Woodward 1972, pp. 1–7.

tology through biomedical technology is part of an aggressive on-going project to evade and abolish the very distinction that will be examined.

Those within Deaf communities differentiate between the simple inability to hear and their self-identification as Deaf. The degree of hearing loss matters relatively little. What is important, and what is deemed primary evidence for membership within the broader community, is the use of sign language.

A, if not the, defining feature of self-identity as belonging to an ethnic or linguistic minority is having and using one's own language. Should those in any given linguistic minority find that their native language is neither approved nor allowed within the educational system into which their children are placed, then this minority would be considered linguistically disenfranchised. In many parts of the world today, Deaf people are still forcibly restrained from using their native languages. They could, indeed they should, be called op-pressed. Deaf writers in some countries have evoked human rights statutes in their efforts to relieve their own situation. Paddy Ladd, a Deaf intellectual living in the United Kingdom, has taken the strongest position, using United Nations documents on human rights to suggest that such treatment of Deaf people constitutes a clear form of what can only be recognized as genocide.[2]

Some terms carry culturally distinct interpretive markers. For ex-ample, a hearing person uses the term "very hard-of-hearing" to refer to someone who is severely hearing impaired or nearly deaf. For a Deaf person, "very hard-of-hearing" means someone who is trying very much to be like a hearing person, even though he or she may be quite deaf. As a pejorative, the phrase describes those deeply invested in denying their deafness or in attempting to "pass" as hearing. The theme of "passing," fraught with ambivalence, com-plicity, resistance, and accommodation, frequently recurs in the poli-tics of identity.

2. Paddy Ladd, "Deaf Culture?" paper presented at the Deaf Way conference, Washington, D.C., 6 July 1989.

The terms *oralism, manualism,* and *total communication* have special application as distinct approaches to education and communication. Discussions of social control of the deaf evolve from a "great methodological debate," which has been explored in greater detail elsewhere, between "oralism" and "manualism."[3] However, the oral/manual controversy is as inadequate a frame as the mind/body split that it reflects. *Oralism* is the name given to those approaches that stress speech and auditory amplification. Oralism further implies a strict and rigid rejection of any use of sign language. Thus oralism is as much an ideology as it is a method, and one with a distinct teleology. As speech was considered God-given, that which separated man from beast, it was a sin to permit the deaf to remain silent.[4] *Manualism* is the name used primarily by the oralist camp to describe those who would allow the use of sign language by deaf people, either in education or in interpersonal communication. *Total communication,* both as an idea and a methodology, was initially proposed as an approach to education and communication combining both speech and sign in a program individually tailored to the particular strengths and weaknesses of a given deaf child. In practical application, however, total communication has come to mean that mix of speech and sign language most convenient to the individual teacher, often with little regard to the strengths or needs of any child. Sign language use in these settings has been shown to be, at best, only "sign-supported speech," which is inadequate to be understood by a child as a complete message.[5] In other words, a teacher, signing while he or she speaks, signs only part of the message. The child sees only these few, widely spaced, and often disconnected signs and does not hear the voice of the teacher. The same studies also show a much higher frequency of mistakes within even this limited signing by these hearing teachers. Hence, "total communication" is anything but total and is very rarely communication.

3. See Winefield 1987, which profiles the battles between Edward Miner Gallaudet and Alexander Graham Bell.
4. Neisser 1983, p. 30.
5. Johnson, Liddell, and Erting 1989.

Terrain of the Terms

Notions of a "Deaf ethnic identity" differ at the respective centers of Hearing and Deaf perspectives. For the Hearing audience, it may be best to engage this through a question. Why would some deaf individuals routinely claim to have been born deaf, despite knowing that they actually became deaf in their childhood years from illness, from the improper treatment of illness, or for other postnatal reasons?

The Hearing person will most likely assume the claim has something to do with the idea of having been ill, with the sense of loss that occurred, or with the circumstances that are clearly "responsible" for the loss. Or perhaps some sense of guilt leads them to insist that they were born with some excluding mark of difference. To the Hearing, deafness represents a loss of communion, the exclusion from their world. In cosmological terms, it is a mark of disfavor. It is Otherness, a stigma to be pitied and, thus, exiled to the margins of social knowledge. Their "silence" represents banishment or, at best, solitude and isolation. Missionary activity and charitable aid are encouraged as the responses morally mandated.

From a Deaf view, the politicized act of claiming a "native" deafness—that is, a deafness by birth—is tied to the positive identity of being "untainted" by the world of the Hearing and their epistemological constraints of sequential sound. The "purity" of Deaf knowledge, true Deafness, that comes from the banishment of this distraction is in Deaf culture a mark of distinction. It is all the better if the parents and even their parents were also Deaf. The agonized writings by Hearing academics and educators have nothing to do with the real interests of Deafness, which are consensually self-referencing rather than concerned with how a "rejoining" or other assimilation with the Hearing might be achieved. Nor do these writings address how an internally generated understanding of Deafness might enhance the Hearing understanding of their own culturally constructed knowledge and power structures. (This latter point, of course, only represents a further appropriation.)

Linguistic and ethnic purity is a trap that operates on similar principles in both Deaf and Hearing worlds. Such boundary setting is one part of the ongoing practices of culture building. It is used to exclude as well as include, but it is often brutal in operation. Nor is it all one-way. Particularly in the United States and Europe, emerging Deaf awareness has led to new efforts to exclude the nondeaf and partially deaf from the Deaf community. New definitions of deaf ethnicity and identity are also providing new methods, frequently linguistic, by which nonmembers or peripheral members (hard-of-hearing, hearing children of deaf parents, parents of deaf children, interpreters, etc.) may be excluded.

These efforts essentialize Deaf identity as a static object of authenticity to be mined or (re)discovered, rather than actively produced. Yet there is no single essence to be discovered, no true measure of authenticity. As Minh-ha Trinh observes,

Difference, like authenticity, is produced not salvaged. If the work of differentiation is constantly engaged and made visible, then even the notions of accumulation and preservation peculiar to western culture-collecting take on a different meaning in a different connotational context. Blindness to the to-and-fro movement between authenticity and inauthenticity in every definition of authenticity leads to a legitimation of a notion of tradition reduced to the past and to a rejection of, or a nostalgia for, so-called lost values. It also leads to an intense fear of an invasion into one's world by the "other"—hence the constant need to reserve access to that world to the "initiated" and the "conformist."[6]

Both sides of this cultural equation are engaging in some of the same practices of boundary setting. Insider and outsider, who can belong? Who can tell which is which? Native versus expert: these terms have resonance well beyond their traditional uses. One can sympathize with the excluding tactics of a newly militant Deafness, as with similar moves within feminism. Each, however, replicates the practices of exclusion against which their resistance took form. Nor do they attend to the gray territory/zones that are dynamic creations of those practices.

6. Trinh 1987, p. 141.

"Under Language Arrest"

Policing of "language" can be achieved in many ways. "Under language arrest" is a phrase rooted in the dominant Hearing society and applied to physiological limitations to producing sound, particularly speech sounds. It appears in medical, audiological, and speech therapy literature as "retardation" or, in a more upbeat vein, "delayed onset" of verbal language. It is, however, a code for a view of language order. The mainstreaming policies for educating deaf children, the understanding of who the Deaf person is, and notions of what are proper approaches to "aid and assist" in the "curative" or "therapeutic" techniques deployed all presume membership in this language order.

From another view, the "language under arrest" is sign language. (Perhaps it was "set upon without delay.") Given starting points both in the physiological model of the body and in the presumption of language-as-speech, no room has been allowed for a visually based modality of language that needs neither such premise. Or rather, such a language would break rules of the dominant order, and, if acknowledged, would be thus an outlaw. An outlaw is something unruly, outside the boundaries of established orders of understanding. Sign languages are situated on the cusp of language and the law. Constables of the cultural order seek to arrest it: an outlaw language to be placed "under language arrest." Although often arrested, sign language is currently a fugitive at large.

In addition to the historically marked suppression of sign languages, the remarkable persistence throughout this century of the oppressive and institutionally sanctioned practices against the category of "the deaf" raises questions simply by their belligerent entrenchment in the face of research, evidence, and the desires of those so labeled. The modern social rights movements of the past thirty years (civil rights, gender issues, racial desegregation, literacy campaigns, etc.) in liberal Western nations fuel a still-growing body of research and resistance by "indigenous" Deaf peoples, much of which presumes the claim to a distinct Deaf ethnicity.[7] Nevertheless, the institutions that manufacture and maintain exclusions of the deaf have been only modestly reformed.

This book is about a particular set of exclusions: exclusions of a way of knowing, a modality of communication, and of a social and human identity. The body of knowledge anchored in the medical model of deafness is rather extensive. Physiological textbooks on hearing impairment and speech therapies fill library shelves. The construction of this protohistory has served a wide range of interests, while suppressing those deemed "insignificant." Critique of this construction has primarily come from those labeled "deaf" or "hearing impaired." Almost by definition, their "voice" goes unheard. Yet, as this work will suggest, careful analysis reveals many more possibilities, many more exclusions, than are immediately apparent.

There are no promises of liberation. Deaf peoples have been dominated and appropriated at will by who label them less than "normal." There is little chance that this will not continue to happen, though it appears that a grounding in the visual terrain of spatial languages may well become valuable in the virtual realities of twenty-first-century optical data and communications grids. As the advantages of a grammaticized vision are incorporated into the metaphors of power and representation, there is little reason to assume that the sources of such knowledge will either benefit or be acknowledged. Indeed, such appropriations happen all the time.

---

7. Deaf people, of any nationality, who employ a fluent sign language seem to assume they will share a common bond with other deaf people who also actively use sign language. The critical factor is that the use of and identification with sign language, or to be more precise, the signing activity, precede any of the other assumptions. It is common, in my experience, to also see deaf people from various nations totally disregard or in a similar fashion dismiss deaf people who are without sign language, either as intellectually impoverished (poor, uneducated, cretins, etc.) or as uninterestingly hearinglike (orally educated deaf who communicate well with no one other than their speech therapists). Even when the signers have no common sign language and must resort back to a simplified grammatical subset of gesticulation, the enthusiasm that assumes common ground animates the exchange and, functionally, ensures its success. These are not isolated incidents but the norm in meetings between deaf people in international social settings.

They usually take the form of constructing a previously excluded culture as though it exists solely to suggest new aesthetic, political, or technical directions for the dominant culture.

The history of yet a further exclusion may also be herein contained.

Signs of Language and Identity

The conditions of "naturalization" into this cultural and linguistic citizenry are unusual. More than 90 percent of deaf children are born into hearing families; thus, fewer than 10 percent of deaf children have even one deaf parent.[8] This means the majority of new citizens are, figuratively, born in the wilderness. Nor is sign language their native language in the sense of being available from infancy, learned from interaction with their parents. Nevertheless, for those sufficiently fortunate to have access to a residential deaf school, sign language is probably the first actual language acquired.

Contrary to the usual transmission of spoken language between generations—passing from parent to child—the primary means of language transmission in the deaf world is within each generation, from their few peers with deaf parents, or at school from those slightly older. For the deaf youths on the street, language is learned from the older deaf survivors on the streets. How—and what— these youth are taught is often through a process we might identify as "abuse." For them, survival is often the only code available.

This basic cultural fact of transmission sets up the beginning of a lifelong gulf of misunderstandings with the hearing world. In most countries, educators of the deaf have limited fluency, at the very best, in the national sign language of their students. As few cultures promote the simple idea that teachers need to learn from their students as much as they need to teach them, it is common to find teachers of the deaf retiring after years of active service—still unable to hold

8. In Thailand, there has been only one documented case of a deaf child of deaf parents. Hence, nearly 100 percent of deaf Thai children come from hearing families.

a simple conversation with one of their own graduates. This is frequently as true of teachers from the oral-only schools as those that used sign language.

That cohorts and, for the lucky few, teachers are responsible for basic language transmission to deaf children, and thus for much of their basic cognitive and emotional development, stems from an earlier abdication by parents. To the hearing family with no previous contact with deafness, a deaf child is a fundamental shock. Moreover, the route most productive of their child's human and intellectual growth is also to them the most counterintuitive. The parents need to focus on the strengths of their child's difference, rather than understanding it as a loss. In effect, the parents need to view their own child as an "other" to themselves, a member of a different culture.[9] Basic kinship ties, as well as the centuries of colonizing discourse built into the modern view of the suppressible other, drive concerned parents to insist that their own child will achieve "hearinglike" status by whatever means required. As a result, the child lands on a continuum whose scale runs from a deaf intelligence to a crippled hearing knowledge. Children, most particularly in less wealthy nations, are lucky if their attainment of whatever point is sought on such a continuum is left, albeit with ample interference, to the schools. For the rest, it is left to the streets.

Because of the pitiful level of actual communication between teachers and their students, few deaf people leave school with literacy skills commensurate with their years spent in the school system. The consequences of this handicap for life success only serve to reproduce and reinforce the idea that deaf people are incapable of "normal" contributions to society.

Underlying these problems is the most fundamental issue, an attitudinal and intellectual barrier: the widespread misconception that

9. This prescription of what parents "should" do when faced with a deaf infant is not easily accepted by the average parent. For example, Bornstein (1990a), a work by a respected expert, concludes fatalistically that while parents should accept the unique linguistic and cultural status of their deaf children, they probably never will.

sign language is not really language. Gesture, code, semaphore, or pantomime, maybe; but language?

Dr. William Stokoe's research, beginning with that published in *Studies in Linguistics* in 1960, began serious linguistic inquiry into various sign languages and their grammatical structures. Such inquiry, particularly in the past decade, has turned into a small but healthy flow of works that have conclusively proven sign languages to be well-developed polysynthetic languages, which are structurally autonomous from the various spoken languages that may exist in their immediate proximity.

So the language of the citizenry is now understood to be a "real" language. But is it only one language? Perhaps the widest popular misconception about sign languages is that they are all alike—international, if you will. This is not true. The World Federation of the Deaf has seen fit to issue an official statement that "there is no such thing as an 'international sign language.'"[10] Sign languages are distinct from each other, in the same manner as spoken languages.

The next misconception is "Isn't that a shame? Shouldn't someone create an international sign language . . . ?" The Deaf community continues to be amazed by this thought. How is it that hearing people, who have no particular barriers between them in their own spoken communication but are unable to accept one single international language, still somehow expect deaf people either to do so or to accept a constructed language imposed by someone wishing to "create" one for their "benefit"? It is a familiar arrogance by which difference is "silenced." But for the Deaf, as with any ethnic or national people, giving up their native or mother language is simply unacceptable.

The third major misconception is that particular sign languages are visual copies of spoken languages: thus American Sign Language must be English or Thai Sign Language must be like spoken Thai. This, too, is far from the truth. American Sign and British Sign Lan-

---

10. The WFD does, however, promote a core glossary in Gestuno, a "Sign Esperanto," for conference use.

guages are totally different from one another, and neither bears any resemblance to the spoken or written English language—and why should they? Unfortunately, there are both linguists and educators who spend years attempting to force artificial constructs of sign language vocabulary to fit the pattern of a spoken language grammar.

While this work is not a study of sign language, the basic details of what sign language is form a crucial backdrop to questions of deaf identity. Sign languages have several important distinctions as a class of languages. Certainly, the most fascinating feature for the linguistic researcher is that they are based on another modality than that of languages traditionally studied. Sign languages are perceived and produced through visual and gestural channels of processing information, rather than through aural and oral channels. The first linguists to approach sign languages reasoned that since vision and hearing function differently, it must be fair to assume that languages based on these distinct functions will have different characteristics. The past two decades of work have proven this initial, although rather tardy, assumption to be wholly correct.

Sign language studies have found well-developed features exclusive to and well-adapted to a language in a manual /visual modality, as well as features apparently shared among all languages. Signs are primarily expressed by one or two hands that perform an articulation in different places on the body or in front of the signer.[11] These articulations include movement, location, handshape, orientation, and nonmanuals. These five aspects of the sign vocabulary occur simultaneously rather than in a serial succession, as do sounds in a spoken language. As the broad category of "nonmanuals" should suggest, sign language is not, as one might think, just the language of hands. Direction of eye gaze, body shifts, shoulders, the mouth, and other parts of the face all participate in producing sign vocabulary. Frequently these nonmanuals are the most critical determinants of meaning, syntax, and inflection. They are also often the most problematic for hearing teachers who cannot bring themselves to use the histrionics necessary to learn beginning sign communications.

11. Brennan, Colville, and Lawson 1980.

As with many inflectional languages, sign languages have a rela-tively free word order. There are, of course, preferred orders and many never-occurring, ungrammatical orders. Examples of the in-teraction between various aspects of a sign would include the simple distinction between a statement and a question, which can be deter-mined by simultaneous use of a forward head-tilt and raised eye-brows. Both could be negated by the addition of repeated sideways head movement.

The above examples of syntax refer to the temporal dimensions of the language—*when* certain aspects take place. Sign languages also have a spatial—a *where*—extension, using movement in different di-rections within a three-dimensional space to convey specific gram-matical significance. This additional use of space is a very special characteristic of sign languages.

Citizenship in the Place of Deafness

Deafness is a country whose history is rewritten from generation to generation. This is partly because of the status of its native lan-guages, partly because more than 90 percent of deaf children are born to hearing parents, and partly because of the curious and spe-cific oppressions that constitute the histories of the deaf. Sign cul-tures, as well as the social "knowledge" of deafness, are necessarily reborn and remade with each generation.

In a sense, they are also reborn from and into a place of ignorance. The common body of knowledge among hearing parents of deaf children is not transmitted through generations of family lore. For most such parents, theirs is the first deaf child to be found in their extended families; thus, just as Deaf cultures necessarily regenerate, so each new generation of hearing parents and experts recreates "knowledge" for their administration of deafness. Each generation of hearing parents seeks out and often reinvents knowledge about the deafness of their children. The scientific texts have been too tightly bound to a mechanistic model of bioknowledge to provide much help. It is no wonder that audiologists and the sellers of amplification techniques and mechanisms (hearing aid salesmen) gained ascendancy as the purveyors of knowledge about deafness in the past century. Each generation falls prey to the hucksters of its age selling promises of new ears for deaf babies, a promise that the difference can be banished, if only for a price. Who pays which price is yet another issue.

Even the supposed "professionals" have acted in seeming ignorance of work already done. Each generation of hearing educators has invented new manual codes to match spoken languages, as if none had ever preceded them, or as if any had ever truly been needed.[12] Only in this generation have any Hearing researchers acknowledged the full linguistic nature of native sign languages.[13] Deafness has been called "an invisible disability" for several reasons: these are just a few.

Key here is that new parents who discover their child is deaf have few native resources to turn toward. Their family practitioner or local pediatrician initially offers hope for a repair to the damaged body. It is a hope never relinquished, and a hope that will be carefully fed by those who would profit. The persistence in denial of its presence is, in fact, presented as a crucial test of faith: as if belief will make "it" go away, and the thingly silent one will speak to them. One staff member of the Alexander Graham Bell Association for the Deaf has been quoted as saying, "They can't hear, but they catch on. Some say there's no such thing as a deaf child. Not if it's done right."[14]

The creation of asylums for deaf-mutes produced virtual warehouses for deaf children. Later, several distinct generations of individuals would experience collection into such warehouses, which later were called schools. While historians have primarily paid attention to the presumed education offered in these institutions by dedicated Hearing people, their actual "product" was the explosive

12. This observation was presented by the author at the People's Workshop at the East-West Center in April 1989; see Wrigley 1995. A recent work examines the history of artificial codes to spoken English; see Bornstein 1990b.

13. See Stokoe 1960, which is widely considered as the seminal work on sign language linguistics.

14. Neisser 1983, p. 32.

growth of language and culture generated by the deaf children and deaf adults by virtue and accident of the warehousing itself.

The "accidental" nature of Deaf culture in no way lessens the legitimacy of either the collective or individual accomplishments of deaf people. The point is that the fragility of the "traditional" channels of cultural transmission, traditional only in the sense of being commonly understood by the dominant Hearing culture (and thus for the Deaf a foreign tradition by definition), meant that different avenues had to be explored. Deaf people, both individually and collectively, have called upon those channels in their own efforts to pass on language, memories, and the collective stuff of "cultures." While it might be said that employing such fragile threads to pass memories to subsequent generations must produce a thin or weak tapestry, it might equally be said that the lack of entrenchment—what is sometimes called the "baggage" of social practices—allows for a freedom in the regeneration of cultural dynamics that other cultures may not so readily enjoy. Recent research [15] in a rural residential school for the deaf in Thailand points to an important tradition of storytellers passing stories and, more significantly, the tradition of the storytelling art itself to younger generations. Such self-education within these institutions has been little studied, but it suggests important avenues of cultural regeneration previously ignored.

There has been a certain safety in the lack of attention given to these processes. As a Foucaultian analysis would predict, increased attentiveness by caretakers within institutional settings usually decreases the opportunities for these activities of cultural transmission to flourish. Thus concern can, and should, be expressed about the possible consequences of making public such mechanisms of cultural integrity. Making visible the "weapons of the weak" [16] may well increase vulnerability rather than strength. This will be a recurring concern throughout this work.

15. Reilly 1995.
16. The phrase is taken from a work of that title by James Scott about resistance and avoidance strategies of peasants in northern peninsular Malaysia (1985).

In the meantime, the deafness of the new child is denied but is neither changed nor aided. It is, in fact, repressed by misplaced hope as each family seeks to "discover" it anew.

The Everyday Invention of Deafness

A small deaf child coming home from school signs to his mother. "Who invented deafness?" he asks. "You did," she replies.

The epigraph above is taken from an upbeat story told in the Bicultural Center's newsletter, a progressive and effective publication by Deaf culture activists. The mother is actively engaged in the intellectual growth of her child. She, too, is growing both in her own signing skills and in her open appreciation of the richness of the language and the culture in which it is found. Her child is being educated in nearly perfect circumstances for a deaf child. There are a very few schools in which both hearing and deaf children are almost equal in number, with deaf teachers actually outnumbering hearing ones. Fluent signing skills are a basic requirement of all teachers, and what is being called a bicultural approach to education is being actively pursued. There are fewer than a dozen such schools worldwide.

Nevertheless, even in these circumstances there is no generational repository; there are no mothers, fathers, or grandparents to offer family lore on the raising of deaf children or on growing up deaf. These resources can be found neither within the extended family nor, in most cases, in the surrounding community. The mother in this scene is correct: her child really is "inventing" Deafness for both of them. Thus, major components of Deaf cultures are regenerated with each successive cohort of children, and the home and family cultures are also in large part regenerated with each successive cohort of parents with newly "discovered" deaf babies. Deaf cultures may be best understood as a product of collaborative and regenerative efforts. Technology has made the same true of modern culture, as well; in neither case, however, is the process of cultural construction easily accepted.

Recent American and European Deaf cultural studies have focused—and indeed very rightly—on the residential schools as the major source of creative Deaf cultures. But this research has generally accepted the structural givens of the institutions, questioning only their methods and staffing. Equally important, its focus has been at the expense of a broader consideration of changing parental demands and desires and how such demands are reflected in school board decisions and administrative policies. These varying demands and expectations too rarely have allowed deaf adults any presence or authority in debates about language and education for deaf children. The situation has changed little since 1880. The "issue" of deaf people has not been ignored: rather, neither the perspective nor particular concerns of deaf people have ever been of interest to those deciding on "the issues."

Even in the last century, serious political debates about the status of deaf people drew wide public attention. The famous series of clashes between Alexander Graham Bell and Edward Miner Gallaudet repeatedly reached the floors of the U.S. Congress. On invitation, Bell also presented his views on deaf people in an address to the British Parliament. Personal interests and political fortunes were at stake, but no deaf person was ever a "spokesperson" on the issues. Not, that is, in any forums in which decisions were actually made. Among the large population of literate and educated deaf, a series of small regional newspapers showcased the opinions and presentations of many leading Deaf Americans.[17] While these papers provide invaluable insights into the diversity and interests of the adult deaf readers of the period, those setting national and state policies on the education, employment, and social positioning of deaf people took little notice of their statements—or their concerns.

Deafness is primarily a visual experience.[18] The deaf child relies upon the sense of vision to communicate and to learn. When a high proportion of the information needed for social and cognitive

17. Beginning in 1849, the number of institutional papers and independent regional journals grew to over fifty by the turn of the century. Known collectively as "the Little Papers," they came to "assume a significance out of proportion to their size" (Van Cleve and Crouch 1989, p. 98).

18. See Erting 1982.

maturation is contained in auditory signals, the deaf child misses out on what other children easily learn. Yet educators of the deaf child focus heavily on the auditory modality, rather than attempting to fulfill those needs through a visual modality.

In the nineteenth century Alexander Graham Bell wrote with vehemence about the persistent and negative effects of deaf children associating with each other (1888). Observing that they taught each other sign language and gained a sense of community with other deaf people that lasted beyond their school years, he concluded that assimilation and social development would never be accomplished unless deaf children were isolated from one another. Bell lobbied tirelessly to modify the education policies of institutions for the deaf, so as to prevent "the formation of a deaf variety of the human race." He was instrumental in establishing a system of day schools that teach speech alone and are infamous among deaf people for their zeal in expunging the use of gesture. Some schools still seek to avoid "contamination" of the learning environment by sign language by not admitting deaf children who already know signs, particularly the children of deaf parents. While boarding schools remain the form of schooling most favored by Deaf activists, trends toward integration into regular day schools are motivated in part by the belief that for deaf people to face the hearing world, they must avoid living in a deaf world.

Like the Augustinian approaching Manichaeanism, the oralist views sign language not as another possible approach to existing problems but as "an alternative possibility of faith that must be constituted as heresy to protect the integrity of the self-identity it threatens through its existence. The indispensability of one conception . . . is established by defining what deviates from it as a heresy that must not be entertained as a counterpossibility."[19] It cannot be allowed as an option.

Thus, the irony is made starkly apparent. Education for blind children focuses heavily on verbal communication, on speaking to and eliciting speech from the blind child. Education for deaf children is,

19. Connolly 1991, pp. 7–8.

likewise, focused heavily on verbal communication, on speaking to and attempting to elicit speech sounds from the deaf child. For the blind child, the policy concentrates on the sense and modality present: hearing and speech. For the deaf child, the concentration is exclusively on the sense and modality absent: hearing and speech. Imagine a school for blind children in which a majority of the learning day consisted of teachers shining very bright lights into blind eyes, while saying little more than "Think color? What color?" Though that seems odd, it is a rather accurate portrayal-in-reverse of mainstream deaf education.

The family life of the deaf child has only recently become a matter of interest. Recent works[20] have focused extensively on the communication skills of the children. Some have also examined the communication skills of the parents, but most have said little about these parents' expectations. The available options change with the shifts in society's attitudes toward difference and the perceived accommodation of those who are different. Indeed, having a signing deaf child is hip in today's politically correct elite circles. While this is nominally better than being hidden from view in the back room or passed off as a servant, as happened in earlier generations, by what qualitative measure has life improved for the child? Yuppie stockbrokers trade in political correctness credits by trotting out their chic "Sharper Image" or "Banana Republic" child to suggest their attunement to late-modern identity issues. Optimally, the child is an adopted one from a poor country, as well. You get the picture.[21]

---

20. See bibliography for a broad sampling.

21. "Lonely Lovely Longs for the Patter of Little Feet," *Star* (17 December 1991). "Marriage and children were the two things Emma Samms said she wanted most in the world last year. Well, things never work out the way you plan 'em. Emma did get married—to London attorney Bart Nagji—but it hardly lasted long enough for the couple to shake off the confetti. Now that the nine-month marriage is behind her, the *Dynasty* dish wants to make motherhood her main course. 'I will consider having children without a man,' explained Emma, 31, who co-founded the wish-come-true Starlight Foundation for terminally-ill kids. '*I'd like to adopt a non-white handicapped child, possibly one with a hearing defect because I can do sign language*'" (emphasis added). The photograph of Ms. Samms presents her scantily clad and provocatively posed.

The other side of this same coin, a faith in bionic medical and technological advances, is also problematic. High-technology neural brain implants are quickly becoming yet another article of faith, promising a fix for the "brokenness" of the deaf ears. Faith in the truth of high science clothes this form of denial in a socially acceptable form of positivism. Again and again, scientific and medical research is complicitous in the techniques of denial.

Most family responses are coded in resentment. Parents, like the advocates of many organized interest groups, most often react to the discovery of their child's deafness by intensely resenting the contingency[22] that has visited this difference upon their own child. Such intensity often is manifest in a virtual reorganization of their own lives around banishing that difference and substituting an approximation, almost any approximation, of a sameness, a simulacrum of that which is deemed lost. The false promise of "There's no such thing as a deaf child. Not if it's done right" speaks both to faith and resentment. Even the political options for acceptance and support of a child's deafness are deeply framed within this resentment of or relationship to contingency.

Language and Location in Deaf Cultures

The significant and defining feature of Deaf culture is the use of an indigenous sign language. While this may seem obvious by now, many still seek to deny that the indigenous sign languages are even language, let alone a crucial feature of Deaf culture. Those making this attempt are almost exclusively hearing. Nevertheless, linguistics research has proven sign languages to be rich, independent language systems.

Deafness, as noted by expert Charles Reilly, is a democratic affliction. Its social identity is unfixed, whether in class, place, or innate gifts. But there are differences in how those who are deaf see themselves. Two important and distinct views mark the ends of a continuum, positions increasingly understood as polar opposites. There

22. Connolly 1991, pp. 16–35.

are those who would deny their deafness and seek to emulate the hearing people that surround them, and there are those who acknowledge their deafness and identify themselves not only with their deafness but through the vehicle of Deaf culture—the distinctive sign languages of native deaf communities. These cultural vehicles have created a separate form of ethnicity with clear markers for self-identification. While lacking racial or national markers, the members of these self-referenced Deaf cultures have no doubts about their culturally distinct identities. Though nominally members of a surrounding dominant culture, they—some but not all—see themselves as apart from it and as members of a specifically "native" Deaf culture.

Deaf cultures in the less affluent world are small communities in which only a minute minority have access to education.[23] The educated do not necessarily form the core of the elite, although education is a strong factor. Wealth from families, charismatic signing skills, physical strength, and employment or capacity to employ are more important than education per se. Educational or training options are highly limited in any case. These communities, such as they are, are limited almost exclusively to urban or regional trading centers. Small clusters of individuals passing mostly unnoticed by the dominant culture that surrounds them, they could be called metaphorically an invisible hill tribe.[24]

23. In developing countries only a small percentage of deaf children ever see the inside of a school. Thailand is well ahead of the average, with approximately 20 percent of deaf children now receiving some schooling. See World Federation of the Deaf 1991.

24. Centuries of ethnic competition, warfare, invasion, and escapes have left pockets of ethnic and cultural tribal groups, often with unique languages, dress, and customs, scattered in the different countries of South, Southeast, and East Asia. These minorities frequently live in adverse conditions in highland and mountainous areas, particularly along borders. Some adopt brightly colored and distinctive tribal costumes, which are marketed in the tourist trade, while others are marked by far more subtle distinctions that are visible only to and among the members of the various groups.

Dominant population groups concerned with internal security have traditionally encouraged these minorities to settle in the border areas, following the adage that "the enemy of my enemy is my friend"; the ethnic minorities act as human buffer

The histories of deaf communities, over the past century in particular, have primarily recorded a direct oppression of their distinctive languages and of their social and cultural identity. This was not always so, as literary deaf communities flourished in eighteenth-century Europe. In colonial America, deaf Americans were among the most highly educated members of their communities.[25] Unfortunately, as part of the pan-European swell of nationalism and the paranoia that accompanied it from the 1870s through the turn of the century, minority ethnic and language groups suffered strenuous persecution. The American "melting pot" policy,[26] whereby immigrant children were required to forgo their ethnic roots and attend English-only schools, also dates from this period. Sign languages, too, were seen as suspect and were repressed where possible. In 1880 in Milan, Italy, an International Convention of Educators of the Deaf—at which only one deaf instructor was present—passed a now infamous resolution banning the use of sign language in the education of deaf children and declaring further that sign languages should be forcibly eradicated. I will not here rehearse the peculiar history of the oppression of sign language, which can be found elsewhere, but it is crucial to understanding Deaf cultures today.[27]

Deaf people remain a disenfranchised linguistic minority in all but a small handful of developed nations, primarily Scandinavian (and there only since 1981), and in a few liberal urban areas of the United States. While Deaf leaders emphasize how much deaf people have in

---

zones between larger traditional rivals. For these reasons, armed camps of rebel insurgents on many borders have been supported with weaponry and financial backing.

Minority populations in rural and remote locations are distanced from dominant cultures socially as well as physically. They generally do not speak the dominant language(s), often are illiterate, and frequently are legally stateless; their children are rarely provided educational opportunities. While they are minorities in their respective countries, they collectively number more than twenty million (not including those within China).

25. See Van Cleve and Crouch 1989; see also Neisser 1983.

26. My father's view of the "melting pot": "Those at the bottom get burned and the scum floats to the top."

27. See Harlan 1984.

common with other linguistic minorities, reasoned ignorance parading under the guise of common wisdom continues to treat deaf people as just another disabled or handicapped group. One anthropologist even suggests that deaf people are only a "damaged subset of the surrounding culture."[28] This view is merely representative of the oppression of deaf cultures and of the unique languages of those communities. Such oppressions are disguised in the full range of scientific and educational discourse and metadiscourse.

This framing further stigmatizes local knowledge with opposed, competing claims. On the one hand, Deaf people are wholly and uniquely defined by their peculiar physical disability or affliction; on the other hand, they can be understood only as a subset defined as a defective part of the dominant (hearing) culture and society. The former position dismisses a category generalized as "human defect" and thus culturally irrelevant. In the latter case, the Deaf are interesting only insofar as they demonstrate how the larger culture treats or relates to the irritant of the minority group's "requirements," perhaps displaying the graciousness of its charity. The "ethnographic circumstances" that constitute the Deaf Thai community, and indeed the very representation of a thing that can be called "the Deaf community," are seen as no more than epiphenomenal, regardless of which view is held. The discursive economy disallows the notion of a "native" Deaf culture by casting that identity as a choice between these two options: either all deaf are alike, and thus to be discounted as statistically insignificant, or all deaf are just like the surrounding hearing culture, except they can't hear. The meaning of "deaf" is based on position in the language order, the category in the standing taxonomy (be it as a charitable concern or as a curse—the mark of external origin). In the juxtaposition of these two views, other possibilities—most crucially, that of difference—have been effectively silenced.

This tension is seldom recognized, let alone resolved. Universalisms in all discourse are fed by the notion that all humans share

28. University of Hawaii anthropologist Jack Bilmes, an "expert" on Thailand, referring to Deaf Thais.

common properties. This search for universals is accompanied by layers of accommodating gestures as well as by various strategies deployed to offset challenges to hegemonic definitions. Yet, indigenous Deaf cultures do suggest ways that we can talk about a "lived universalism" of Deaf experiences, while we also recognize distinctions among local "ethnic" (in the word's more common usage) Deaf cultures. They may mirror certain aspects of the surrounding dominant culture, but they also have epistemological roots by which these aspects have been legitimately "claimed" or "understood" from within the native and indigenous Deaf experience. On these certain grounds an indigenous Deaf culture may represent an ethnic "authenticity" based on claims fully equal, if not superior, to those of the Hearing population living around them.

Such a suggestion is warmly received in Deaf gatherings, but hearing audiences deflect it through discursive evasion. Discussions of ethnicity that presume to include indigenous deaf peoples generally recognize as cultural traits only those visible aspects of the surrounding local culture and signs of deference that local deaf citizens adopt; these are the traits "provided" to them. In the case of many educational institutions that are rigorous in the disciplinary enactments of institutional procedures, this limited recognition is clearly valid.

One of the unique features of Deaf culture is that no "place" claim is available for community self-identification. Many nativist social movements and other indigenous organizations make claims of a "special relationship" with place or "the land." Religious notions of a special stewardship over the land are often invoked as part of such relationships. These concepts of place are heavily laden with both Western romanticized ideas of nature and the socially constructed realities of natural resources. The very notion of the indigenous—native as opposed to foreign—takes physical place as a key part of its legitimizing ethos. This has proven convenient in some cases, contentious in others. As is increasingly being understood, most of these claims have little basis in historical or environmental details of the actual "stewardship," whether previous or current. Nevertheless, the "we-were-here-first" approach to native claims, though opposed to the "we-have-divine-sanction-to-subjugate" approach of colonists, similarly rests on a mythological basis. Yet not even fictitious claims of native rights to a place are available to native deaf communities. The deaf are an invisible and widely distributed minority, as the democratic nature of deafness would suggest. The circumstances of the Deaf as a cultural minority, however, make it clear that place is not intrinsic to a nativist identity.

There are competing experiential and hermeneutical perspectives of this "freedom" from place. One is of a freedom by and of choice: the leisure, as it were, to be unburdened by the requirements or demands of attachment to place. This is experienced each time surplus production allows another child of an agrarian family to attend school. Another is a freedom only in negation, through the experience of exclusion from access to place. The corresponding example would be any agrarian worker made landless, through any set of events. Of course, other areas would provide other examples of "freedom" through exclusion or inclusion.

It is not that place has no intrinsic value, nor that great rewards are not returned from certain experiential investments, but rather that multiple values and contrasting experiences compete for the opportunities to construct what "meanings" are available for such investments. Every marking off of a "place" requires and is built upon an exclusion. Such exclusions may or may not be related to a physical or geographical place.

Modern Life in Both Deaf and Hearing Cultures

Deafness, in its socially constructed relationship with Hearing culture, is defined by barriers to communication and to participation. In this framing, it has a great deal in common with poverty. Lack of access—to timely information, to basic education, to decision-making processes—and a total disregard by those with authority for their specific local concerns are faced by deaf and poor people alike. The dreams and desires that have led other disenfranchised minorities, as well as the deaf, to band together in mutual self-assistance are remarkably similar.[29]

29. See Morse, Rahman, and Johnson 1995.

The key demand of language rights, that distinctive ethnic mother tongues be used for education and communal life, is often made also by poor minorities. Nevertheless, the overt subjugation of the sign languages of native deaf communities has continued with little change over the past century, while similar oppressions of other linguistic minorities have been greatly reduced, at least on purely linguistic grounds. While the formal authorities continue to disregard the concerns of minorities generally, the state apparatuses that maintain the exclusions of deaf people are both more explicit and more rigid than those applied to the poor.

Deafness and poverty are also coupled in a much more immediate way. The experience of deafness in the developing world, in the absence of family support, is almost always connected with underemployment and poverty. This is not particularly surprising, but it means that the deaf are thus doubly excluded. Self-representation and self-help are often the only avenues remaining. Unfortunately, the community often totally lacks the experiential base of such forms of expressive representation. Having been cut off not only from the decision-making processes that have directly affected their lives but also from the very details and information that may have preceded and informed these decisions, deaf people in the developing world have had little experience in any public arena. They are both information and process poor, in a very real sense. Self-representation and self-help require both information and skills in public consensus building. In any body of people so long denied access to information and to participation in decision-making processes, such information and skills are extremely rare.

This description paints the experience of deafness as one of victimization. While this is certainly not true by definition, in practice victimization is very much a part of the lives of many deaf people. The descriptions above are part of the context in which and from which the claims to an ethnicity are emerging. But the stories are not necessarily negative. Skills, talent, and initiative are also part of the deaf experience. However, as with those in poverty, the defining criteria of success have more to do with how opportunities are structured than with any individual "virtue" or "merit." Both poor people and deaf people are too often on the wrong side of the structural equations.

In 1982, a training seminar was conducted among the first deaf "employees" setting up a handicraft workshop, under what would later evolve into the National Association of the Deaf in Thailand (NADT). The agreed purpose was to develop a worker-management style of operations; but none of the staff initially wanted to participate in management decisions. To them, optimal circumstances meant only that such decisions were explained, not that they should or would be expected to have an active role in actually making them. When it was made clear that decisions were to be participatory, the staff initially participated reluctantly; absentee rates were often highest on staff meeting days. When major issues were on the agenda, the workshop was often empty. After these meetings became part of the daily schedule, they became more difficult to avoid, but many staff members came late until the experience of participation became more common.

The seminar clearly illustrates the effects of limited access to information and processes. When it began, the staff did not distinguish between "money" and "budget." After the concepts were understood, vocabulary emerged to make these distinctions, as well as many others, for operational purposes. The point is that the experience of the workers, not their language, was impoverished. Following the basic training of these first workshops, and with the help of several summer interns from the Stanford Business School in the mid-1980s, the Silent World Workshop became and has remained a freestanding business. Since 1985, it has operated totally on the staff's acquired commercial skills, Deaf managed and without donor financial aid.

Down and Out on the Streets of Bangkok

Deaf "communities" in the less wealthy nations are mostly found in urban settings, as rural deaf people migrate in search of both employment prospects and other deaf people. Isolated linguistically from the surrounding dominant culture, they focus their attentions primarily on each other. Thus, village or small town attitudes and atmosphere are found even in large urban settings.[30] Within these "small towns," bickering, gossip, manipulation, exploitation, jealousy, and spite are the norm. Alcohol abuse and violence against women and gay boys are common. Funerals and the infrequent holiday parties are the few occasions on which groups intermix. Fights are not uncommon at such events, usually provoked by money and personal slights. Scandalmongering is a favorite pastime.

Certainly such positive behaviors as sharing, cooperation, and mutual assistance occur, but it is equally important to observe that those whose lives are dominated by negative experiences often focus on negative emotions, and that they find many more outlets for negative emotions than opportunities for positive experiences. The Thai Sign Language, for example, is extraordinarily rich in descriptive and evocative vocabulary for negative experiences, big and small, precisely because the population base has such extensive familiarity with negative life events.

The urban Deaf community of Bangkok is marked by disparate groups, roughly analogous to "gangs," although only some fit the Western urban model. Groups of disadvantaged deaf gravitate toward leaders, be they those who can employ them, those who are charismatic, strong figures, or those with resources to lend in time of distress. Loose alliances develop among the leaders for various reasons, including old school ties, financial dealings, or simple affinity in style. Intrigues to expand power, influence, or economic control are the stuff of everyday life. In these regards, the elite of the urban Deaf communities mirror the elite of the surrounding dominant Hearing community, at least in motive and vice.

"Elite" here, as well as more generally in less wealthy nations, usually refers to those who have homes, enjoy family support, and have had access to education. Unfortunately, as noted earlier, this is only a very small percentage of the Deaf. The rest are poor and get

---

30. These observations draw heavily from Thailand, particularly from Bangkok, a city of over eight million.

by either by living in the servant quarters of large estates or in sweat-shop dormitories, or by living on their own, on or near the streets.

The influence of petty capitalism among the urban Deaf popula-tion in Bangkok, primarily through street vending to tourists, has produced social changes that will be examined in detail in chapter 4. Here, brief comments about everyday street life illustrate not so much details of Deaf culture as the options available to the Deaf and the position of deafness in a world insistent upon denying its exis-tence; these are some of the manifestations of that denial. Street ven-dors, selling a typical range of tourism trade goods, compete vigor-ously with each other. Deceit, malice, and greed are the primary social virtues developed in this setting. While the income is remark-ably good during high tourist season, even the most successful ven-dors lament the mind-killing environment in which they work and the attitudes it fosters. The best and brightest of the educated, the most motivated of the uneducated, and the street deaf with no other choices are all drawn to vending to deal with corrupt police, street thugs, thieves, weather, and the incredibly thick air pollution as they work alongside some of the world's worst traffic jams.

More than a few know they are working in horrible conditions that are affecting them both physically and psychologically. One young woman told me of her desire to "wash the tacky contamina-tion of the street from her [entire] body" at the end of each day, while also observing how difficult it was even for her friends to avoid changing under the steady onslaught of visible corruptions. (She worked as a vendor on Patpong Road, the famous tourist bar and prostitute district in Bangkok.)

Yet vending has provided the first major entrance into the econ-omy for many urban deaf. Previously, the nonprofit financing of the self-representative body, the NADT, paid wages that were higher than had ever been available before, comparable to those of a mod-estly paid civil servant, but a smaller number of individuals were in-volved. Moreover, recent vendor income has been much higher. While NADT wages ranged between Baht 2,500 to 7,000 ($100–280) per month, mostly at the lower end of that scale, the street vendors have monthly earnings from about Baht 4,000 ($160), for a paid assistant, to Baht 12,000–15,000 ($480–600), for individual stall holders. Several multiple-stall owners are clearing in excess of Baht 100,000 ($4,000) per month in the high season. They dress and talk quite poor, however, to fend off the malice and revenge of their competitors. The current and past two presidents of the NADT are also stall owners on Patpong and Silom Roads.

As was noted at the outset, Deafness is a distinct ethnic identity and its members are prone to the same strengths and foibles, joys and sorrows, as any "normal" human community. While some ethnographic-like aspects of Deaf cultures will be examined, this is not the topic of the work. It is a study of exclusion and inclusion, of the availability and administration of acceptable identities, and about the construction of perceptions by which certain chosen differences "matter" more than others.

2
Hearing Deaf History

A telephone is ringing. A call to consciousness, to a sense of connection and one of disconnection. There is no such thing as one telephone. The ringing only proves that. No other technology born in a search for a missing other has done so much to exclude the other found. The telephone was invented to create speech for the deaf. Telephones and deafness: it is a story of ironies.

The reason I chose to call this chapter "Hearing Deaf History"[1] is that much of what is being pawned off as "Deaf history" sounds remarkably like narrative forms of Hearing history in which only the names and details of auditory status have been changed. Painting psychohistories of great men struggling to attain a place in the history of hearing civilizations has little or nothing to do with portraying the historical circumstances of Deaf people living on the margins of those hearing societies. Such Deaf history is a deception, merely reinvoking and reinscribing the domination and exclusions that have more often been known as the "markers" of Deaf peoples' historical experience.

Harlan Lane's *When the Mind Hears*[2] is a work that should be read by all who are interested in the circumstances of deafness in early America. Whether or not it should become the "origin" story of all Deaf history is a very different question, which raises the

1. A much earlier version of this section was presented to the Eleventh World Congress of the World Federation of the Deaf in Tokyo, 2–11 July 1991, and appears in the published proceedings. It was also published as "Die 'Deaf History' der Hörenden; oder: Strategien zur Rettung der Andersartigkeit," *Das Zeichen* 23.7 (1993): 14–19.
2. Lane 1984.

general problem with Western assumptions about the primacy of all things European and Western: the rest of the world has no history, except as the West deigns to provide it or as it originated in Europe.[3] So, as much as I respect the scholarship of Lane's work, I prefer a rather different reading of his text.

The work is highly readable, impeccably footnoted, and an important addition to scholarship about events in Deaf history. It has been very popular, in part because of its narrative style. For a community in need of and ever eluded by origin narratives—a description that equally well fits all late-modern humanity—Lane's pious morality play features both the oppressions widely perceived by deaf people in their own dealings with hearing societies and the nobility of some of the finer efforts to resist or surmount such exclusions and rejections. The book's confident voice soothes readers with the psychological reassurance of both a wholeness ultimately available and the natural strength of resistance to perceived injustice, offering great inspiration for a telos of recovery of pure origins. The appeal, however, is part of the problem. Lane's reproduction of so many kitsch forms of social order and so many restrictions slides by inadequately questioned, as the book remains complicit with too many other social injustices.

When the Mind Hears is a type of work that Michael J. Shapiro would call a "pious biography,"[4] a work infused with the saint-making language of religious hagiography. With pious awe, the long road of hardship endured is seen to have been strewn with signs or markers of the greatness to come. This allegory or morality play also seeks to be an origin story: the genesis of "where it all began," in an unsullied past to be reclaimed. It is less like the Bible, in which the hand of God is seen in markers big and small, than like the saga of a typical American frontier hero, which emphasizes the strength of individual character. Struggle, forbearance, perseverance, destiny: it's a great plot line. It sells well. Surely, the epic film version will be forthcoming.

3. See Wolf 1982; see also Bhabha 1994.
4. See Shapiro 1988.

The processing of history into myth—and myth into history—is a traditional accoutrement of popular mobilization. Perhaps Shapiro's treatment of Benjamin Franklin's autobiography will provide a useful illustration. The correspondence surrounding Franklin's decision to write an autobiography clearly documents that he was encouraged to cast himself as an ideal model to form the appropriate American character. Beyond just exemplifying the ideal character, the work was meant to valorize the context within which such a character ought to function. In short, the autobiography was constructed as no less than as an advertisement for America. As one of Franklin's friends advised: "All that has happened to you, is also connected with detail of the manners and situations of a rising people." It is important that the social structure of America at that time and the opportunities for success were presented as just and fair, in no way excluding those not well situated to take advantage of those opportunities. In other words, the autobiography also served as an apology for the wide range of social injustices that were thus rendered silent and invisible.

The parallel with Lane's pseudo-autobiography of Laurent Clérc as instantiating the biography of a rising people is clear. Like the Franklin biography, it is a first-person narrative about success and about the importance of hard work and perseverance in achieving it. Like other "destiny narratives," the story treats every episode in a life as a sign of future achievement and of a great people being born.[5] While the background of the struggles for sign language rights is well presented, the story questions no other aspect of social relations between Gallaudet and Clérc, or between society and its Deaf members. At best, Lane's treatment of Deaf history reproduces the standard pieties of a dominant social order, though in the guise of a story of struggle against a particular aspect of that social order.

I would also add that as an "origin story," it reproduces the usual Euro-American perspective, which suggests that the history that comes from Europe is the only history that matters. Not only is Deaf history seen as dependent upon the attention of the Hearing to

5. Ibid., p. 57.

"discover" and script it, but also those discoverers must be the Hearing of Europe and North America. In certain quarters of the developing world, these notions of Deaf history are simply more examples of the colonial violence by which the West denies the very existence or history of "third world" peoples.

One can say that there are two types of biographies, or rather two points on a spectrum. At one end there are biographies that support the management of various control- and allegiance-producing institutions; at the other end are those that provoke thought about the existing system of truth or about the political power and authority systems that these truths support.[6] In other words, some biographies paint vividly scenic backdrops for the heroic sagas they tell. Others point at the details of oppression such rosy backdrops paint over, generally laughing at the grand sagas as pompous, pious, and very self-serving. My sympathies are largely with this second camp.

Hence, my critique of Deaf history starts with a different view than the usual story of origins. I see in the tale of the Abbé de l'Épée an attempt to present some sort of Santa Claus to the Deaf, who brings with him the attention, the surveillance, the administrations of and by the Hearing. This was a gift? Actually, it is more useful to see the Abbé de l'Épée as a kind of Christopher Columbus on a voyage to "discover" the Deaf World. In employing this metaphor, I borrow from Tzvetan Todorov's demonstration that the "New World" was not so much discovered as imaginatively preconstituted by the Spanish conquistadors. What was already there was a source of gold for wealth and a source of souls for the church. What was required was a justification for the exploitation of both. Columbus found the balance in an assumed reciprocity: he and his men would bring religion and take gold.

Todorov shows clearly how the beliefs Columbus held about the world influenced his interpretations. He compares the two sides of Columbus's character, both navigator in search of truth and interpreter who confirms truth presumed in advance.[7] This duality is par-

6. Ibid., p. 65.
7. Todorov 1984, p. 19.

ticularly evident in the discovery of Cuba, which, for Columbus, had to be Asia. "He has his conviction, namely that the island of Cuba is a part of the continent [Asia], and he decides to eliminate all information tending to prove the contrary."[8] When contrary evidence does appear, Columbus discounts the source of the information. This has also been the standard practice of Hearing interest in the Deaf since the Abbé de l'Épée: search for the "truth" known in advance and discount the sources of any contradictory evidence. Like the "Indians" before them, the Deaf have routinely been dismissed as a possible source of accurate information, in addition to being routinely rounded up and excluded for administrative convenience.

The most significant component of the contact narrative regards Columbus's own views of language and, consequently, of the Caribs. In one passage, Todorov examines the relationship between these two understandings. On the first voyage, Columbus writes of his desire to take six Caribs back to Europe "so that they may learn to speak," which, Todorov notes, shocked his translators in Europe sufficiently that each later "corrected" the text.[9] But Columbus consistently refused to believe that the "Indians" (as they were imagined by the Spaniards) even had a language that was their own. Todorov presents Columbus's choices when confronted with a foreign language: to recognize it as language, but not different, or to acknowledge its difference, but not admit it is language. These views, of course, are remarkably similar to the attitudes of some educators of the deaf. Sign languages are most often considered by hearing officials either to be only a manual form of the dominant spoken language or to be a set of gestures, pantomime, or semaphore signals without distinct linguistic status.

Columbus continued to use the evidence before him to confirm the ideas he wished, regardless of how contradictory it may have been. Indeed, Columbus was torn, because those ideas themselves were contradictory. He needed to see the Indians as similar to the Europeans, so that they could adopt the customs he brought, most

8. Ibid., p. 21.
9. Ibid., p. 30.

particularly Christianity. At the same time, he needed to see them as different, so that a relationship of superiority-inferiority could be used to justify exploiting the wealth he sought.[10] The relationship sounds familiar to most Deaf activists.

Todorov finds the perceptions and attitude of Columbus essentially similar to the modern relations between colonist and the colonized. There is in his description an echo of Homi Bhabha, who applies a Hegelian master-slave structure to colonialism and notes that the "ambivalence of colonial authority repeatedly turns from mimicry—a difference that is almost nothing but not quite; to menace—a difference that is almost total but not quite."[11] The master-slave relationship, like the Hearing dominance of the Deaf, restricts the subordinate to a simplistic contrast between the mimic, which might be called a quality counterfeit, and the menace, an "otherness" so very threatening . . . except for (because of) the vague resemblance.

This contrasting construction, as different and the same, recurs in issues raised throughout much of the discourse of otherness and difference. The question of "passing," a strategy of safe passage by which codes of assimilation with a dominant culture or other are assumed, is fraught with ambivalence and tension. The question of belonging, be it either to the dominant culture or to the self-identified community of an excluded group, is under constant negotiation. To pass may be necessary in certain instances, yet it appears to be achieved at the price of an ethnic death,[12] a denial. This "achievement" is part of the paradox of identity.

As with other minority or self-identified communities, Deaf people must struggle with coping strategies that, though unsatisfactory, may be needed to fulfill short-term requirements. The perpetual question for each deaf individual is not how "hearinglike" he or she is, but how successfully does that person negotiate each

10. Ibid., p. 45.
11. Bhabha 1984, pp. 125–33; see also Bhabha 1994, chap. 4 (quote from p. 91).
12. See Quintanales 1983.

encounter with hearing institutions and with hearing people, with and without authority. The acceptability of different coping strategies is debated within Deaf culture. Nevertheless, the dualism of mimic and menace frequently frames each negotiation in ways that never allow any adequate purchase on identity outside that limiting framework.

As Columbus found, the contrast is a conflict. Either they are human, or they are different. If they are human, then they are not only equivalent but the same as (the dominant) "us." This leads to an assimilation that both denies and crushes difference. So, they are different. But it is a difference understood as inferiority, which legitimates their exploitation and marginalization. Both, as Todorov points out, are based on an egocentric "identification of our own values with values in general, of our I with the universe."[13] In neither case is a distinct otherness, a difference that is not a mirror image or imperfect copy, acceptable or possible. The "history" of the hearing "discovery" and colonization of the deaf is directly analogous here. As was true of the Europeans in their conquest of the Americas, the hearing assume their values to be universal; there is no place for values that presume deafness.

I present this contrast as an elaborate gesture to put huge quotation marks around the Abbé de l'Épée's "discovery" of the world of the Deaf. All that was really "discovered" or of interest was the mentality of the dominant hearing society of that time. The Deaf provided a wonderful opportunity for the Abbé de l'Épée to enter the public discussion of popular theories about the origins of language and about the "natural state" of man. European society of the day was fascinated with these questions. The Hearing were interested in the Deaf only as a reflection of themselves; there was little interest in Deafness or in Deaf people. The gift of the Abbé de l'Épée to the Deaf was, as noted above, attention, examinations, discipline, surveillance, administration, and colonization by the Hearing.

This appropriation sought grounds for conversion, and conver-

13. Todorov 1984, p. 42.

sion is at the core of Deaf history. That which is now called "history" begins with the first efforts at conversion; what precedes is only "prehistory." This conversion was not only religious, sought by a priest, but linguistic, as he tried to create the first manual code of the written language—a far more significant conversion, which is still being contested. It must be deemed "successful" in that "deaf history" now almost exclusively comprises its moments. While the Abbé de l'Épée never denied that the deaf were communicating among themselves using already existing signs, the historical narratives have found it generally convenient to mark the "beginning" of sign language from the date of his first artificial replica or simulacrum, a manually encoded version of the hearing language.

This legacy, as indirectly described in Lane's *When the Mind Hears,* is carried forward by the champions of the following generations, Thomas Gallaudet and Laurent Clérc, who deliver it unto the New World: a new identity. The genesis is claimed. It is a new birth: the "origin" of Deaf culture. This particular idea of Deaf culture and the current notions of Deaf identity would appear to be the end product of a progression that began when deaf children were rounded up and placed in the asylum. In France, this isolation of the deaf was part of a major seventeenth-century social movement— "the Great Confinement"—to confine a wide range of those labeled as deviant.[14] From the asylum to the institution to the school, the ultimate goal was to produce a deaf person acceptable to the dominant society.

The asylum. The institution. The school. Deaf identity. Does Deaf history recount the success of this progression—or is it about the margins where control has failed? Isn't Deaf history really about the small land wars at the margins of society and self-identity, exactly where the Hearing administrations of the Deaf through these institutions don't quite succeed in controlling or suppressing Deafness? Isn't Deaf history more about the resistances to subjugation and oppression than about the success of the institutions into which Hearing people put Deaf people?

14. See Foucault 1965.

A Genealogy of Deaf Identity

In order to better address such questions, I would like to examine certain themes that have remained fairly consistent in the Hearing domination and administration of Deaf people since their historic "discovery" by the Abbé de l'Épée. Like Christopher Columbus before them, the Hearing who "discovered" the Deaf did not recognize the meaningful difference in the ways of being and the unique languages of the Deaf; rather, they moved to appropriate that difference for Hearing purposes, simultaneously denying its significance to the Deaf. There is a consistency that underlies the Hearing administration of Deaf people, regardless of the policies or methods they have pursued—even those ends and means that seem directly opposed.

Thus I find the great "oral-manual debate" to have been—and to remain today—an argument primarily between two camps of the Hearing that seek the same goal: the creation of a Deaf identity acceptable and convenient to Hearing social and administrative concerns. Below, I have laid out the broader categories by which the Hearing administration of Deaf lives since the time of the Abbé de l'Épée may be more critically understood.

Production and Administration of Deaf Identity

Traditional	Modern/mainstream
1. Separation (from society)	Separation (from their peers)
2. Isolation (as a type and group)	Isolation (from each other)
3. Denial by exclusion	Denial by dispersal
4. Objects of Christian salvation	Objects of scientific inquiry

The side marked "traditional" should be easily recognized as the historical experience most often associated with being Deaf. Beginning with the Abbé de l'Épée and his successors, Deaf people were rounded up and placed into institutions, first called asylums and later called schools. The institutionalization was seen, in part, as a means for society to control those who were different. This separation also "protected" society from contact with those deemed "afflicted." Saving souls was another accepted, and profitable, reason given; it satisfied dominant assumptions about a direct link between speech and divinity while aiding in the competition for the nobility's lucrative patronage.

Deaf culture, as a product of the Deaf institutions, was an accident: an unintended and undesired result. It was certainly not planned by those who set up the institutions, and much of the second column demonstrates Hearing administrative attempts to control those unintended results. The goal, if not the practice, remains the same: to suppress and deny the meaning and significance of difference.

The other side of this chart, marked for convenience as "modern/mainstream," shows the current approach to managing Deaf people. For this "successful" refinement, we should credit Alexander Graham Bell, who recognized that segregating Deaf people from society produced side effects—well-adjusted, fluent, and intelligent signers who preferred to choose their friends from others like themselves. Therefore, reasoned Bell and his associates, Deaf people should be separated: not from society, as had been the practices of the institutions, but from each other.[15]

The second line is closely related to the first: separation achieves isolation. It was commonly believed that society needed protection from "infection" by social ills that difference usually implied. This was also a period of public obsession with manners, with proper dress and behavior. Hence, Deaf people were seen both as "undesirable" and without social "refinements" in behavior. Arden Neisser's observations about oralism mirror the public obsessions of this period:

Oralism was a nineteenth-century idea, with its enthusiasm for apparatus, its confidence in the future of technology. It was reinforced by the Protestant ethic of hard work, unremitting practice, and strength of character to overcome all of life's afflictions. It flourished in the framework of Victorian manners (and Victorian science), and reflected a deep Anglo-Saxon antagonism toward all languages other than English. (Bilingualism was considered bad for the brain.) Oralism was consolidated during that period in history when the Welsh language was banned from schools in Wales; when

15. Bell 1884; see also Bell 1898.

Victoria as Empress of India made English the administrative language of the subcontinent; and when the great immigrations began, bringing foreign languages and cultures to America. Ties among English speakers were strong and there was a movement to standardize the tongue. The model for Victorian gentility was an immobile one, and a large part of "teaching the English how to speak" was directed at the elimination of gestures. Gesturing was something that Italians did, and Jews, and Frenchmen; it reflected the poverty of their cultures and the immaturity of their personalities. Sign language became a code word with strong racial overtones. It was seen as a foreign system, the invention, moreover, of a medievalist French priest.[16]

The segregation and social training of deaf children were seen as socially desirable goods by the enlightened among the Hearing. Society was protected from contact with this contaminant, and the Deaf were given the "opportunity" to improve themselves. Deaf education has long focused almost exclusively on behavioral training to produce Deaf people acceptable to Hearing society, although these institutional goals are rarely stated so explicitly.

As social shifts led to economic and administrative reasons to "deinstitutionalize" inmates of asylums and residential institutions, the unintended results of group isolation of Deaf people (that is, intelligent and articulate Deaf people) became more visible. This visibility, coupled with Alexander Graham Bell's and others' belief in eugenics—that movement to "improve" the human species through controlled breeding—lent support to a new demands to "re-isolate" Deaf people, but now from each other rather than from society.[17] This isolation has not yet been fully achieved through what we know as "mainstreaming," although it has been relatively "effective."

The desired separation can be achieved in more than one way. For the oralist, mainstreaming has a broader goal: deaf children will "pass" as hearing, thus becoming "acceptable" as hearinglike persons. Nevertheless, separate oral-only schools may still be required to accomplish this goal. "Separation from each other" may also be gained, despite physical proximity, by highly restricting options for

16. Neisser 1983, pp. 29–30.
17. Bell 1884.

communication. *Separation for the purpose of creating sameness is mainstreaming; separation in recognition of unique difference is not.*[18]

The general theme of "isolation" is heavily deployed, as "the tragedy of isolation" often appears as a dramatic image of some cruel and horrible fate inherent to deafness. This was and still is used by medical and institutional authorities to justify policies, including invasive surgical experimentation, that forcibly accommodate the deaf child to hearing social needs. This theme has played well from the financial standpoint of these interests, even when their efforts result only in an enforced isolation of a different type.[19]

The meanings of deafness are rooted in social relations, and most social relations are clearly dominated by institutions and technologies that assume hearing. Certainly I am excited by moves to fashion more positive social relations that assume, or even emphasize, Deafness. Such are among the most affirming practices of proclaiming "D" (uppercase) forms of Deaf cultures. These forms can and should be centered on and explored for possible distinctions unique to Deaf social relations. Still, these relations are heavily burdened by the historical contexts in which Deaf identities have emerged, as outlined above. Nor does the denial of coping strategies labeled "d" (lowercase) aid the discussion, as such a denial locates the meaning of difference in the individual rather than in the social relationships in which individual actions are set.

It is a stark dualism—good Deaf, bad deaf—that does little to help individuals in their daily lives. Nor does it help illuminate the wider range of strategies employed by individuals coping with exclusion and the many faces of oppression in their daily lives. In simple terms, the dichotomy of "d/D" is so crudely drawn that, while initially useful, it now serves to silence the full range of d/Deaf people's

18. See chapter 6 for further discussion.

19. "Ideally, the Clarke School [a famous oral-only school for the deaf] expects that all their graduates will associate exclusively with the hearing. In addition to their historic hope of improving the gene pool, these associations are seen as providing deaf adults with continuous opportunities for practicing their oral skills, thus turning friendships between deaf and hearing into permanent speech therapy situations" (Neisser 1983, p. 128).

experiences. It also plays into a strategy of domination by pitting Deaf people against deaf people as these labels are actively policed.

Historically the management of Deaf identity has thus shifted between two contrasting but related strategies. In the traditional approach, which began with their "discovery" by hearing people, deaf people were excluded and isolated from society as a group. Though a distinct Deaf identity was denied through removal from society, it was facilitated through this physical warehousing of deaf people together. In the modern approach, exclusion and isolation are achieved through dispersal—by mainstreaming, a watering down of the group identity in order to deny the unintended results that isolation as a type has produced: the "accident" of Deaf culture.

Here again we might observe that the motivations of the conquistadors and of the "discoverers" of Deaf people seem not so very different, nor do they seem very different today. While conquering missionaries sought to save souls to justify the stealing of gold, the Abbé de l'Épée sought a pious justification for his use of Deaf people both to demonstrate popular theories of language origins and to curry royal favor and public popularity. He achieved that popularity only late in life with his public displays of Jean Massieu, the predecessor to Laurent Clérc.

It is an open question whether today's scientific examinations seek to "save" Deaf culture's "soul" in order to expropriate it as an object of curiosity or they simply seek "scientific facts." Yet for those tempted to feel better about the scientific agenda, I would repeat an old adage: You cannot begin as an object and hope to become a subject.[20] The object of the deaf body, as the site of scientific exploration, resonates with the colonization of subject peoples as well as with the use of laboratory animals for developing new technologies. As speech became synonymous with language, the search for the origins of language turned to the body of the deaf; medical researchers sought both to discover language's neurolinguistic source and to reproduce it via technological innovations applied to deaf ears.

---

20. Ms. Manfa Suwanarat, co-compiler of *The Thai Sign Language Dictionary*, reacted to this saying by noting, "Anyway, the verbs have all the fun."

But even in the theoretical framing of such medical research the desire has been not for language production but for language perception. Language has been identified less with speech than with hearing.

One of the skeletons in the closet of contemporary linguistics is that it has lavished attention on hearing but largely ignored speaking, which one might say was roughly half of language, and the most important half at that. Although there are many detailed theories and models of language perception, and of the comprehension of heard utterances (the paths from phonology, through syntax, to semantics and pragmatics), no one—not Noam Chomsky, and not any of his rivals or followers—has had anything very substantial (right or wrong) to say about systems of language production. It is as if all theories of art were theories of art appreciation with never a word about the artists who created it—as if all art consisted of objets trouvés appreciated by dealers and collectors.[21]

Here Daniel Dennett clearly rehearses the conflation of speech-plus-hearing as synonymous with language, but he also observes the lopsided approach within that limited frame. The scientific and medical research on the source of language became obsessed with the technological reproduction of hearing. Whether language might be produced or perceived through any other modality of cognitive perception is a question apparently left unasked. But no effort has been spared in the search for the source of language perception, whether those explorations sought the technical terrain of mechanical replication or the inner terrain of invasive surgical experimentation on the bodies of deaf children.

Identity, be it Deaf or any other, is not a discovery; it is an achievement in an exchange of discursive economies. Some aspects of our identities are easier to achieve than others. Many are produced and assigned by the society we inhabit as part of a broader system of exchange. Our differences are given meaning within a discursive economy that we are urged to know as "natural." One obvious example is gender, the socially constructed and established difference between male and female. But these constructions, be they gender

21. Dennett 1991, p. 231.

restrictions or normal/abnormal distinctions,[22] benefit certain interests at the expense of others and are not always accepted by
all—or even available to all. Other ways may ambiguate, and thus
threaten, accepted meanings. In such cases, the "achievement" of
identity, which sometimes is ambivalent, becomes more visible.

I believe that both Deaf history and Deaf identity are products
more of resistance than of accommodation to dominant social
meanings, though they remain dependent upon an interaction with
the dominant. But the grand stories of traditional Deaf history have
more to do with accommodation and assimilation than they do with
resistance, for in these versions the resistances serve only to legitimate the institutions that heroic figures established and have left behind. And, as I suggested earlier, these institutions are today still
serving very different purposes than those described in the great
stories.

I must observe that little of this terrain has been examined by
what Deaf history calls the "great debates." Whether the approaches
are oral, manual/signing, or total communication, whether the
schools are residential or mainstream, the basic administrative techniques and the achievements of Hearing productions of Deaf history
have been left untouched and continue in operation. Indeed, the
tradition of Deaf history has been a highly selective one; only certain
events and meanings are chosen for emphasis and celebration, while
others are neglected or excluded. These selected meanings and
events have been repackaged and are now presented as pious and
moral allegories, which further suggest that the social fabric in which
this selective tradition is placed is fundamentally fair and good. I
intend here to raise strong questions about this selectiveness.

Endearing Kitsch

The "standard" history of the deaf—that is, the narrative that is
passed off as history—is one of endearing kitsch. The story invariably begins in Paris of 1756 with the Abbé de l'Épée, "an ordinary,

---

22. See Minow 1990, chap. 5.

bookish, neighborhood priest, [who] simply took an interest in a small group of deaf children and began to instruct them. . . . A small school developed, grew, received a modest amount of royal support, and after the Revolution became the world-famous National Institution for Deaf-Mutes."[23] Quaint and pat, this is a heartwarming story, full of struggle and sacrifice, perseverance and achievement, disappointment and reward, triumph and tragedy. Yet its piety has more to do with the interests of the storytellers than with those of the supposed "subjects" of the story.

But there are two ways of telling this story. One is seemingly straightforward and factual, both in framing events that lead to discovery and in its logic, which produces the necessary means to educate and incorporate the previously downtrodden. It presents a one-way street, an inclusive vision for joining humanity with the help of goodness and essential human values. The medical model, a subject of many debates between disabled rights activists and rehabilitation professionals, falls under this heading.

The second way enjoins you to enter the perspective of the deaf others, both prior to their discovery and throughout the projected story of trials and tribulations along the path to gain entrance to the promised "world of the hearing," if not to the promised land. This play on words is not without its own irony, for these are not "landed" others who can, if only in an ontology of historical identity, be rooted in a place or in the search to return to one. Deafness as a location[24] might be understood only as a percentage—a relationship but not a place. Deaf ethnicity might be thus understood as an incidence ratio, an identity arrayed in time rather than space. While otherness is still about unequal relationships, "place" no longer plays a part, as it did for Columbus, in constructing absolute otherness.

It is in adhering to this key interpretive referent/anchor that Todorov's analysis of a sixteenth-century traumatic encounter differs from our considerations of identity formation at the end of the

23. Neisser 1983, p. 18.
24. In this usage, can we say that *hear/here* represents more than a homophone?

twentieth century.[25] Even in that earlier "place," any attempt at pure contextualism,[26] that entering into the internal perspective of a discovered people in order to perceive a pure understanding, is a strategy that provides only a mirror image of a previously one-way street. It seeks understanding so that a conversion might be more easily effected.

Deaf history is about such conversions, and it comprises the narratives of their desires. As we have seen, Deaf history only "begins" with the first efforts at conversion. Yet the "facts" of these histories do not pass entirely unchallenged, either within the internally privileged frame of facticity or from the external context of practices such facts have enabled. Appropriated and exploited for purposes entirely external to themselves, the deaf have been "silenced"[27] more than once and often given voices not their own. Authentic voices, in any sense of the phrase, are in short supply. Signs are plentiful, but the code by which the dominant readings might be challenged is unprivileged and disenfranchised. Still, the storytellers leave hints of how the threads of the tapestry might be rewoven, and further hints of how the new looms might be glimpsed. As was noted earlier, no liberations are promised, but the questions resonate deeply and in

25. As the notion of "place" becomes porous, it is useful to attend to the "epistemologies of purity" that Connolly reads from within Todorov's framing. He shows that the quest for purity in standards to contain an established structure of faith is delicate. The modernist exchange of image-rooted commodities and the location of information identities in the dataspace of the 1990s show remarkable parallels. These parallels are particularly visible in the very fragility and delicacy of their structures and foundations. In each case, the monumental efforts to sustain them become remarkable not because of the efforts expended but rather because the great expense is invisible to those most called upon to it. In the coming century, the same will be true of maintaining your citizen datafile. These relations will be further examined in chapter 5.

26. Connolly 1991, pp. 40–41.

27. Use of the term *silencing* to note the exclusion of other points of view is highly in vogue in academic circles. Given the heavy baggage of "silence"—so drearily applied to the "silent world of the deaf" and other such metaphors—becomes either hermeneutically rich with irony or epistemologically (and acoustically) misleading.

unsuspected arenas. They resonate in the political silence of sound knowledge. The narratives that pose these questions are worth a second look.

The history of the deaf is a "story of discovery" much like that of Columbus and the "New" World, in that it was partially a re-discovery, partially a conquest, and most certainly an appropriation. In his examination of the fifteenth-century encounter, William Connolly explores the limitations of the English terms available by which the relation between "discoverer" and "discovered" might be described.

The simple word "discovery," then, does not capture the relation between Columbus and the world he encountered. Neither does any other single word in English: words like "invention" and "constitution" give too much impetus to the initiating side; words like "dialogue" and "discourse" give too much to a mutual task of decipherment to promote common under-standing; words like "conquest" and "colonization" underplay the effects of the encounter upon the self-identities of the initiating power. All these words, in the common ranges of signification, reflect one or another of the epistemologies of purity; each projects a "regulative ideal" that seems to me not only unattainable but dangerous to invoke *in any simple or unam-biguous way*.[28]

The codes by which this newer appropriation was achieved alter-nate between the same codes of conquest and conversion deployed for understanding the "New" World. The code of conquest de-ployed with the deaf justified assaulting the "natural" state of man in order to discover the "civilized" man within. The code of conver-sion brought the word not to but from their previously soundless lips. As was true in the case of Columbus, these two codes have op-erated in tandem to appropriate the deaf for purposes other than their own. The ironic utility of deafness for the hearing is clear in several stories.

The histories recounted in even the most "sympathetic" and morally uplifting versions have been depoliticized and neutralized to deny the resistance and escape that have been crucial in produc-

28. Connolly 1991, pp. 37–38; emphasis in original.

ing those meager stories of "success" now proclaimed cheerily and piously by the discoverers. Both "history" and "discovery" are among the terms that routinely shift in meaning.

Two eighteenth-century thinkers should be mentioned as particularly relevant to these stories and to the historical positioning of visual/gestural language forms. One is J. G. Herder (1744–1803), who is generally considered the originator of sociolinguistics or, if one prefers, the key source from which later discussions of the relationship between language and identity flow.[29] The other is the Abbé de Condillac (1715–80), who studied with John Locke. Condillac, though almost forgotten in the academy today, wrote an essay on the origins of language that was taken very seriously during its time.[30] Herder produced an important critique of the designative nature of Condillac's argument; but Condillac's *Essay* provided the justification for the Abbé de l'Épée to establish the first asylum for the deaf in 1765, on the basis that Condillac's theory demonstrated language as sufficiently designative to be available for instruction to deaf-mutes. The theory fit the common perception of deaf-mutes as being totally without other forms of language. The public experiments conducted to demonstrate these ideas turned on two distinct notions: the "original nature" of man, which fed popular fascinations with civilized destiny, and the Christian salvation of souls previously thought "lost" without the Word of God. Each of these found expression in the desire for the forbidden experiment.

The Forbidden Experiment

Itard sensed that the Wild Boy was not an idiot but a special kind of missing link, a creature in whom one could observe how a human being may fail to develop into a socialized adult because of lack of stimulus. If this "animal" or "infant" could be restored to the human capacities of his age level, then the tabula rasa theory of learning would gain persuasive proof. Itard

29. J. G. Herder, *Treatise on the Origin of Language* (1772).

30. Abbé de Condillac, *An Essay on the Origin of Human Knowledge: Being a Supplement to Mr. Locke's "Essay on the Human Understanding"* (1746). His collected works comprised twenty-three volumes.

believed that he had stumbled upon the possibility of performing a crucial experiment—in effect, the forbidden experiment.
    —Roger Shattuck, *The Forbidden Experiment*

On January 9, 1800, a naked boy, whose every action suggested an animal more than a human, was captured near the village of Saint-Sernin in southern France.[31] He appeared to be about twelve and could not speak. He had apparently survived in the wilderness of the region, through several harsh winters, for five or six years. Due to the precise yet coincidental timing of his appearance, occurring when it did at the end of the eighteenth century and birth of the nineteenth, he would become a phenomenon of passionate fascination to the minds of his age. Like many other subjects—and objects—of knowledge exploration, he would die in obscurity, abandoned when he no longer appeared likely to prove the great theories of that age. Yet the disciplines erected around him and tested on him continue today, both in special education for "learning disabled children" and in teaching methods such as those used in Montessori preschools around the world.

The newly discovered Wild Boy seemed to be the perfect example, or case, that might provide the missing evidence of the natural state of man. From all appearances, nature itself had delivered up the long-desired product of the "forbidden experiment"—the experiment that would "separate an infant very early from its mother and let it develop in nature, with no human contact, no education, no help."[32] The underlying motive for conducting such an experiment is to validate speech as the "natural source" of language. Montaigne wrote, "I believe that a child brought up in complete solitude, far from all intercourse (which would be a difficult experiment to carry out), would have some kind of speech to express his ideas, for it is not likely that nature would deprive us of this resource when she has given it to many other animals. . . . But it is yet to be found out what language the child would speak; and what has been conjectured

31. Much of the brief story of the Wild Boy in this section is taken from Shattuck's *Forbidden Experiment* (1980).
32. Shattuck 1980, p. 44.

about it has no great probability." [33] As will be seen, the discovery of the Wild Boy was timely, in more ways than one.

The experiment had been tried before. Herodotus reports that in the seventh century B.C., the Egyptian pharaoh Psamtik isolated two infants in a mountain hut to be cared for by a servant. Since the purpose of the experiment was to find out what language men speak "naturally," without education, the servant was instructed on pain of death not to talk to his charges. The first reported utterance was the Phrygian word for bread. Shattuck wryly observes, "We are not told what language the servant spoke—or refrained from speaking." [34] The Holy Roman Emperor Frederick II repeated the experiment, also in hopes of discovering man's "natural language." The children died before producing any recognizable speech. And a third trial is said to have been made in the early sixteenth century by King James IV of Scotland, wanting to demonstrate the ancient origins of his country. As predicted—and presumably arranged—the Scottish children began to speak "very good Hebrew." [35]

All this, of course, was before the Papal Bull of 1537 declaring the "savages" of the New World to be human and thus worth converting to Christianity. It was also before the advent of the Enlightenment notions that were fueling the interests of European society at the beginning of the nineteenth century. Moreover, those interests remain and have inspired numerous films, plays, and books celebrating the "case" of the Wild Boy of Aveyron. The best of the films is François Truffaut's 1970 *The Wild Child* (*L'Enfant sauvage*), in which Truffaut plays Itard, acting for the first time in one of his own films. Roger Shattuck's *Forbidden Experiment: The Story of the Wild Boy of Aveyron* (1980) and Harlan Lane's *Wild Boy of Aveyron* (1976) also present this story of the most famous of a brief series of "wild" or "feral" children discovered in late-eighteenth-century Europe, when fascination with the origins of language and the natural state of man was most intense.

33. Montaigne, *Essays* 2 : 12; quoted in Shattuck 1980, p. 44 n.
34. Shattuck 1980, p. 44.
35. Ibid., pp. 43–44.

The popular press of the day covered the progress of these feral children—and the deaf students of the Abbé de l'Épée. It is more than coincidence that the institution to which this most famous of the feral children was assigned shared the grounds with the first asylum for deaf-mutes, the National Institute for Deaf-Mutes in Paris. The "study" of the Wild Boy presents a portrait (in its representational form) of the foundations of special education. It is yet another origin story whose piety serves more than one function.

Powerful ironies emerge from the relation among "Victor" (as the Wild Boy was called for only a few years before again being known simply as "the savage"), the search for language origins and the natural state of man, and the deaf children with whom he shared an institution and with whom he was allowed almost no contact. The Wild Boy never learned to speak. He could apparently hear, but he responded only to the few sounds that ever interested him. He could produce sounds, but he never uttered a complete sentence. He made what was considered remarkable progress in written communication through methods that are still in use.

Nevertheless, when he failed to learn speech, or to speak at all, after five years of effort, Itard abandoned him. While an "action language" of simple pantomime served well for basic interaction, great labor had gone into those years of attempting to make him speak. *Speech became the sole measure of Victor's "humanity."* When he failed, he was given into the care of the servant housekeeper in a small house nearby and allowed a simple pension; he then disappears from history. He died without note some twenty years later in that same little house near the great institute.

One of the most remarkable ironies of this story is that the Wild Boy was never instructed in sign language nor allowed the opportunity to interact with the hundreds of deaf youths his own age who lived within the same greater institutional compound to test whether signing would have opened a channel for further communicative advances, or indeed whether he would have benefited from the increased social interaction. Here is another lesson from that period still relevant today: this remarkable propensity to exclude an obvious option immediately at hand, in the several senses of the phrase, continues in practice without sufficient reflection or justification.

The empiricism of Locke and Condillac greatly inspired this period, particularly in the area of reform. If physical circumstances form or determine human life, then changes in those circumstances will result in changes in those lives. These efforts were now guided not by Christian charity but by philosophical beliefs about how humans develop into "civilized beings." The reformists who entered into the insane asylums—in particular the man sometimes called the first psychiatrist, Dr. Philippe Pinel[36]—also noted one group of misfits, often confined with the insane, who deserved different treatment: the deaf-mutes. "Reform could not heal their physical flaw, but a new environment in which they could use a sign language of their own would restore them to a place in society."[37]

Whether the Wild Boy could have signed is less significant here than the events that brought him to such rapid prominence and the lingering obsession with speech as the source of language. The story of the Wild Boy of Aveyron is a narrative of the efforts and the codified methods of Dr. Jean-Marc Gaspard Itard. It is not about Itard himself but about the presumptions made, the institutions erected based on those presumptions, and their subsequent endurance. The institutions in place still generally acknowledge their descent from Itard's written works.

Itard was a student of Philippe Pinel and, like many of his peers, was intellectually influenced by the political theories of Locke and Condillac. Condillac had personally praised the Abbé de l'Epée for his work in training deaf-mutes in sign language. Itard was a medical intern of twenty-five when he came to the National Institute for Deaf-Mutes in Paris. He was working at a hospital nearby and decided to respond to a posted position to aid with the "savage boy" recently arrived in Paris and placed into the institute. The Abbé Sicard, successor to the Abbé de l'Epée, had declared the Wild Boy an "imbecile" and wanted no part of him. But the minister of the

36. Pinel (1745–1826) is a legendary figure in the emergence of the field known as medical psychology.
37. Shattuck 1980, p. 59.

interior, Napoleon's brother, had placed him there with a stipend, so an assistant was sought.

Itard was armed with Locke's and Condillac's theory "that we are born with empty heads and that our ideas arise from what we perceive and experience."[38] Condillac, in particular, had used the imagery of a statue being brought to life by sense impressions. This resonated well with older myths: "He [Itard] had become Pygmalion, the legendary King of Cyprus who fell in love with the ivory statue he was carving. In answer to his prayers, the gods turned the statue into a beautiful living maiden, whom Pygmalion named Galatea. Itard's scientific and emotional attraction to the Wild Boy must have been powerful. He was drawn to the black sheep, to the stone the builders rejected. Here was a lost soul to be rescued."[39]

The timing of the "discovery" of the Wild Boy was crucial in determining both his meaning to those who discovered him and his significance in the development of institutional methods of treatment and education. Yet the coincidental nature of that timing carried further irony. The end of the eighteenth century found France, as well as much of Europe, exhausted from a period of great upheaval. The French Revolution and the subsequent Reign of Terror were past, but the struggle to constitute a new order was not yet complete. In December 1799, Napoleon Bonaparte took over the government of France without bloodshed, and voter approval of Napoleon's constitution was overwhelming. With the restoration of civil liberties, a group of sixty scholars, doctors, explorers, and naturalists founded the Society of Observers of Man. It was only several weeks later that the story of the Wild Boy, the "Savage of Aveyron," appeared in the press. As Shattuck puts it, "He had come on stage just as the eye of the storm passed over."[40]

38. Ibid., p. 73.
39. Ibid., p. 75. I would add that "the stone the builders rejected" is a key metaphor in Enlightenment traditions. It was based on the legend of the keystone for the sacred vault of King Solomon's temple, wrought by a worthy fellow of craft, which was first rejected but later recovered.
40. Ibid., p. 50.

In the calm of that storm Victor would surge to fame, yet he would die in obscurity. But the "forbidden experiment" lives on in the late twentieth century in the notions of oralism and hearing sciences for educating the deaf.[41] Deferring any other channel or modality of information to the deaf child is little different than putting the child with the herder and demanding no words ever be spoken, so that we might see if the "natural" will be discovered through some spontaneous emergence. It is but the old experiment in new and modern garb.

Don't the medical research and surgeries undertaken on deaf children attempting to recreate sensations of sound that might resemble, but which admittedly do not match, "hearing" further promise that which cannot yet be delivered, that which is still only a promise? Isn't the hope, and its scientific rationalization, rooted in the same desire that drove Herodotus to banish the child to the shepherd's hut?

Language and the "Natural" State of Man

Crucial legacies of Itard's study of Victor—both the philosophy of language that informed it and the institutional structure that emerged from it—remain, essentially unchanged, in the politics of Deafness and in Deaf education today. Arguably, the fully distinct French Sign Language (LSF) that developed in this asylum was an accident, an accident resulting from the warehousing of so many deaf people and having nothing to do with de l'Épée's intention to demonstrate the validity of Condillac's theories of language. Yet Condillac's discursive framework has tenaciously continued to inform the political struggles between Deaf people and those who still seek to administrate them.

The "Great Communications Debate," in a somewhat simplified reading, takes place entirely within the framework left by Condillac's

41. For example, the College of Social and Behavioral Sciences of Ohio State University has a Division of Hearing Science.

theory, although the perspective of Deaf leaders toward the issues is very much expressivist, in the tradition of the language theorist Charles Taylor.[42] More precisely, it is not so much Condillac's direct legacy as the institutional imperatives lingering from his work and the work of de l'Épée that constitute the terrain upon and within which the argument is still being pursued. The "great debate" refers both to the larger running war between advocates of sign language and advocates of speech for the deaf, which began with l'Épée and Condillac, and also, as noted earlier, to the specific feud or rivalry at the end of the nineteenth century between Alexander Graham Bell (of telephone fame) and Edward Miner Gallaudet (son of the founder of the first permanent school for the deaf in the United States, the American Asylum for the Deaf, and himself the founder of Gallaudet University), which was widely followed in the popular press of the day.[43]

Deaf historians (and historians of the Deaf) writing about the teaching methods of l'Épée have nearly always acknowledged, if only in passing, that his approach is profoundly inappropriate for understanding the distinct attributes of sign language, but gratitude that he created the first formal school always overrides a deeper examination of the conflict inherent in his philosophy. It is worth further noting that these historians also fail to mark the shift from "asylum" to "school," at best merely footnoting that the first schools for the Deaf in America were also called asylums.

Condillac, as Herder points out, assumes an original relationship between expression and its signification; that is, he assumes it is already understood what it is for a word to stand for something. Herder argues that a reflective awareness is necessary for, in fact inseparable from, language: words must come first. The interesting historical detail is that the Abbé de l'Épée had several very successful Deaf pupils who became highly literate, developed clear enunciation (as opposed to speech per se), and were renowned throughout Europe. Jean Massieu, the most famous of these students, was seen as

42. See Taylor 1987.
43. See Winefield 1987.

proof of Condillac's theory, as he had been found deaf—meaning he had had no language as it was philosophically understood—but had been given language and the enunciation skills so important to the understanding of language. But Massieu in fact proved little; for though he had been illiterate and speechless, he was very clever, and his own careful observations had formed his understanding of the function of language. His performances for the royal and noble courts of Europe were carefully scripted to support the favored theories—and to gain fortune for his teacher. His own writings, and more particularly those of his brightest deaf student, Laurent Clérc,[44] gave a very different picture of this process than that presumed by their "benefactors."

The great utility of the "discovery" of the Deaf by the hearing priest, and their later colonization by Alexander Graham Bell, was to produce the telephone. As part of an intriguing analysis of language and desire in Bell's relationships with his deaf mother and deaf wife, Avital Ronell notes, "The telephone was borne up by the invaginated structures of a mother's deaf ear."[45] But while this may have been the first of the telecommunication technologies to be borne up from the body of the deaf, it will not, judging by current experimental surgery, be the last. Like the fertile land "discovered" by the Christian explorers to be taken from the pagan natives, the fertile terrain of deaf bodies was also "discovered" by Christians and later appropriated for commercial exploitation. These linkages are further explored in chapter 5.

The great utility of the discovery enacted by Columbus was to initiate ownership of the continent. Relying on laws repudiating even its own claim to legitimacy, the United States has never renounced the claim to colonial ownership of America, the sole legitimacy of which was rooted in Old Norman law.[46] When the United

44. Laurent Clérc was the Deaf Frenchman who, together with Thomas Gallaudet, founded Deaf education in America. Note that the hearing guy got the university named after him. The deaf guy, Clérc, got a statue on the campus grounds . . .

45. Ronell 1989, p. 4. Ronell provides a Heideggerian and Freudian discussion of personal relations with the telephone in modernity.

46. Williams 1990, pp. 305–08.

Nations International Year of Indigenous People was declared, the date was deliberately postponed a year—to 1993—to avoid coinciding with the five hundredth anniversary of Columbus's first voyage to the "New World." Some ironies are simply too great to bear.

The "place" of deafness is one of irony. The policies that constrain education and social identity for people who are deaf present curious anomalies when contrasted with the treatment of almost any other difference found in societies. On examination, the ceaselessly vigorous suppression of this difference appears strangely archaic. At first, these policies may seem part of a "natural" response to a clear biological distinction. But the consistency of denial, the enormous efforts to constrain and forcibly modify the body, and the continuing refusal to allow those so defined and labeled as deaf to present their own claims to truth are oddly out of sync with the rest of the postcolonial, late-modern world. Almost no other social or physical difference is so thoroughly controlled through a policing so naturalized and so unnoticed by those not subject to its gaze. At a time when tolerance of a broad array of identity differences has become commonplace and even is promoted (though perhaps as a distraction from other social injustices), the intensive administration of deaf identity is unusual.

An entire industry of speech therapists and hearing aid salespeople, together with their medical alliances, prey upon the ignorance, fear, and emotions of parents who, discovering their child is deaf, will pay anything to remove that difference. Pay they do, yet the difference remains, however distorted by the interventions. "Oral" histories of the Deaf, more appropriately called "visual" histories, are filled with the bitterness of Deaf adults at their treatment as children by medical "experts," at denials of their deafness, and at the stunted educational curriculum that results from oralism.

Yet this network of encoded interests, although key to enforcing denial and parasitic upon it, is not the most significant construction upon the body of deafness. Our understandings of language and communication technology have needed a convenient other to appropriate. Like the otherness confronted and invented by sixteenth-century Christians, this form of otherness is "often constituted as the innocent to be converted, the amoralist to be excommunicated, or the indispensable Jew to be enclosed in a ghetto and used occasionally as a counter to consolidate consensus within the canon."[47]

The history of deafness is one of appropriation by the hearing. Those aspects of deafness not appropriated were further relegated to the category of the insane, both as a means to further ignore inconvenient details and as another indirect form of appropriation.[48] The history of deafness has been sometimes referred to as the escape from classification with the feeble-minded and the insane.[49] While that description is partially correct, this study seeks also to point to other details of that history it leaves out.

The colonization of deafness by the hearing represents an enormous investment in particular worldviews and in the technologies that further create and sustain such views. Here, as with all heavy infrastructural or colonial investments, divestment and decolonization deeply threaten established interests.

47. Connolly 1991, p. 39.
48. See Foucault 1965.
49. Neisser 1983, p. 281.

3

A Curious Place for a Colony

"Mr. Ness, Mr. Ness. You put Capone away, and now we hear they're gonna repeal Prohibition. What will you do now?"
"I think I'll have a drink."
—The Untouchables

Reinscribing Colonialism

Eliot Ness was seemingly able to accept a fundamental shift in worldview in midstride. Few of us are as poised or willing to make such shifts so readily. The shift from Prohibition, at least for a revenue enforcement officer, might suggest the old line, "Everything you know is wrong." Yet his loyalty to the juridical order itself provided a sufficient anchor in a sea of turbulent change. If the law now deemed it legal to have a drink, he was ready to have one.

Other events have demanded epistemic change without the benefit of such sure anchors. The discovery of the "New World" is one obvious instance of anchors being continually sought as the old ones were cut loose, but other events, some not so momentous, have also been significant. The telescope, for example, didn't itself lead to a major industry, but it helped create the foundation for the Industrial Revolution by offering a window into the invisible world of distant objects, thus changing our sense of humanity's place in the universe. The discovery of what were called "feral children" in the late eighteenth century evoked the myth of Romulus and Remus as they were proclaimed as new evidence of the "natural state of man." The recent emergence of human retroviruses invokes a new locus of surveillance of blood purity, sexuality, and the body.

Prohibition, Columbus, the telescope, a "wild boy" in Aveyron, and HIV/AIDS. Each changed humanity's view of the individual in relationship to the surrounding world. Each involved a reinscription of a dominating form of knowledge over a newly discovered "place." Though not the same, each disturbed and unsettled long-held convictions. Yet in every case the familiar readily reaches out to recolonize the unconventional.

Colonialism may be described as an unequal power relationship between two or more groups in which "one not only controls and rules the other but also endeavors to impose its cultural order onto the subordinate group(s)."[1] This colonialism, a relationship of duress, is produced in an economy of identities available to domination. The traditional geopolitical history of colonialism is a pious narrative that supports systems of dominance, authority, extraction, and marginalization. The heroic bits are good entertainment, but the whole is a misleading account that privileges particular interests. Such heroics presuppose their own need for security, while the menacing threat of some absolute other is an open call to central casting. Colonial history cannot be easily generalized, but there are central themes. Phillip Darby, in a study of British and American imperialism (1987), notes three primary motivations: power politics, moral responsibility, and economic interest. The goal of cultural reformation of those considered backward, inferior, or pathetic informs each of these motivations, which are further underscored by a politics of fear. Both cultural reform and fear resurface in the internal colonization of difference in modernity, particularly of the deaf.

The traditional history of colonialism presents its advance as an inevitable part of early industrial expansion and economic development. But, as Merry observes, the history of colonialism is being rewritten as "one of resistance and struggle. . . . In late nineteenth-century British thinking, advanced peoples had an obligation to help

1. Merry 1991, p. 894.

those less advanced, to provide guidance and instruction and even to rule them. . . . Nevertheless, there was constant resistance . . . , evasion, secret worlds of noncompliance."[2] Native cultures, or marginal cultures that would become nativist, found strength in the ambiguities such resistance and noncompliance made possible.

The emerging historical interest in such oppositional strategies in colonialism also serves to highlight similar strategies by marginalized peoples within contemporary dominant cultures. The depoliticizing language of social services, which focuses on structure and distribution rather than on the processes of oppression and domination, is being increasingly questioned. In particular, the constitutive nature of such depoliticized language is being rejected because it reflects only a particular economy of interests. The suppression of certain identities, exclusions driven by fears remaining from an earlier epoch, exemplifies the shifting as well as arbitrary value of specific differences and their meanings.

In *On the Genealogy of Morals* Nietzsche observes that we donate the world, then forget we were the donors.[3] We invent a fearful god; then live in fear. Having forgotten our earlier invention, we then explain our fear by inventing a god. Michael Shapiro makes use of Kakfa's story "The Burrow"[4] to denaturalize the politics of fear that fuel modern security and identity discourse. As he observes, "one cannot understand the contemporary, fear-driven discourse about 'national security' outside of the context of what is thought to be at stake, of 'who' it is that must be made secure." Its significance can be made known only through the politicized "questioning of the complex interrelations between a practice of inquiry and the historical practices out of which it emerges."[5] We (a dominant unnamed "we" of a hearing normative frame) learn to perceive speech—and its congenital root, hearing—as synonymous with language; we then diligently eradicate contrary evidence and those who might bear it.

2. Ibid., p. 896.
3. Nietzsche 1900.
4. Kafka 1971.
5. Shapiro 1992, pp. 125, 127.

The colonization of deafness and people who are deaf curiously persists in the shifting economies of identity. The conflation of widely varied physical distinctions as "disabilities" requires a health and medical model of difference. If deafness or other physical disability was not a mark of God, either of holy wrath or of disunity with a cosmic order, then it became the salient category in the medical-scientific way of knowing.[6] In that model, deafness is a naturalized category, but this categorization is coming under attack. These challenges insist that naturalization itself is a phenomenon with a history and a geography, and it cannot remain an unquestioned manifestation of "the natural order of things." This process of naming, conflating identity with an unambiguously defined body, becomes invisible when the act of making the distinction disappears and only the distinctions themselves remain. In this way boundaries, and the identities formed within them, take on an air of inevitability—it becomes possible to think of them as having no history and requiring no explanation, as simply "the way things are."[7]

The choices open to those so "naturally" categorized have generally been limited to accommodation, integration, and assimilation. These options are usually understood to represent strategies available for coping with dominant categories, yet they are more accurately understood as societal practices, tactics that reinscribe distinction and domination. Works putatively representing the attitudes, aptitudes, and social positioning of those in other "disabled" categories are dominated by the theme of desired readmission to membership in the dominant order. These writings are rooted in the genre of grand salvation and (re)union narratives. Certainly here they perpetuate a disenabling, perhaps more accurately called a "disabling," model of value.

Most works focusing on cognitive and expressive development of language in blind children, as well as much of the sociology on blind

6. Foucault (1980) makes this observation regarding sexuality, as well: sexuality shifted from the domain of sin to that of health.

7. An interesting discussion of this point is offered by Kathy E. Ferguson and Gili Ashkenazi in "Gender Identity in Star Trek," a paper presented to the Conference on Popular Culture, Lexington, KY, March 1992.

adults, concentrate on the paradox of their metaphorical compensation for visual and sight-based vocabulary and idioms.
In the narrative progressions of these works, personal adjustments and accommodations are part of the cost, and an imagined
reinclusion and acceptance (as "nearly normal") are represented
as the prize.[8] Those who are Deaf, however, generally don't quite
agree with this "one-way street" conception of the odyssey to become acceptably "normal"—in their case, hearing. As often as not,
the deaf person is unwilling to deny the cultural identity available—
as Deaf—in order to join this odyssey. Others, who only discover
later in life the deception they've been sold, are often bitter about
the sham.

The social isolation as a group or class, as individuals were institutionally named and warehoused as "deaf," fed the processes of
self-identification. These processes required accommodation to the
paternalism of the hearing society and of the keepers of the institutions. Paternalism in any historical setting defines relations of
superordination and subordination. The strength of paternalism
as a prevailing ethos increases as the members of the community
accept—or feel compelled to accept—these relations as legitimate.
The driving impetus, in the historical circumstances of the deaf, was
framed in health and medical terms as a need to protect and secure
society from infection while simultaneously a need was claimed to
provide protection, instruction, and moral direction to these poor
unfortunates. Such circumstances also engender their own spirit of
resistance. This process is most easily perceived within the institution of slavery: "Accommodation itself breathed a critical spirit and
disguised subversive actions and often embraced its apparent opposite—resistance. In fact accommodation might best be understood
as a way of accepting what could not be helped without falling prey
to the pressures for dehumanization, emasculation, and self-hatred.
In particular, the slaves' accommodation to paternalism enabled
them to assert rights, which by their very nature not only set limits

8. R. Scott 1981; see also Landau and Gleitman 1985.

to their surrender of self but actually constituted an implicit rejection of slavery."[9]

The institutionalization of the deaf was not an act of enslavement, but the relationship between keeper and the kept was certainly marked by a paternalism not unlike that which accompanied the American experience of slavery. What developed was a complex and ambiguous kind of paternalism that was accepted by both keepers and kept—but with radically different interpretations. Accommodation and resistance developed as two forms of a single process, for accommodation to the paternalism of the institutions served as a crucial tactic of evasion that enabled the development of Deaf culture. The process continues today, although it is still under attack. As the asylums for deaf children shifted their disciplinary techniques to blend those of the hospital with those of the nationalist school, new systems of ordering were reproduced to colonize this subaltern group to the common good. The methods of surveillance, the scheduling of time, the regimentation and ritualization of life, and the uncompromising control of the body in action or repose that emerged from the tactics of the nineteenth century remain the dominant features visible in current approaches to educating deaf children.

Again, while the institution of slavery is not being directly compared to the institutionalization of deaf people, the use of accommodation as a tactic of resistance in both systems is striking similar. It reappears even in rights talk, in which assertions of rights at once accept the power of the dominant to grant rights and simultaneously confront that power with ever-increasing demands based on the paradox of subordination within the relations of paternalism.

The slaveholders established their hegemony over the slaves primarily through the development of an elaborate web of paternalistic relationships, but the slaves' place in that hegemonic system reflected deep contradictions, manifested in the dialectic of accommodation and resistance. The slaves' insistence on defining paternalism in their own way represented a

9. Genovese 1974, pp. 597–98.

rejection of the moral pretensions of the slaveholders, for it refused that psychological surrender of will which constituted the ideological foundation of such pretensions. By developing a sense of moral worth and by asserting rights, the slaves transformed their acquiescence in paternalism into a rejection of slavery itself, although their masters assumed acquiescence in the one to demonstrate acquiescence in the other.[10]

While escape from the category of the insane, to which the deaf were long consigned, has by and large been granted by the purveyors of recent scientific discourse, the institutional practices and policies associated with that category are still generally in place, though they are being increasingly challenged. Still, the resilience of the order enacting that domination has been remarkable. Even the language in which reforms are posed reinscribes the old code, as is explored in further detail in chapter 6. Both challenge and resistance reflect the dynamics of accommodation and resistance within the late-modern discourse of rights talk and security, identity and sovereignty: "Systems of sovereignty and exchange have submerged some cultural identities and political affiliations, e.g. those based on ethnicity or gender or coevolutionary status, while enhancing others, e.g. those based on private property relations, male-dominated families and states, historical conquests, and post-war territorial settlements. Terrorism, illegal drug trade, pre-conquest ethnic identifications, changes in gender relationships, and the demand for sustainable development all challenge prevailing paradigms of sovereignty, national integration, legitimate exchange, and human-nature relationships."[11]

The previous chapter investigated the narrative framing of pious and heroic "discovery" histories of the deaf. This work does not recover and secure a more "authentic" history but investigates how domination and oppression of certain identities, or ways of being that are inconvenient to dominant orders, have been maintained. The themes it traces are likewise reproduced within the consensual

10. Ibid., p. 658.
11. International Studies Association, 1993 annual meeting theme statement, "The Enterprise of the Americas," drafted by Michael J. Shapiro and Hayward R. Alker, Jr.

communities formed by the use—and the experience—of these tactics. While the continued colonization of the Deaf by the Hearing is
my primary concern, the reproduction of domination of the d/Deaf
by other d/Deaf people should not be ignored.

Investigating the ways in which individual and group selves are
created, sustained, consolidated, and appropriated in and through
exchanges with others, Michael J. Shapiro deploys an "entrepreneurial" frame to examine the exchange of recognitions within a
given economy of codes. Identities are about boundaries, but the
selection and choices of boundaries and the relative weight assigned
to the differentiations are consensual to the extent that we participate in their recognition. Identities are, in effect, commodities for
exchange in the marketplace. In the souk or bazaar we find the free-
market trading in identity futures, simply another of the commodities available in the postmodern economy of recognitions. The
bodies these identities are sometimes attached to are similarly commodified. In the free-market network economy of recognitions,
nothing is "natural," except for a price. Differentiations may be
marked in this code as items of contention (objects of haggling) in
gaining recognition of appropriate exchange value (sold for a good
price). The entrepreneurial justification merely gives agents the
sense of freedom to present whatever "goods" can be conjured as
wares in the greater arena of identity exchange. Identity, like money,
is a form of confidence game.[12]

Thus, the disabled and the aged represent temporality, reflecting
the fragility of the identities on sale. All people will become, are in
the process of becoming, aged, disabled, and dead. No escape is
available. Hence, the circulation that establishes and depends on a
mediated notion of an identity exchange value would preferably
deny or ignore the aged and disabled, as their presence compromises
codes of both purity and use/sale value—unless read with yet other
codes. Western discourse, while complicit with the economies of

12. This is a process of convincing others you are who you aren't, that you have
what you don't, and that they should give you what they shouldn't, whether that be
belief or money. A related activity is choosing a public persona from the available
markers.

identity exchange, offers some traditional countercodes. One such anchoring code, discussed in chapter 6, is found in the modernist practices of rights talk.

Vital Signs

Why does the shopworn phrase *vital signs* offer such fertile ground for interpretation? The question is more than just rhetorical: it calls for a careful look at the metaphors by which we know our world, and, more particularly, by which the hearing know the deaf. The root of *vital* comes from the Latin word for "life," and in its modern usage means "of, characteristic, or necessary to life." While members of the deaf community strongly agree that Sign, as a generic term for the indigenous sign languages native to respective Deaf cultures, is synonymous with cultural life, that is not how this phrase is usually understood. Vital signs more commonly represent an epistemological code of a physical and mechanistic "understanding" of the body broadly known as the *medical model*. The irony in the phrase, however, is that this mechanistic/medical model has remained the dominant framework by which the hearing world knows the deaf individual as "defective," a body less than complete. Hence, the medical model would say that in a deaf individual certain vital signs, in this case the sense of hearing and a fluency of speech, are absent or defective. From the perspective of the deaf individual, Sign, the only linguistic experience directly accessible, is the most important "sign of vitality" present. Yet the institutions that have been formed on the medical model are structurally committed to denying this second interpretation.

To question whether such a view is true or false is pointless. More important is determining to what extent such a discursive economy, this way of understanding embedded in the very language of the medical model, has legitimated policies that then enforce, and literally create, the "reality" of deaf people as defective. This description of the physical world and of the phenomenological characteristics by which the inherent "qualifications" of an individual to participate are determined, while seeming to illuminate reality, is in fact only one interpretation—an interpretation that silences other ways of understanding. The exclusion of deafness and deaf people is as direct as it is exemplary.

The "factual" accounts by which the hearing come to view the "task" or the "requirement" of a deaf child to confront a "hearing world" are seen by many Deaf adults as an archaic narrative of social control, a historically constructed domain of administrative convenience that has been disastrous in its impact on human lives. The birth of modern medicine at the end of the eighteenth century, resulting from the epistemological shift documented in Foucault's *Birth of the Clinic* (1973), spawned the modern medical understanding of institutions, including the asylums created for deaf-mutes, as medical reformatories. The institution of deaf education has been structured by its entanglement with a legendary history, one that confuses and identifies a desired "should" with the "is" that must be. Sound, and hence speech, becomes seen as the only possible basis for understanding and the transmission of understanding, rather than as merely one view of "reality." This is but another way of noting a teleological project.

The "deaf-mute" or the "deaf and dumb" have been a creation of the eighteenth century, much as the "delinquent" was a product of the same efforts.[13] As juridical discourse began to expand its concern beyond crime and punishment to the psychology of the perpetrator, the category of the criminal was created. As the intellectual curiosity of the eighteenth century about the origins of thought and language gave way to the rush to establish institutions to maintain the "defective," the categories of affliction were stratified and isolated in the larger taxonomy of discourse. The "deaf-mute" were placed into a category from which they have never quite escaped.

Deaf people are different than hearing people. They can do anything hearing people can do, except hear. The first statement is what we might—without theoretical digressions into theories of facticity—call a fact. The second comes from a bumper sticker. In bumper sticker epistemology, it, too, could be considered truth. If one truth

13. See Foucault 1979.

claim seems more "natural" than the other, you may thank the medical model.

The first claim requires a physical body; the second requires a social body. Each body is a socially circumscribed and discrete entity that inhabits a particular space or location. The dominant paradigm here is that of the sovereign state and national identity. The subject of these sovereignties, and the object of nationalist identities, is the bounded agent of rational self-reflection and autonomous action. Within this nesting of paradigms the personal terrain of the body is defined as private and, thus, inconsequential to the realm of the civic. In that move, the body is simultaneously marked and dismissed. The consequences of governance for the common civic good upon that terrain are also defined as private, and therefore beyond any consideration of responsibility possibly inherent in the sovereign state. Social services to ameliorate demands and unwanted consequences, which are defined as incidental or epiphenomenal, are produced as "benefits" of supplemental bounty or providence rather than as the point and purpose of governance. In periods of low external threat, in order to mobilize the public the internal needs and demands themselves may be defined as a "crisis" or as "urgent" concerns. Still, no basic responsibility of governance is at issue, only the necessity to support the state so that future external threats to the nation might be contained. Because the topic remains national security, the circumstances and practices responsible for producing the "crisis" are dismissed, as are those directly affected by its production. Note how we make and distinguish facts and subjectivities.

The fact of deafness is, however, not questionable. There are people who do not hear. Some are born that way, some are not. Some become deaf late in life, some early. What that means, however, when the audiological, physiological, and neurobiological scientific descriptions are taken into account, is part of a biopolitic that is increasingly transboundary. Deafness is a way of being that is both unfixed and inadequately contained within conventional borders of Hearingness. It is a way of being that demonstrates the limits of the sovereign model of nationalist boundaries and cultural identity.

The marginalization of those who are deaf is not overtly the goal or purpose of the sovereign state. Deafness has already been defined and remanded as a medical artifact; hence it needs no further attention. Those invested in the sovereign model would insist that no relation exists between deafness and the sovereign state. But we are concerned here with the practices by which a social way of knowing is naturalized, made into fact—the questioning of which is made to seem unthinkable. The questioning of what appears beyond question is a key component of political inquiry. This is such an inquiry.

People who are deaf are hearing people with broken ears. If we could fix the ears, they would be hearing. This common logic is indeed common, but not necessarily logic. Black people are white people who have dark skin. If we could fix the skin, they would be white. Women are men with the wrong genitalia . . . ; and so it goes. Such crude reversals reveal a social fabric of practices by which we know what identities are both available and acceptable. As suggested by the examples, these are by no means innocent but are tightly coded in a hierarchy declared natural. While these codes are increasingly contested, some codings, such as those of Deafness, have remained so well anchored in the nineteenth-century models of the physical and social body that they have been little questioned until very late in the twentieth century. The insistence on the superior status of medical truth helps support the sovereign state. Genealogies of purity are rooted in a hierarchy of the body.

Until recently, the deaf have been strictly incidental within such paradigms. It is, in part, the lateness of their emergence from the furthest peripheries of culture that draws attention to the very success of the maintenance of their exclusions. Populations whose identity claims exceed the sovereign boundaries are objects of a Manichaean logic. Bodies that don't match the aesthetic, nationalist, or linguistic hierarchies are particularly vulnerable to the Manichaean shift: that is, as they do not conform to the canon of acceptable bodies, they necessarily embody an absolute heresy. If their identities cannot be tied to another sovereign and geographical place, they are pathological objects of scientific knowledge.

William Connolly recasts that shift through a series of questions:

What, though, are the compulsions that drive a church, a state, a culture, an identity to close itself up by defining a range of differences as heretical, evil, irrational, perverse, or destructive, even when the bearers of difference pose no direct threat of conquest? What is it in the terms of interaction between competing identities that fosters the probability of this response by one or both of the contending parties?

To pose this question is to reterritorialize the problem. . . . It is to engage the problem . . . residing within human structures of personal identity and social order. Anyone who poses a single, simple resolution to it will almost certainly get it wrong.[14]

As discussed in chapter 1, more than 90 percent of deaf children are born to hearing parents. That children can be born into families unconnected with their "native" identity disrupts the fixedness of the identity of any baby. It disrupts notions of what it means to be native, as well as notions of what—or where—it is one can be native to. Being native is a product of sovereignty. Deafness, the label attached to a broad collective view of those ways of being adopted by peoples who are deaf, is deeply enmeshed with a struggle against the sovereign model's Manichaean reduction of Deafness to a pathology.

Like toxicities that know no borders, the social practices of modernity and their effects have leaked through the boundaries of sovereign states. Defining the meaning of being Deaf is part of a struggle against the toxicity of pathological models of the body. The struggle against that model of knowledge, by the Deaf and by other marginal bodies, occurs within the ambivalent domain of postcolonial relationships with science, capitalism, and the security concerns of the state.

There are other marginal identities that equally trouble notions of sovereignty. Some are produced by the state to justify the expenses of its own upkeep; these include terrorists, drug lords, and welfare cheats. Others are produced by the state's maintenance procedures but are unwanted. Globally these include all refugees; however, each sovereignty reserves its special ire for the particular pariahs that serve to reinforce and reproduce its specific boundaries. These might include neighboring states and their citizens, but almost al-

14. Connolly 1991, p. 3.

ways one or more internal minority "types" are required. Each type's definition and meaning are socially constructed, but these constructions are often "supported" with evidence from the medical and scientific realm of "fact." Race, gender, ethnicity, and class are among the traditional hierarchical categories of demonized types. Each is a subset of the larger hierarchy of bodies. "Race and gender are not prior universal social categories—much less natural or biological givens. Race and gender are the world-changing products of specific, but very large and durable, histories." [15]

As modernity's firmest anchors become more porous, a hypercirculation of social markers of the normal and acceptable is required. Deafness as a medical condition is socially inconsequential to what might be called the "larger concerns" of the state. Deafness as a cultural identity disturbs or is inadequately contained within the usual nationalism of sovereign identity, but it generally can be dismissed. Yet the consequences of a visually linguistic modality, a way of being that valorizes radically different linguistic channels or modalities, overtly threaten crucial anchors of language and social meaning. Better to deny such differences than to consider the consequences the confrontation opens.

The question "What is deaf culture?" thus has a porosity of meaning. This does not rule out the very real concerns it raises in terms of specific lives and the effects of public policies on particular people and their families. An analogy can be drawn with environmental concerns, which have very real consequences on individual lives and life in general; a fundamental principle of eco-diplomacy is an understanding of our world as a single biosphere, as deeply intertwined as it is infinitely diverse. The drive to divide, conquer, exploit, and master nature and its bounty has left a trail of devastation only now becoming visible. The realm of the social has been likewise crippled (consider it a meaningful pun) by the maintenance and surveillance demands of the sovereign state.

The global awareness of eco-diplomacy is radically opposed to the West's classic belief in the earth as a boundless gift of God, the

15. Haraway 1989, p. 8.

source of natural bounty to be harvested and exploited, a food chain and a resource hierarchy with "man," and indeed specifically men, securely on top. The phrase "it's a hearing world" likewise represents a global view, but it is not one that acknowledges either the diversities or the interdependent reciprocities implicit in a transborder biopolitics of bodies. It is a product of an older tradition that projects identities as resources of the state in a distinct natural hierarchy, some simply of higher market value than others. Situated well down the hierarchy, deafness is a low-order resource (or menu item in the social services food chain), available for extraction as needed.

Thus, a politics of marginalization manifests itself as a form of resistance: a self-conscious solidarity produced by the shared economy of sign language communication, much like the initial effects of other communication technologies that also produce communal or consensual bonds—from early telephones to the virtual reality of postmodern computer hackers. Deafness is not just a medical phenomenon but a form of produced marginality. Nor is justice just about distribution, but rather it is about center and periphery, resistance and complicity, marginalization and normalization.

Models of Subordination and Domination

Institutions, and their representations of the state, are the productive sites of the "place" of national identity. One learns how to be a citizen through relationships both with and within schools and administrative agencies. The location teaches acceptance of the codings by which success or failure is assigned within these relations. Basic brutalities accompany the administrative control of "inferior" peoples. Inferior, in the relational sense, may be taken as broadly as "all who are not superior," but it is obviously a heavily coded word here. The brutalities that underlie the broader usage are fundamentally similar and are vividly portrayed in the postcolonial coding of deaf identity.

The residential school, like the asylum that preceded it, represents an entity, outpost, and microcosm of the state. This is part of the state's continued insinuations of itself into modern identity, but the remnants of earlier practices in the place of residential schools for the deaf allow us to perceive the logistics and brutalities of mismatched tactics. These practices have survived due only to the framing of this colonial outpost as so "isolated." The asylum that became the school is so far away, out on the borders of social welfare anthropology, that, like the missionaries, it has been forgotten. But, having been noticed, its survival may be in doubt, as the active attempt to dissolve these institutional relics through the mechanics of distributional mainstreaming suggests that this window may soon close.

As increasingly sophisticated state surveillance overcame the isolation of each group that had thus understood themselves collectively through their difference, so identity surveillance provided improved registration and monitoring of every individual's economic and social relations to the state. Records, cases, credit, and credentials produce the data. As the volume of information available to the state on individual identity increases, and as relationally linked data from enhanced tax mechanics improve the tracking of credit and capital, the state is required to return in social services less in payment for the net gain in surveillance and "security." The reduction in "special" services is justified on the ideological grounds of equality and impartiality. The downside is that maintenance costs of the data collecting, processing, and security (a subdivision of national security) increase beyond the moneys freed by slashing social services. Nevertheless, the state gains by not providing social services that might support and produce creative difference. This reflects the political options of domination and the state's management of difference as it maintains itself.

Mainstreaming, the dispersal of groups under tighter measures of specific individual achievement—measures that promote both accommodation to the dominant mores and recognition by and within the state—is also cheaper for the state. The state has competing demands for its tax revenues, and distributive responses make small and quite inadequate outlays look more significant. Many types of differences formerly isolated have been dealt with through dispersal, in modern times mostly by default. Some aggregations are self-selected, ethnic, historical, and landed. Those in the dominant majority have been penetrated by various forms of resident otherness. Most such internally produced "othernesses," be they socioeconomic, genetic, or imaginary (body or language), are effectively and efficiently managed through the pursuit and naming of external otherness—or otherness constructed as external.

Residential Deaf schools appear culturally problematic to different audiences for very different reasons. To the self-identified Deaf community, the residential schools for the deaf increasingly are becoming an option only for the wealthy. The common image of large tax-supported institutions for the maintenance of (those portrayed as) the unproductive and unsightly children of difference is largely negative. This is particularly the case when mainstreaming is presented as a way to decrease government spending and to reduce the number of those visibly dependent on the state, both popular conservative goals.

Mainstreaming is also part of the politics of the "worthy poor" and the ethic of "fitting in." Charity, best if strictly private, is the preferred government policy. Children of the poor who are deaf will be in overcrowded schools with underpaid and undertrained teachers who have no spare time to learn, let alone use, sign language. (She or he will probably be remembered, briefly, as that sweet or shy child, though occasionally uncontrollable, who left the school early.) These deaf children will not do well in school, nor will their options improve as they grow older. The residential setting will be exclusively the private domain of children of wealthy parents. In many ways, this will return deaf children to the opportunities of about the late seventeenth century, when only the deaf children of noble landed families received thorough educations. And as in that century, the remainder of the deaf are absorbed invisibly, the modern equivalent of subsistence-level peasants.

Normalizing Justice

Social movements that are seeking recognition of their difference most often make claims for both rights and social justice. Inherent limitations within the framing of rights talk will be discussed in chapter 6; here we will consider how calls for social justice also are often diverted into less politicized areas.

Iris Marion Young, in *Justice and the Politics of Difference* (1990), observes that "contemporary theories of justice are dominated by a distributive paradigm, which tends to focus on the possession of material goods and social positions."[16] In the international arena, for example, USAID shifted its focus on program funding to what were called the "Basic Human Needs" less because of humanitarian concerns, as the program language that accompanied the policy suggested, than because of two self-interested motives: to deflect attention away from opportunity structures favorable to both U.S. foreign policy and U.S. corporate investment interests, and to deflect criticism of USAID's dismal record in directly implementing foreign assistance programs. Redefining the terms of discourse and restricting the discussion of development to matters of distribution make the allocation of scarce material goods, such as resources, wealth, or jobs, the sole topic of concern. Stripped from the discussion are the decision-making processes and the institutional contexts by which the very inequities of such distributions are both produced and maintained. Moreover, the Basic Human Needs agenda, like the distributive paradigm it reflects, makes such "needs" appear as static items or goods to be addressed strictly through improved logistics rather than as the results and products of social relations and political processes.

But reducing justice to the problems of distribution disguises more serious forms of oppression. Young explores five manifestations or "faces" of oppression: exploitation, marginalization, powerlessness, cultural imperialism, and violence. Viewing oppression rather than maldistribution as the formative practice of social injustice is key: for while "distributive injustices may contribute to or result from these forms of oppression, . . . none is reducible to distribution and all involve social structures and relations beyond distribution."[17]

16. Young 1990, p. 8.
17. Ibid., p. 47.

Thus the object of oppression, as well as the supposed beneficiary of the improved distribution, must be considered. This object is modern identity, and its study must analyze the range of differences that are allowable in its formation. Young's project raises questions about practices that seemingly address social needs but structurally reproduce the oppression of difference. Like the "goods" in supposed need of better distribution, identities are not static items but products of social relations and political processes. Yet the ideological framework in which social justice is upheld as an ideal reproduces this distributive paradigm in its conception of an impartial unity. Not only is impartiality an impossible practice, but even dedication to it as an ideal has adverse consequences: "The ideal of impartiality, a keystone of most modern moral theories and theories of justice, denies difference . . . [and] serves at least two ideological functions. First, claims to impartiality feed cultural imperialism by allowing the particular experience and perspective of privileged groups to parade as universal. Second, the conviction that bureaucrats and experts can exercise their decision-making power in an impartial manner legitimates authoritarian hierarchy."[18]

Young traces how "impartiality" emerges out of the Enlightenment ideal of the public realm of politics, which was viewed as advancing toward "the universality of a general will that leaves difference, particularity, and the body behind in the private realms of family and civil society."[19] The claim to a common good, which is reproduced in the call for community, is seen to transcend particularities and difference and, at the same time, to justify the exclusion of those people and groups who are identified with feelings, reproduction, or the body. Gender, race, age, and disability provide disqualifying distinctions from the impartiality of this common good. Obviously, only certain ideal types and interests are allowed to provide the ground of the "common."

This critical approach to traditional moral theory derives in part

18. Ibid., p. 10.
19. Ibid., p. 97.

from feminist theorists[20] who reject the division or distinction between public, impersonal institutional roles in which the ideal of impartiality and formal reason applies, on the one hand, and private, personal relations that have a different moral structure, on the other. Once this public/private dichotomy is questioned, the very notion of impartiality is seen as inadequate. Some writers, though not Young, have explored the role by which ideals of "impartiality became tied to impersonality"[21] in the spread of colonial legal systems, examining how this ideal, applied to those who occupy positions of authority as well as to those who are seen as subject to that authority, underlies the processes of domination.

The underlying conflict within the ideal of impartiality is most clearly manifest in programs and policies of "equal treatment." This principle produces the legal framing of "the least restrictive environment," a phrase first used in a legal ruling on the deinstitutionalization of mental patients and then, as tradition and history would suggest, applied in law and policy to people with disabilities. In education, the "least restrictive environment" was seen simply as release from the schools, the same buildings formerly called asylums. Yet paradoxically the "fair inclusion" sought here is mechanical; it can only be achieved on the common ground of "the normal" if difference is denied. Young's critique is pointed: "The politics of difference sometimes implies overriding a principle of equal treatment with the principle that group differences should be acknowledged in public policy and in the policies and procedures of economic institutions, in order to reduce actual or potential oppression. . . . Some fear that such differential treatment again stigmatizes these groups. . . . [T]his is true only if we continue to understand difference as opposition—identifying equality with sameness and difference with deviance or devaluation."[22]

20. I am grateful to a range of teachers and writers; here I draw in particular on Kathy Ferguson, Judith Butler, Donna Haraway, and Gayatri Chakravorty Spivak.
21. Merry 1991, pp. 889–922.
22. Young 1990, p. 11.

As the mainstreaming of deaf children clearly illustrates, the question of fair inclusion should revolve around equal access to the content of curriculum rather than physical dispersal among other children. When the difference of deafness is obliterated, through the insistence on both a social identification as "hearinglike" and an oral-centric modality of communication, then fair inclusion understood as access to curricular content is functionally denied. As the modern linkage of place and identity might suggest, fair inclusion as practiced in the mainstreaming of deaf children is primarily concerned with where the children are being educated rather than with what opportunities to learn they are being offered. Of course the paradox of impartiality returns, yet again, in the public realm of social possibilities: the public good is not affected by where these deaf children go, but public interests must define what they are.

Difference becomes a static, unchangeable feature, although creative evasions and resistances develop as features of cultural response. The physical inclusion of the disabled child is part of the distribution of access; it is the material good of being allowed among the "normal." The denial of their difference, emphasized through the accommodating gestures to "special needs" that further reproduce the static clarity of the child's identity, ensures the ultimate exclusion of the adult from the political processes that define the social relationships available.

Within the larger genealogy of deaf identity, the mainstreamed child also exemplifies how the suppression of difference both supports claims to community and meets the needs of that community. Because notions of purity are often the driving force behind a community, those differences that either threaten or call into question such purity must be dealt with severely. Any otherness seen as outside must be excluded; any otherness seen within, among those who claim unity in their difference, must be suppressed. The social goal of heterogeneity, which seems to be an essential part of democracy, is not served by the oppressive desires of unity or purity. However, the crucial role played by these ideals in providing an impetus to knowledge and in legitimating action is most vividly demon-

strated in the dedication to eradicating deafness and culturally elimi-
nating those who might visibly manifest it.

Outlaw Ontologies

One reason that the clash between the Old World and the New
World is a recurring theme is that the literal distance between the
two suggests the vastness of the divide. But, appearances are misleading; here, as more obviously in the case of the Deaf and Hearing,
the crucial divide was one not of geography but of meaning. For the
Deaf, there was never an Atlantic Ocean providing a buffer, even if
only temporarily, to suggest that an originary place was a significant
marker of purity. Clearly, the clash is of ways of being. The language
of the Deaf is not the only outlaw.[23]

Much deafness, in the narrowly medical frame, occurs or is acquired in early infancy through illnesses or injuries. Many other
cases occur prenatally, induced either by maternal illness or by phar-
maceuticals. Strictly genetic deafness is rather unusual, as the genetic
code for deafness is quite recessive. It is also common: nearly 25
percent of the human population carries this gene.

The deaf are distributed somewhat randomly throughout all human societies, and nowhere have they existed in their own place.[24]
As Deafness is a culture characterized as an incidence ratio, its "natives" are colonized anew with each generation. From the perspective of this dispersed citizenry, the consensual collective now calling
themselves "Deaf" can use their distinctions to claim "native"
status. The claims resonate well with other distributed and disembodied identity productions of the postmodern era. Still, while options for collective identity proliferate, individual options shrink. For

23. See chapter 1, "Under Language Arrest."
24. Though in 1855, Mr. J. J. Flournoy proposed that a Deaf Commonwealth
be established in the unclaimed territories of the western United States. Heated
exchanges over the proposal drew national attention at the time. See Turner 1856,
p. 118; Van Cleve and Crouch 1989, pp. 60–70. See also Douglas Bullard's *Islay*
(1986), a novel on the theme of a separatist Deaf State.

like other identities whose security has been undermined in the late-modern age, the native status available to those who are deaf is under assault. Unlike those other identities, deafness is being attacked directly by specific weapons that include the most sophisticated tools of medical science and surgery. As an identity within the medical taxonomy, "deafness" is well secured; however, that medical identity "legitimates" deafness as a target for ultimate extirpation, by whatever medical, surgical, or management techniques may be required.

Biogenetics, including the field loosely described as "genetic engineering," loudly and publicly promises "the end of human genetic defects." Congenital deafness is one of the "defects" most highly targeted in this research. Research into implant technology, the biomechanical techniques of neuroprosthetics, has also focused extensively on the attempt to recreate "hearing" via neurological brain stem implant technology.[25] Thus deafness is seen as difference that "should" be ultimately abolished, whether through shorter-term tactics—policies of educational assimilation and practices of acoustical amplification—or through permanent neurosurgical "repairs" and the ultimate dreams of genetically engineering a "purified" gene pool.

Assimilation means that deviance is absorbed into the requirements of the socially dominant. Difference becomes a focus as part of the attempt to overcome it, the desire to incorporate it into our next level of inclusivity. As long as efforts are made to breed "them"—be they attitudes, attributes, or anatomies—out of existence, surgical techniques of biomechanical adaptations will continue to be developed. As the "problem" of deafness is localized onto the individual body to be "adapted," the medical taxonomy as the model for deaf identity is reproduced and assured. The logistics of the medical framing of deaf identity reflect steady efforts at absorbing and eventually eradicating deafness, even as the besieged body of

25. A "1991 Discover Award," announced by *Discover* magazine in December 1991, was presented to the director of auditory implant research at the House Ear Institute in Los Angeles for development of the Auditory Brainstem Implant. The FDA has awarded a "new product development" grant to this project ("Talking to the Brain" 1991, p. 74).

culture flowers more brightly. In one of the darker possible views, current Deaf culture is the final flowering of an exotic species whose identity is destined to wither and fade into extinction. Such a "conquest" is the stuff of Nobel Prize fantasies in medical schools and labs. At least some Deaf leaders see similarities with other laboratories that once engaged in eradicating troublesome identities.[26]

Thus banished to the margins, situated on the cusp of language and the law, deafness is increasingly an outlaw ontology, a hunted existence, an experience or way of being that, by definition, evades the biopolitics of the new eugenics. Some believe that deafness has always been an outlaw ontology, but one whose fugitive status was generally ignored. How long this fugitive will keep evading capture is increasingly in question. What is not in question, however, is that the attempts to eradicate deafness will continue to intensify, and the ever-refined techniques of surveillance make the risk of extirpation more real than ever before.

The Sites of Marginality

Silenced. We fear those who speak about us, who do not speak to us and with us. We know what it is like to be silenced. We know that the forces that silence us, because they never want us to speak, differ from the forces that say speak, tell me your story. Only do not speak in a voice of resistance. Only speak from that space in the margin that is a sign of deprivation, a wound, an unfulfilled longing. Only speak your pain.

—bell hooks, *Yearning*

Opposition is not enough. In that vacant space after one has resisted there is still the necessity to become—to make oneself anew.

—Paulo Freire, *Pedagogy of the Oppressed*

There are two faces of marginality. The first is an exclusion or oppression imposed by another; the other is a site of resistance, a strategy of choice whose strength is determined by the site chosen. While the "locations" of these faces may be coterminous, their

---

26. Paddy Ladd, a Deaf intellectual living in the United Kingdom, calls medical research efforts to eliminate Deafness and the Deaf as a people a clear form of genocide. See also chapter 1.

meanings are very different. Before we explore those spaces chosen or claimed as sites of resistance, it is important that we get an idea of how the modern deaf child experiences that other site, daily life mainstreamed in a hearing school.

The following passage is worth quoting at length for its richly textured glimpse into that daily experience. This narrative of imprisonment, which comes from a 1988 short story by Christine Wixtrom, "Alone in the Crowd . . . ," mirrors the isolation reproduced by institutions in the setting of dispersion. It is included here as a grounding presence.

It's a Monday in May, near the end of the school year. The classroom door is open, and the hearing students are pouring in, greeting their friends and talking excitedly about their weekend experiences. The deaf student slips in silently, sits down alone and buries his head in a book as he waits for class to begin. He cannot hear the buzz of activity and conversation around him. He was not a part of the weekend activities. No one speaks to him. He looks up as a girl he likes comes up the row to her seat and drops her books down on the desk. He ventures to speak softly to her, not noticing that she is already talking and joking with a guy across the room. The deaf student finally captures her glance and asks his questions, but the girl doesn't understand what he says. (His speech is slightly impaired, and the room is noisy.) After two more repetitions of "How was your weekend?" he is rewarded with a perfunctory "Oh, fine!" before she turns around and gets wrapped up in a detailed secret exchange with her best girlfriend, who sits right behind her. They giggle and talk, glancing up once in a while to catch the eye of the boy across the room. The deaf student rearranges the papers on his desk.

Finally, the teacher begins to lecture, and the lively conversational exchanges become subdued. The hearing students settle into pseudo-attentive postures, reverting to subtle, subversive communications with those around them. The deaf student, in his front row, corner seat, turns his eyes on the interpreter. He keeps his focus there, working to grasp visually what the other students are effortlessly half-listening to. The teacher questions a student in the back of the room. Her hearing friends whisper help. Their encouragement boosts her confidence and she boldly answers the teacher. Satisfied, the teacher moves on to question someone else. The first student joins those whispering to the boy who's now on the spot. He picks up the quiet cues and impresses the instructor with his evident mastery of the subject. A peer support system of companionable cooperation helps keep everyone afloat. However, only those with sensitive hearing and social support can tap into this interwoven network of surreptitious assistance. When a pointed question is directed to the deaf student, he is on his own. No student schemes bring him into the "we" of class camaraderie. Instead, when he speaks, the students suddenly stop talking and stare. But he is oblivious to the awkward silence in the room. He is verbally stumbling, searching for an answer that will pacify the teacher; and yet not be too specific. He strains to minimize the risk of opening himself up for embarrassment of saying something that has already been said, or something that misses the mark entirely. While he is still speaking, the bell rings and the other students pack up and start moving out the back door. The deaf student, his eyes on the teacher, doesn't notice the interpreter's signal that the bell has already sounded. The teacher smiles uncomfortably and cuts him off to give last-minute instructions as the students pour out the door.

. . . In the next class, the first five minutes are set aside for the class to practice sign language. The deaf student has been hoping that the sign lessons would provide at least a sparse stock of signs that students could use with him. The presenter demonstrates how to form the signs. A few students follow along, hesitantly imitating these gestures which seem so strange to them. But most of the students just take advantage of a little more time to pass notes, whisper together, and strengthen established friendships. Although they have had almost a year of exposure to signing, the deaf student is still waiting for the day when someone, sometime, will approach him for a few words of simple conversation. . . .

. . . As class starts, the teacher returns papers she has corrected. The deaf student hopes he won't be singled out again as "different." At the first of the year, he had been one of two students in a class who received the same poor grade on a test. The teacher had suggested to the hearing student that he work harder; then he had asked the deaf student if he wanted to move to a less demanding class. It seemed that people suspected that he might be "dumb" as well as deaf. Perhaps it was the same assumption that led another teacher to react with amazement when the deaf student earned an "A" grade on the first exam in his class. Thankfully, today his paper is returned without incident, and the rest of the period passes uneventfully.

During the afternoon, there is a rally in the gym. The deaf student arrives early, choosing a seat on one of the lower bleachers, where he will be close enough to see the speakers and the interpreter. Students stream in through doors on both sides of the building. It isn't long before the bleachers are jam-packed with talking, laughing, cheering students. The building is fairly bursting with spirited shouting, dynamic energy, and animated conversations. But no one talks with the deaf student. Set apart by silence, he cannot enter the world of words around him. Only an observer, behind a quiet barrier, he is alone in the crowd.[27]

This excerpt, whose somewhat stylized tone emphasizes victimization and the solitary pathos of the "different" child, presents a stark contrast to the usual positivist presumptions about the "joys of mainstreaming" that parents and educators so deeply desire to believe. Their understanding of the "mainstreaming experience," mediated through the epistemology of that belief, has no connection with the experience of the deaf student, to whom such mediations are unavailable.

Although many minor aspects of this story might not ring true, the general sense of solitude and marginality—not selected but imposed through the isolating act of mainstreaming itself—surely does. Even with the specialized "support" of an individual interpreter,[28] the deaf student is stranded without peers. It is a chilling picture of the power of naturalized patterns in social construction to exclude and marginalize. Marshaling defenses and resistance tactics becomes increasingly difficult when virtual solitary confinement, fashioned within the swirling context of a public school, becomes the primary experience of "education." While the student does not suffer the overt hostility of, say, racism, he or she endures a marginality that is both unchosen and relentlessly oppressive. It is little wonder that representative organizations of Deaf people the world over, including the World Federation of the Deaf, lobby strenuously to preserve the residential Deaf schools. Such demands have little to do with the facilities, the formal aspect of the education available, or the "opportunity to learn to fit in" and everything to do with the residential school being a place of social and cognitive identity formation and the space of cultural life and resistance. A marginality chosen simply seems better than one imposed.

This story also allows us to reenter the domain of accommodation and resistance. The mainstreaming of deaf children is predicated on

27. Wixtrom 1988, pp. 14–15.
28. Only deaf students "get" their very own adult to follow them around all day.

deprivation: as part of a strategy of assimilation, deafness is denied. Deaf advocates simply call it child abuse. For the deaf child, it means entering into a communicative desert of visual white noise. While in one sense it is intellectual and emotional dead space, the mainstream environment is equally a flowing cacophony of motion and imagery, of semiotic signs only partially moored. Though there is no true "master code" for reading any flood of information and events, education is primarily concerned with imparting the specific code set of the dominant culture. Alone in this zone of communicative white noise, the deaf child lacks the metacode of beliefs by which this direct experience is mediated and social competence achieved. Nor are other meaning codes made available. For a child faced with seemingly random images and the data of unrelated events, the main "lessons learned" are fear and the stress of isolation in a crowd.

Because the intellectual and peer stimulus that deaf children receive in the mainstream setting is severely impoverished, the self-generation of resistance tactics is ruthlessly suppressed. Such tactics are not reinforced, because, in an economy based in recognition, they are not recognized. Rarely does a mainstreamed deaf child see Deaf adults, and certainly not adults acting as what might be called "role models." Any such adult who might make possible a visible recognition of difference or who might reflect an unsanctioned meaning of that difference is either absent or relegated to the margins. While the margins are where cultures of difference generally draw their strength, it is the function of internal colonialism to render these margins unavailable. As the framework of my earlier argument suggests, *mainstreaming may be understood as a structural response to the cultural margins sustained by the residential schools.*

Wixtrom's story continues a certain vein of victimization that can be taken beyond its immediate terrain. The deaf child in the mainstream setting lacks the resources needed to respond intellectually or emotionally to experiences that fall into the broad category of assimilation. Yet the human spirit is enormously resilient, notwithstanding strenuous efforts to break it throughout history. Among the many deaf are a substantial number of quite "normal" people who would claim to lead satisfying lives. More than a few have been quite creative in their life pursuits, and some have prospered as well as returned much to their communities. Organizations and many social and civic activities dot the geopolitical map of Deaf "communities." There are also deaf people educated exclusively within oral-only systems who have achieved what they have desired in life. I am presuming no one essential Deaf experience: instead, my inquiry examines the practices that produce the context of the dominant experiences available and thus establish what it "means"— what it can mean—to be d/Deaf.

The dilemma of accommodation and resistance resists any simple resolution, although some steps for improving the options for deaf children and adults clearly emerge. The first is to break away from the "either/or" choice, presumed by both educators and parents, that demands an exclusive modality of language, sign or speech, be made available to the deaf child. It is just as important to refuse the pernicious rephrasing of this duality as "which first?"—the notion that should efforts fail to impart speech, then signing is always "available" as a fallback.

Recognizing the features of difference that matter is part of the attentiveness to possibilities and open spaces in which learning and lives take place. What is most interesting about deaf children is not that their ears don't work, but how quickly they learn through visual modes of language when they have the opportunity. Yet, as is noted throughout this book, education for deaf children still focuses primarily on the status of their ears rather than on the avenues open to their learning. Even when modality of access does become an issue, the discussion is limited by the obsession with purity; and these policies, too, are determined by questions of "how" (the technical aspects of that modality) and not "what" (the content delivered through that modality).

Generalizing about deaf culture is as problematic as generalizing about deaf people. Nonetheless, one important response to marginality has been the attempt to stake out an alternate center. Many Deaf representative organizations claim a "lived universalism," and a certain aspect may be achieved by those inhabiting the margins of those bodies. The national associations and the global body of national associations, the World Federation of the Deaf (WFD), host conferences, symposiums, and, especially, global congresses that are important sites of cultural performances, events that transform Deaf sociocultural awareness and regenerate cultural practices. Such regeneration and transformations, however, emerge primarily in spite of these organizations, not because of them.

The organizations themselves, as opposed to the events they catalyze, are frequently rigidly hierarchical in structure, patriarchal in nature, and ritualistic in their strict adherence to the Western procedural formalisms they share with the organizations of the dominant culture that they hope to "influence." Managerial control is tightly policed by an old guard elite. While the orderly procedures for elections of officers appear to be democratic, these proceedings are effectively open only to the elite and candidates are necessarily those with sufficient wealth to support their involvement. These bodies are, in effect, no more than shadowy simulacra of the colonial institutions they mimic.

The events that surround the formal assemblies, however, take little notice of elite rituals. For example, at the World Congress held by the WFD every four years, the public presentations, the theatrical events, and, even more important, the restaurants and coffee shops in the general vicinity are the actual loci of attention for the majority of those attending. These are the sites of cultural reproduction and spontaneous celebrations of a consensual communal identity.

The sheer infectiousness of the spirit of spontaneous and voluntary group solidarity that surrounds these international events is difficult to convey in writing. The gatherings of the past decade have each generally exceeded five thousand persons. The Deaf Way Conference and Festival, an independent event held in Washington, D.C., in 1989, was attended by approximately six thousand people from more than eighty countries. More than 350 sign language interpreters worked the proceedings. Art exhibits, theatrical performances, and social receptions were the furiously fertile terrain of cultural reproduction and regeneration. Yet these cultural centers of gravity were external to the formal programs of each of these grand gatherings. The sea of ecstatic people cared little about the procedural events of the General Assembly; they were there because of the entertainment and, more important, the social interaction with both new and old acquaintances. The location of Deaf culture was here.

The first sizable large Deaf culture "event" I ever attended, the Ninth World Congress in 1983, held in Palermo, Italy, was an overwhelming experience. The Sicilian touch in organizing the events, plus the local residents of Palermo, made the experience as close to an early Fellini movie as could be imagined. More to the point, in the swirling chaos of excited strangers eagerly approaching anyone observed to be signing—the semiotic marker of citizenship—I experienced the feeling of not belonging among them, even as I joined in the signed conversations. When asked if I was deaf, I felt the surge of desire to say, "Well, just a little . . . ," as if the ambiguation would make the "difference," would let me "belong."

The cafés were overrun each night with large and small groups of deaf people who constantly kept an eye open for new arrivals who could be incorporated into the discussions that filled the visual space of the restaurant. It was there I first heard/saw many of the great jokes deaf people have about the curious behavior of hearing people. The few tables of hearing people were self-contained little worlds, with occupants who spoke only to each other and glanced furtively at the emotive visual gesturing among the tables surrounding them. All the deaf laughed at them, noting, "Isn't it odd that they always leave a restaurant having met no one new?" They were right. It is odd.

Deaf people at these restaurants clearly distinguished between private conversations and the social opportunity to engage another group of signers, but they also noticed how hearing people rarely pursue the second option. Hearing people might explain this by arguing that deaf people have fewer opportunities to meet with other deaf people. From the Hearing perspective, this may justify their own behavior. However, from the Deaf perspective, the explanation simply indicates further the impoverishment of the Hearing's social mores regarding communication with new and different people. The politics of inclusion and exclusion are evoked in the distinctive patterns these attitudes create. Call it an epistemology of restaurants.

This socializing among widely various peoples, who represent the full spectrum of class, race, nationality, age, sexual preference, political inclinations, skill, and gifts, is occasioned by the shared modality of their communications. Not all efforts to connect are successful. As has been noted, there is no one "international" sign language, and cross-language miscommunications are sometimes vastly amusing. These spontaneous jokes are often embellished and quickly become anecdotes that themselves expand the Deaf cultural reservoir. However, the years of attempting to communicate ideas to disinterested hearing people provide a vast array of communicative strategies and ad hoc tactics that deaf people share, and know that they share. These fallback techniques serve to prime the pump in moments of lost connections, in establishing shared vocabulary or in regaining a consensual ground. Once the vocabulary and ground are established, the level of linguistic exchange moves rapidly beyond what a similar mix of monolinguals of various spoken languages could ever hope to achieve.

As the only hearing person among some of these international groups of socializers, I felt oddly jealous of their sense of belonging to a spontaneous universality. It felt odd not because of the sense of belonging itself. Western tradition is filled with pious narratives that reproduce attachments to place and to social notions of the common good. What felt odd was a spontaneous sense of universal "citizenry" that did not require a physical place. Like the link between speech and language, the connection between location and belonging suddenly was shown to be unnecessary.

It is precisely because of its marginal status, its rarity and its exclusion, that the use of sign language becomes "value loaded" to those native to it (whatever their personal audiological status). The oppression, regardless how unnoticed by the dominating culture, adds luster to the excitement such gatherings occasion. That luster, however, signals both resistance and oppression. Signing becomes "special" precisely because it is outlaw, its fugitive status a marker of a delicate balance of survival. Attaining marginality is a bitter achieve-ment. The flower may be bright, the fruit might be sweet to the taste, but the plant is rooted in and nourished by violence. Celebra-tions of native culture and ethnicity in historical fairs and boutiques equally partake of this paradoxical relation with oppression. Differ-ence, as a static commodity, increases in exchange value as its rarity grows. Artifacts are bought up, captured, or incorporated in the pro-cess of assimilation. The trade in these artifacts of cultural status and identity distributes oppression.

While deaf people hold experiences in common and Deaf identity is marked by the physical register of sign language, the sense of "citi-zenship" inheres in a process, in social relations. This citizenship is not a static commodity of deafness or of sign language as a modality: it lies in the social exchange of recognitions reproduced through signing. It is the immersion in the exchange, into and through the modality of the visual-gestural language, that produces this sense of citizenship that needs no place. The desire of the deaf for immersion in the communication grid as a means of "becoming" resonates with the postmodern experience of information more generally. This communicative "citizenry" may soon represent the only expe-rience of community.

Deaf Colonialism: Exclusion and Inclusion in Deaf Identity

Exclusion and inclusion are both experiences and practices in the achievement of identity.[29] Deaf culture is yet another terrain in which these occur. More particularly, I address here recent shifts in the boundaries that frame the interpretive meanings of Deafness, examining the strict policing of membership in what is called the "Deaf community" and the claims to authenticity by constables of cultural purity.

29. An early version of this section was presented as a paper with the same title to the Eleventh World Congress, WFD, in Tokyo, 2–11 July 1991. It was later published as "Kulturimperialismus unter Gehörlosen: Aus- und Einschluβ in Deaf Identity," *Das Zeichen* 27.8 (1994): 38–43.

I tread on sensitive ground. My aim is to point out new forms of exclusion as well as to describe older forms that both fade and reappear in current discussions. I hope to raise new questions about the current ways of talking about Deaf culture and Deaf history. Inasmuch as I perceive the current writings on Deaf culture as conceptually limited, my criticisms are meant to open up new avenues in the hopes that Deaf thinkers will make use of these criticisms to explore such new avenues. As an "outsider," I cannot. While I can see new barriers being erected and can talk about them, I do not presume to tell "the Deaf" what lies beyond these barriers. Here I return to an examination of several key terms in the popular discourse on Deafness. These terms include "Deaf identity," "Deaf culture," "deaf" versus "Deaf," and, perhaps most problematic of all, "Deaf community."

The first vexed notion is that of "Deaf identity." Who is Deaf and who isn't? The early (re)stirrings of Deaf Awareness were very exciting. Yet, just as the popular movement of Deaf Awareness was taking off, there was a new and very powerful move to restrict the terms by which individuals could consider themselves "Deaf." Historically, hearing society has used various social and legal means to exclude deaf people. Therefore, if you were so excluded, you might not yet think to be proud, but you did not doubt that you were deaf—nor that you were excluded. Then came the distinction between those people who actively identified themselves with the experience of Deafness and others who sought to accommodate themselves to the Hearing society through denial or self-suppression. Those who self-identified were "Deaf," while those who sought to deny or evade were merely "deaf."

Thus, a distinction between "deaf" and "Deaf" (lowercase versus uppercase) was "agreed upon" that has now become part of the "common knowledge" about Deafness. This marking of polarities appeals primarily because of its ready emphasis on the position and choice of the autonomous individual regarding how he or she self-identifies. Thus, an individual person is either "Deaf" or "deaf" depending upon his or her exercise of "free will" or autonomous choice of inclination. This, we might note, is a very Western and traditionally liberal notion. Indeed, the obsession of modern Western cultures with the autonomous individual complicates many issues of Deaf identity, including the presumptions of oralism and mainstreaming, because it locates the problems created by difference in the individual rather than in the social practices and relations we accept as "normal."[30]

Even more recently, however, yet another set of distinctions has been used to identify those who are considered "truly Deaf" or part of the "natural Deaf leadership." Pointing to the "fact" of a natural position of elites in society, certain writers, including Deaf writers, now declare that it is *only* Deaf persons born of Deaf parents and also having Deaf siblings who qualify to be part of this "natural Deaf elite." Leadership accrues to such individuals "normally," as the facts of their birth create a "native" form of Deafness.[31]

I have very serious reservations about this construction of "natural" leadership, as should most Deaf people. I will explain my own reasons briefly, but I would first suggest one other reason why I think most Deaf people would also want to reject this line of thinking. The overwhelming majority (more than 90 percent) of all deaf people have hearing parents and, consequently, *do not qualify* for this exalted status of "true Deafness." They simply aren't Deaf enough, on a scale of purity. *Or perhaps, more precisely, they are like the peasant class supporting a newly defined nobility.* Given the rigid and very hierarchical form of most organizations of the Deaf, including the WFD, which tightly police participation and access to leadership roles through formal procedures, I suggest this peasant-noble metaphor is not so far afield.

No sooner had a new Deaf Awareness and Deaf Pride been declared than redefinitions occurred affecting over 90 percent of those who would have thought themselves to belong; if not wholly excluded, they were clearly restricted or pushed yet again to the margins. Shifting the boundaries of the interpretive meaning of Deafness (upper case) *evokes* a strict policing of member identity in

30. See Minow 1990.
31. Stokoe, Bernard, and Padden 1980. See also Padden 1980.

what is called the "Deaf community." Even as one form of exclusion is escaped, another is *invoked*.

This notion of a "natural elite" is a perversion of the idea of pride in the Deaf experience. If circumstances of privilege over others are seen as normal or natural, then the oppressions that sustain such privilege are justified. By claiming special exemption from the usually negative understandings of the label "deaf," those who maintain they are a natural elite because of their "privileged" birth actively reinforce those negative connotations. For all except those in the natural elite, who we now understand make up a special "class," the negative assumptions about deaf people are confirmed. Claimants to this elite status thus buy into the interests of the institution in exchange for its exclusive privileges.[32]

Further discussion of the "deaf/Deaf" distinction can help clarify this point. As noted earlier, the appeal of this distinction was its focus on the individual. The strategy is to separate oneself from the group that has a negative label and to demand treatment as an individual. Yet this response leaves in place the negative meaning of the label, even if that one individual is denying its application to him or her.

As a strategy of individual resistance, this tactic has been used by other oppressed minorities, as well. U.S. Supreme Court Justice Thurgood Marshall once wrote in a decision, "Members of minority groups frequently respond to discrimination and prejudice by attempting to dissociate themselves from the group, even to the point of adopting the majority's negative attitudes toward the minority."[33] Marshall had in mind the hidden impacts and injuries of race and class, but the analogy is clear. Hearing domination and oppression of Deaf people have produced many types of coping strategies—including attempts of Deaf people to act like and pass as Hearing people, for various reasons. *Yet, the "d/D" distinction is now used*

---

32. This intimate relation between elites of the center and the periphery is well documented in the traditional literature of political science. The classic work on this subject is Galtung 1971.

33. See *Castenda v. Partida*, 430 U.S. 482, 503 (1977) (Marshall, J., concurring). See also Sennett and Cobb 1972.

primarily to exclude those who have failed to select the politically correct coping strategy.

This criticism does not deny that the distinction had utility when it was first made. It called attention to negative and positive coping strategies. Or rather, it used a positive view of difference to declare certain strategies positive and others negative. Those labeled "Deaf" called upon the positive features of difference in defining their self-identity, while those labeled "deaf" were those who sought to deny or evade the difference. However, that distinction was only one step: we must move beyond it to examine more closely the social relationships that produce or require coping strategies based on negative views of difference. This might suggest that those previously labeled "deaf" not only belong to the community but may be in greater need of support, both social and material, in coming to terms with their self-identification.

Hearing-identified "deaf" people will not all automatically become Deaf-identified, but if they are no longer excluded—even in retaliation for their supposed "collaboration" with the Hearing oppressors—they may well come to see their own experiences of being deaf more positively. A reverse flow of appreciation might also occur from "d" to "D," for Hearing-identified deaf people may have discovered useful strategies of declaring and maintaining dignity and self-esteem, not to mention achieving objectives, while immersed in their Hearing-dominated environments.

When the seemingly clear division between "d" and "D" is reexamined, there appears a large gray area—an open ground of individual experience, of personal perspective. When the distinction refers only to given moments, to particular tactics within circumstances that are very local, then we see that much of who we are rests on social meanings we supply from those available. For coping with the "hearing/public" contexts of their lives, Deaf people have (or should have, but usually don't have) the full arsenal of tactics and strategies contained within the spectrum of d/Deaf experiences. The denial of what are called "d" forms can be a powerful tool for calling forth the positive meanings of personal experiences of difference—for emphasizing the best of what are called "Deaf" ways. It can also be equally powerful in oppressing those caught in opportunity structures that have denied them the privilege or luxury of options now deemed "politically correct." In effect, the d/D dichotomy plays into the strategies of domination by pitting Deaf people against themselves over labels assigned to alternative strategies for coping with the dominant Hearing cultures.

Similarly, when Deaf people who have been born into "strong Deaf" families—those families with a high incidence of "native-born" Deafness over successive generations—claim elite status, they twist the vagaries and contingencies of life into a naturalized order of right and thus justify the exclusion of the majority. While we might notice that a small number of people in the world are very rich and many are very poor, this state of affairs need not be "ordained by God," nor necessary or natural. It is, rather, totally human-made, wrought through brutality and oppression. Recasting the given as the necessary is a time-honored technique used by the powerful to justify their positions. Deaf people need not adopt it to exclude and oppress other deaf people.

To be sure, deaf children of Deaf parents are blessed with early access to full linguistic models and to Deaf cultural experience transmitted across generations. (These best-case circumstances, in which pure signing linguistic roots and material security coincide with cultural wealth, are sadly more rare than we might hope to believe.) Theirs is not, however, the only "authentic" experience of Deafness. That such children are more articulate and initially better adjusted to their social surroundings may well be true in some cases. But by no means should we conclude that such children are either the only "natural" leaders or the only "truly Deaf" people. On the contrary, we might judge that such benefits as these children have had ought to be made available to as many other deaf children as possible. Build on their good fortune, yes; but the attempt to naturalize particular family circumstances as a birthright to an elite position is a self-serving political maneuver based on an exclusionary tactic. It uses evidence that should benefit all to justify new barriers that will maintain privilege.[34] These self-proclaimed Deaf elites behave as though deaf-ness were a turf they have conquered, a field of power where they can maintain authority and presence and can reap rewards *only* if there are *only a few* present, if they are always a rare commodity.[35]

The claim to an elite status for a minority of Deaf people rests on an essentialist argument that assumes a "Deaf essence" shaping all Deaf experience. The multiplicities of Deaf lives, however, challenge the idea that there is only "one" legitimate Deaf experience. Hence, in referring to the mythical "elite Deaf experience"—enjoyed by Deaf children with both Deaf parents and Deaf grandparents, and with many Deaf neighbors as well—we can value and cherish the meaning of this experience without essentializing it. We can recognize its power for individual growth without needing to silence other experiences as "inauthentic." Support for the positive aspects of Deaf Awareness requires a process of decolonization that continually opposes reinscribing notions of an "authentic" Deaf identity. To rephrase that, and to paraphrase a position taken by bell hooks in a racial context: by ignoring the differences among Deaf people and claiming a further elite status, relatively privileged Deaf people are able to claim identification with all experience of Deafness while also assuming special authority to speak for Deaf people quite unlike themselves.[36]

Such blindness to diversity is unfortunately common. In a recent article, "The Sociolinguistic Aspects of the Black Deaf Community," Anthony Aramburo expressed great surprise to discover that Deaf people of color label themselves primarily by race. African Americans identified themselves as "Black" first and as "Deaf" second. The exceptions seemed to be those Black Deaf children who had been institutionalized in almost totally White residential schools.[37] This used to be called disparagingly the "Oreo syndrome," by those who did not consider it a positive thing at all.

34. This has, in fact, been used quite nicely by a few well-known Deaf names to advance their personal positions as spokespersons for all Deaf experience.
35. See hooks 1990, p. 101.
36. hooks 1984, pp. 43–65.
37. Aramburo 1989.

While such surprise is best called racist, I am sure that both the author and his editor would be hurt by this characterization, so amazed do they seem not to find their newly discovered "unity" in Deaf identity. Among writers of color, however, their reaction would seem perfectly normal—a "normal" example of the unconscious racial silencing in mainstream social movements. In this regard, the Deaf Culture movement appears to be no better.[38] African-American and African-European Black children who are deaf are reminded daily of their identities as members of a racial minority that is excluded by the majority. These reminders are both institutional and personal, and they are more deeply embedded than the reminders of their Deaf identity. A deaf Black child can appear to be hearing by simply not signing, but she or he cannot appear to be White. In this Western society, *that* is the more meaningful difference.

The self-identification processes that proclaim as positive features previously labeled negative are as crucial in the fight against racism, sexism, and class divisions as they are in the movement for Deaf Awareness. But the notions of Deaf identity and Deaf culture must, therefore, be equally attentive to the varieties of experience that make up what is called Deaf culture—or rather, what ought to be called Deaf cultures. Otherwise, a Deaf culture that adopts without question the privileged perspective of the Euro-American, White, patriarchal, heterosexual, educated, middle- and upper-class male is as exclusive, as oppressive, and as dominating as that against which Deaf leaders say they are fighting. Being freed from one stereotype while reinscribing a full host of other equally oppressive stereotypes is certainly no liberation.

These concerns resonate with special force in the discussion of "Deaf community." The ideal of community is very powerful, and very ambiguous. Many aspects of that ideal are positive and reaffirming. Many of the Deaf envision a life free from Hearing domination and oppression, a society that rejoices in the shared

---

38. See cover story, "Deaf Minorities: Looking Back, Moving Forward," in *Gallaudet Today*, Winter 1990–91.

experiences of Deafness and the dreams of its members. The call to a Deaf community has been a very popular one. Indeed, most conversations about Deafness and Deaf culture now unreflectively use the term as if it were an understood norm and a unified or unifiable whole.

While I am eager to support its positive aspects, I do have serious questions about the actual effects of this claim for community. I recognize how problematic it is for me, as a White, Western, Hearing male, to make these critical comments. But as I have already made clear, my purpose is constructive without presuming to be prescriptive. By pointing to new barriers or practices of exclusion as they emerge, I hope to make them easier to recognize and consciously engage.

In practice, the ideal of community often operates to exclude those with whom the group does not identify. Thus social difference is denied, repressed, and excluded, both on an auditory/signing spectrum and through techniques made familiar by the dominant culture. By claiming an ideal of "unity" in a shared whole, proponents of community deny the multiplicity and heterogeneity, the different ways of life, that are the reality of Deaf people the world over. Certainly there is comfort in a self-enclosed and unified whole, but such comfort is achieved at the expense of those who are on the margins of or otherwise excluded from that unity. Those who are not White, who are not living in the rich nations of Europe, North America, or the so-called developed nations, who are not middle or upper-middle class, male, or heterosexual, who don't "qualify" for membership under the active policing of distinctions between deaf/ Deaf, or who primarily identify with some difference other than deafness: none of these are fully acceptable to a "unified 'Deaf' community."

Certainly Deaf people have often experienced being excluded from "community." What has not been so clear is that some Deaf people, or self-selected groups of Deaf people, can practice the same exclusions in positing their "Deaf community." The key point is that those committed to an ideal of community tend to value and enforce homogeneity.[39] For most people, a community is a group that shares a specific heritage, self-identification, culture, and set of norms. While some articulate Deaf people insist that all the Deaf share such heritage, culture, and norms, it takes only a moment's reflection to realize that other differences—of race, class, local or national culture, gender, education, or other characteristics—may be more significant than the ideal of a uniform or unified community allows.

As more than one writer has suggested, a "myth of community" can readily operate to produce and implicitly to legitimate racist and class-bound behavior and policy. By its nature, it produces exclusionary results. Leadership of the Gallaudet "Deaf President Now" movement was conspicuously White, for example. How many non-Caucasians are there in leadership positions in the American Deaf community? How many third world Deaf people of color are leaders in the WFD? How many women head national associations? No conscious or purposeful racism or sexism need be at work; the nearly absolute absence of these marginalized individuals is clear enough.

My attack here is not, as it may seem, on Deaf culture, but on general problems that also happen to apply to Deaf culture, albeit in particular ways, problems that can and should be dealt with directly. Several writers observe that "new" communities often have the atmosphere of cliques; they keep leadership circles small and unchanging, and they keep potential new members who are "different" out or in acceptable positions of subordination. This certainly occurs in Deaf organizations, too. The implicit group goal of mutual identification often reproduces and enforces a homogeneity (a politically correct—"Deaf correct"—sameness) that conflicts with the organizations' formally stated commitments to difference.

There is an underlying paradox in these internal tensions. The claim of a unified or unifying "Deaf" identify or perspective rests on a simplification, an essentialism, that denies much of the very fabric of the experiences of most Deaf people. Deaf people fall into

39. Young 1990, p. 234.

every category of race, gender, ethnicity, education, economic class, and nationality, and they vary in sexual orientation, physical condition, and other sources of assigned "difference." Assimilation, imitation, and the role of rebelliously-exotic-other are not the only available options and never have been. Yet the calls for a "Deaf culture" frequently threaten to suppress this multiplicity and displace it with a single perspective. As Audre Lorde has noted of the experiences of Black women: "There is a pretense to a homogeneity of experience covered by the word 'sisterhood' that does not in fact exist."[40] Neither is there any one d/Deaf experience.

Building relations of group solidarity is a political project of constructing and affirming a positive group identity. These are crucial steps toward confronting cultural imperialism and discovering things about oneself and others with whom one feels affinity. Nevertheless, people who try to enforce that strong sense of mutual identification in their zeal to affirm the positive meaning of group specificity are likely to reproduce exclusions very similar to those they already confront.[41] Thus, as discussed earlier, by ignoring the differences among Deaf people within and among nations, relatively privileged Deaf individuals can claim to identify with all experience of Deafness, while also assuming special authority to speak for Deaf people quite unlike themselves. *The 'certainty' of "Deaf culture"— in the singular—hazards a new arrogance: the projection of one certain form of Deaf culture, one experience, and one kind as the model for all.*

The World Federation of the Deaf, as the institutional representative of Deaf associations worldwide, has shown itself to be particularly insensitive to many of these issues. As it continues to be dominated by White, Euro-American traditions, the primary model is, as noted earlier, strictly hierarchical, patriarchal, static, and formalistic. The WFD has continued to ignore the objections from the developing nation members of the WFD that its arrogant efforts to create a new "International Sign Language"—motivated almost

40. Lorde 1984, p. 116.
41. Young 1990, p. 236.

exclusively by economic concerns regarding costs of interpreting—continue to wreak havoc on their own efforts to research native languages. In attempting to have their cake and eat it, too, the WFD seems blissfully uninterested in the damage caused by ignorance of such native languages in the name of a gesticulatory Esperanto, formerly called Gestuno and now repackaged as "International Sign," complete with disclaimer—something like a cigarette package health warning—of linguistic status.

This "International Sign" is routinely acknowledged not to be a true language, but a grab bag collection of polyglot vocabulary woven by whoever is speaking. Only those familiar with the western European or American context can make sense of its limited vocabulary set. This restriction to a controlled vocabulary effectively silences political rhetoric by continually redirecting discussion to only officially approved topics, debated in approved vocabulary.

The resurgence of Deaf Awareness, Deaf Pride, and Deaf cultures has been achieved by revaluing difference. By recasting the meaning of Deafness in positive terms, by reclaiming the authority of directly lived lives, Deaf people the world over are making clear political claims to self- and collective determination. As Deaf people move to recenter their perspective as a norm, I seek merely to call attention to new forms of exclusion lurking in the wings. Rigid hierarchies of organizations, restrictive or hidden rules for participation in decision making, patriarchal forms of privilege, conscious and unconscious racism and nationalism, and sexual divisions of labor and reward all lie in wait for Deaf culture: these issues must be confronted.

There are many Deaf cultures. A view that is attentive to the many faces of oppression will better understand the Deaf experiences of marginalization, exploitation, powerlessness, cultural imperialism, and violence—from within as well as without. Deaf history and Deaf culture appear truly "different"—born at the margins of the dominant Hearing societies, claiming strength from the margins,[42] and often existing in opposition to some of the dominant society's deepest assumptions. Because Deaf culture claims its strength from this

42. See hooks 1990.

location, it should, at least theoretically, be possible for the Deaf community to come to terms more easily with other forms of being and experience at the margins and to be much more positive in its celebration of differences. But such true acceptance of diversity can only be achieved through a rejection of pious narratives, the Hearing histories of great glories foretold, which promote the exclusion of every other form of difference but their perceived own.

4

Merit Accounting in a Karmic Economy

Identities are built upon layers and layers of habitualized gestures, postures, expressions, responses, attitudes, descriptions and anticipations. These layers readily become more-or-less frozen into place, a "sedimented corporeal style."
—Judith Butler, *Gender Trouble*

An Oppositional Ethnography

This chapter, while discussing aspects of life in Thailand, is not an ethnography in the traditional sense; rather, it presents the available ways to "be" a Deaf Thai, what might be called the conditions of possibility. There is no essence of "the Deaf Thai" to be unveiled or discovered, but only particular practices that constitute options available to Thai children and adults who are deaf. The specific mix of options emergent in late-modern Thailand, influenced by historical progressions, by import and adaptation of institutions and procedures, and by intruding popular media, circumscribes what can be called Deaf Thai culture. This culture, like others, is composed of the patterns of recognition among the individual identities of its members. But, as this view would suggest, if that mix of social practices were to shift or be altered and additional options made available, then what is called the "culture" would change accordingly. Such critical framing of the discursive economies that constitute traditional ethnography, an approach currently called "critical anthropology," displaces the colonial sureties and conventions of the discipline.

In keeping with that shift, this foray into the lives of Deaf Thais seeks no final unity, even as it pursues an engaged activism to build

117

cooperative relations and self-representative organizations among those who might seek such a self-identifying "community." Yet that very activism and the observations of circumstances and opportunity structures available lead me to criticisms of this community as well as admiration for the individuals working toward it. Much of my criticism focuses on the closed system of codes that produce restrictions on life choices. While in some of my examples I describe the life circumstances of particular individuals, my purpose is to invoke an oppositional viewpoint in reading these codes. As noted at the outset, I am not deaf, but I am puzzled by certain aspects of the social relationships both between hearingness and deafness and between hearing people and deaf people. In particular, examining the former opens up or reveals questions about seemingly arbitrary restrictions on possible ways of being. Through processes decidedly more political than biological, some distinctions are named as crucial to identity, others are deemed marks of exclusion, while others are merely ignored.

I am no doubt open to the charge that in some respects I have appropriated the experiences of others. Yet I hope I neither essentialize nor dismiss real people with lives fully their own. In my engagements and observations of both personal and collective coping strategies, I have found instances of both creative managing and craven acquiescence. In neither case, however, do I contend that any strategies deployed or identities assumed represent any "essence" intrinsic to Deafness in general or to Thai Deafness in particular. Both realms of possible responses are equally worthy of exploration, as they exemplify strategies and identities available within prevailing structures of opportunity and surveillance.

It is my intention that questions raised here might loosen—or induce others to loosen—restrictions previously moored securely within entrenched practices. Nevertheless, I realize that exposing either coping strategies or weaknesses in administrative surveillance may, in turn, lead to tightened control over identity options. This prospect is particularly likely in the context of schooling and institutional life. Within the academy, such an outcome is generally referred to as exposing or compromising the "weapons of the weak."

The phrase is borrowed from a book of that title by James Scott (1985) about resistance and avoidance strategies of peasants in northern peninsular Malaysia. My own reading of his work does not lead me to agree that any unique resistance strategies were revealed and thus compromised, although he describes a richly woven fabric of life in an agrarian community. So, while researchers should be concerned about divulging the admittedly shrinking and sometimes fragile techniques of evasion and omission available to the dispossessed, I am unconvinced that either Scott's work or mine does so. I would prefer to think that the opposite outcome—that is, promoting such techniques—is even more likely.

This chapter contains several distinct voices. One will address the programs of donor agencies in establishing modest financial assistance channels to support grassroots empowerment efforts. For a detailed summary of the institutional history of education in Thailand and the current status of the educational opportunities for Thai deaf children, the reader is referred to works by two of my colleagues.[1] These areas are framed in the traditional language of institutional goals and objectives.

Primarily, however, this chapter focuses on vignettes that do not support these dominant narratives; instead, they present images of lives that have emerged from, or fallen through, the cracks and fissures in the institutional edifices. Such spaces, and the escapes or leakage through them, neither require nor demand the response of a better containment, but rather make visible those fixed boundaries that might be just as well (re)moved. One exemplary use of these "weapons of the weak" would be applying rights talk strategies to aid the newly visible inhabitants of spaces among the cracks and fissures. These inhabitants speak in their own voices.

The following section briefly introduces the reader to the streets of Bangkok, capital of Thailand, a country never overtly colonized by foreign powers. While Thailand has adopted and adapted many aspects of Western culture, including educational institutions and their practices, such borrowings have generally been mediated by

1. Reilly 1995. See also Suvannus 1987.

the particularities of Thai interests, perspectives, and history. Some of these particularities will be examined below.

Bangkok: "Only for the Privileged Fews"

Bangkok is a highly cosmopolitan city of roughly ten million people. It possesses as wealthy, varied, and typically self-obsessed a societal elite as will be found anywhere on the planet. The Oriental Hotel, voted the world's finest hotel for over a decade running, has nearly a dozen world-class five-star competitors in the city. These form a rich setting for international and Thai socialite feeding frenzies. It can be fun, but our concern here is with the hard work of such scenes: charity.

This is an elite-driven society, with no apologies offered for the prestige and lavish privilege enjoyed by both old, landed nobility and the new economic nobility of the various military and trading dynasties. Advertising, a major feeder on Thailand's decade-long double-digit economic growth, produces signs and images that directly stress elitist themes. New buildings compete with names not merely hinting at but proclaiming ever-escalating degrees of refined exclusivity. With enormous billboards and full-page ad spreads, one large property development announced, "Only for the Privileged Fews." The developers insisted on keeping this wording as it was. While recognizing that "fews" is nonstandard English and technically a mistake, the Thais saw several distinct "fews" available to be "privileged." This made perfect sense to them and presumably to their customers—the project has done well. The real point, however, is semiotic: "exclusivity" is one of the most highly prized signs of status, particularly when available for grand public display.

Fashion shows, and the concomitant displays of attendance, are a major staple of the fund-raising benefit season. The cooler months of the year are called the "high season," as social calendars are especially full. Nevertheless, events by which the wealthy might parade onto the tabloid social pages take place throughout the year. The largest events support the old-line foundations, mostly under royal patronage, but even the smallest parties are produced in support of this or that charity for photo spreads in the local papers. Such public display is an active part of life for the Thai social elite. Actual contact with the objects of this charity, however, is even more actively shunned by the majority of those attending such events. Since the few "programs" or what might be called "services" available to Thai Deaf or indeed to any Thai with disabilities are provided under the guise of charity, the construction of these events significantly shapes the constrictions on possible identity options for those who might avail themselves of such "charity." One can imagine social circumstances changing sufficiently that there would be no need for these benefits.

For charity is not the goal of these events. Those seeking to be beneficiaries of the funds raised struggle with a conflict between public perceptions of "development," which focus on concepts of empowerment, and perceptions of "charity," which focus on assistance to the "worthy" poor; but those who host and attend these events have little interest in this set of issues. Their concerns are balanced between the mutually incompatible objectives of status and merit. The notion of status needs no nuanced introduction here, as the markers at stake are the mundane signs of wealth, privilege, and exclusivity.[2] These markers, or rather the claimants to them, play a significant role in the success of fund-raising events, as well as the success of attempts to leverage any resources to those actually in need. It is these claimants who concern us here.

For example, society women may be honored by a formal title of ranking created by the Royal House of Chakri, the ruling dynasty of the Thai kingdom. The actual royal decorations, and most certainly their ultimate source, are highly revered. As some of the lower royal order decorations, and the many step rankings within them, are determined by the various bureaucratic mechanisms of the state, they often function as status markers within the bureaucracy and in the public arena. These awards, although royally approved, are granted by the officials of the government machinery.

The desire of society women for certain coveted ranks is widely

2. See Ewen 1988.

lampooned in popular Thai culture. The award of a certain rank within one of the higher royal orders entitles a women neither born nor married into a royal lineage to be addressed as "Khunying," an honorific generally translated as equivalent to the British "Lady." One higher rank, "Thanpuying," analogous to the British "Dame," is possible.[3] This higher ranking is rarely given to a person of common birth. In a society still deeply attached to stratified patron-client patrimonies rooted in the social life of the old royal Thai aristocracy, and still attached to a widely revered monarchy, these titles are highly prized—and coveted.

Women who fancy themselves as deserving high honors may lurk around social development programs in search of activities and achievements for which they might claim credit. Some spend their lives in this fashion. A few succeed; many do not. Popular satires depict public events being actively sabotaged by schemers who would rather see such efforts fail if they are not to be credited with the success. The actual objects of ridicule, the greed and desire of the social climbers, are clearly targeted; the lampooning is certainly not directed at the source of the award.[4] There is also wide recognition that such sabotage, both active and indirect, does occur. The crucial point here is that efforts at self-representation have no place at all in such machinations.

Merit Mining

The notion of "merit" in traditional Buddhist theology is complex. This brief overview does not attempt to present the theological

3. The Most Auspicious Order of Chula Chom Klao. The ranks of fourth class, lower grade, and fourth class, upper grade, designate a woman as "Khunying." The rank of third class is addressed as "Thanpuying." Ranks above this class are generally reserved to members of the royalty.

4. I should make absolutely clear that no disrespect or criticism of Thailand's highest symbols is contained in this work. As a member and officer of two of the Royal Thai Orders, one created by King Mongkut and another created by King Chulalongkorn, I could harbor no such intent. I have also known wonderful people engaged in creative and generous efforts to improve social and political conditions who have been granted honors, as well as others who have actively avoided credit and recognition.

framework; instead, it offers one view of the popular Thai attitudes toward the traditional values inherent in the notions of merit and merit making.

Theravada Buddhism, also known as Hinayana Buddhism, adheres to the original Pali scriptures, stressing the duty of the individual to observe the Eightfold Noble Path in the search for nontheistic enlightenment.[5] The Theravada approach teaches that until enlightenment is attained, attempts to help others will be entrapped within the cycles of desire and suffering. In contrast, the Mahayana approach teaches a re-donation of any merit gained, whether good will or deed, to the benefit of all suffering beings. The Mahayana goal is thus a seeking of universal release for all beings from the endless cycles of suffering and rebirth that the Hindus call *samsara*. The Theravada is considered the "purist" school, for it teaches an austere practice by which a limited number will find direct enlightenment.

In Thailand, although the official religion is Theravada Buddhism, the older animist traditions of spirit belief deeply invade all aspects of the religious life, most particularly in notions of reincarnation, otherworld spirits of the dead, and spirit afterlife.[6] Nevertheless, there is an overarching belief that good deeds will garner merit and thus ensure a better life in the next incarnation. All thoughts, actions, or deeds that observe the noble truths produce merit, a sort of karmic capital, which is stockpiled toward the ultimate goal. Likewise, any thoughts, actions, or deeds that violate the principles reduce the accumulated merit and contribute to ill-fortune, either in this life or the next.

In such a view, accidents never simply happen, but are just deserts. The question is never why something has occurred, but only why now? Any piece of good fortune, of course, is seen as due or even expected. All merit is accumulated in what might be termed a "spiritual trust fund," which may be drawn upon within this life or applied

5. The Eightfold Noble Path of Buddhism comprises right understanding, right thought, right speech, right action, right livelihood, right effort, right mindfulness, and right concentration.

6. See Tambiah 1978.

to the luck of rebirth. As with other trust funds, however, the "executor" is not the beneficiary. One does not know if rewards will come in this life or in the next. In the more traditional sense, merit making is about far-sighted sacrifice, deposits in bonds that may or may not make you rich, that you cannot choose to redeem.

Any attempt to change Thai social attitudes toward deafness must confront Theravada notions of merit and rebirth, which focus strictly on the individual, rather than on the social as in the Mahayana tradition. Thus, any marked birth, be the mark a disability, female gender, poverty, or merely unattractive appearance, is seen as a karmic product due: just rewards for insufficient merit gained in a prior life. The victim bears full blame. Responsibility for pulling oneself up by the bootstraps, so to speak, is not restricted to just this life alone.

While the more learned Thais generally understand a "better rebirth" in moral or allegorical terms, the common Thai will usually see it in purely material terms. Thus, the rich and privileged are somehow seen as deserving their good fortune because of what must have been good deeds in previous lives. The opportunity to make merit—by, say, hosting a feast or supporting a temple—traditionally represented the average Thai's highest goal in life. If the rich are envied, it may well be as much for their ability more easily to make merit than for the wealth they possess. Lottery winners are distinctly viewed as being rewarded for good karma from past merit stockpiles.

That the rich put on shows of patronage is thus seen as simply a carryover from their gracious behaviors in earlier lives; such acts are not required but merely are an afterglow of that merit. The rich may be appealed to on this basis of a respect due to a sacred judgment of their own merit. Such requests from the poor or less fortunate are phrased as recognitions of the superior status and merit of the wealthy, which naturally mean they must be generous. This moral jujitsu is consistent with Scott's representation of the "weapons of the weak" in the distinctive Islamic culture of neighboring northern Malaysia,[7] and there it is added to moral claims for patronage. The

7. J. Scott 1985.

Thai claims are usually framed in a discourse of "fairness," as opposed to "rights."

A truly "good" person, one reborn into a position of wealth or power who also exhibits a special charismatic graciousness or *baramee*, is highly prized because of his or her high spiritual merit (and not because of the particular generosities that may be exhibited through that graciousness). This teleological underpinning dovetails nicely with traditional patronage systems of loyalty that are an overt part of Thai discourse and political practice.[8] The expectation of assistance from the wealthy to the poor is thus framed not in the Western notion of "entitlement" but rather in karmic terms of merit and *baramee*.

I must stress that I am looking at aberrations within the practices of merit making and patronage; many Thais make merit by doing good without seeking praise or recognition of their contributions. Compassion is understood to be a profitable state of mind, and helping others represents a form of saving, albeit in an intangible account, for another future. A traditional Thai teaching instructs one "to gild the back of the Buddha," or to put the gold leaf where it will escape public notice but pay the homage due. Its purport, of course, is to do good deeds without expectation of public recognition. Many Thais practice their beliefs in such a way. I must make this clear, even at the cost of some repetition, because my particular observations are of those who demand, either with or without subtlety, popular notice of their merit-making efforts. They are a small but highly visible minority who also have considerable impact.

Merit making is not a neutral activity. In popular discourse, it is often framed in win-lose terms. Socially minded Thais seeking personal advancement learn early how to prospect for potential merit and opportunistically to mine it out. Merit mining is a process of extracting positive value by (re)confirming the negative "mark" assigned to an other. The most valued "ore" is the one most clearly marked negative, as the merit lies in the image of a positive reversal effected on the crude negative material. Those who most "deserve"

8. Hanks 1962; see also Sombat Chantornvong 1978.

such attention are not those in greatest "need" nor even most likely to benefit from some imagined assistance, but those who provide the best mirror, who will most brightly reflect the act of supposed "generosity." Merit may be said here to be a value of imaginary candlepower. The act is merely the candle, but its brightness is directly proportional to the understood "markedness" of the object on which it falls. Like money, merit has no intrinsic value; its worth resides entirely in its image. The episteme is merit accounting in a karmic economy.

The formal and informal rituals by which this karmic accounting is pursued are rich and varied. One of the most common phrasings of Thai interest refers to "the benefit" of individual action. The seeking of merit is thus often seen as a selfish activity, one that attempts to serve only the active agent's acquisition of merit. This framing, however, is certainly not the only one, as a brief digression will make clear.

The historical uses of selfishness are entangled in knowing and identity formation.[9] To recognize cultural distinctions in the use of selfish/selfless claims, let us consider some examples of differences between Thai and Western assumptions. Thais have been observed, in the limited anthropological literature that devotes any attention to the topic, to ascribe engaging in social relationships to selfish motives, and even parents refer to childrearing in terms of reciprocity (i.e., the children will take care of me when I am old). Thais are, in fact, highly suspicious of the selfless claims of Westerners about their own engagement in social relations, often dismissing them out of hand. Development project workers have usually noted that villagers more readily accept them when they describe their reasons for being

9. "Selfish interest is radically posed as coming before knowledge, which it subordinates to its needs as a simple instrument; a knowledge, which is dissociated from pleasure and happiness, is linked to the struggle, the hate, and the spitefulness directed against it until it arrives at its own rejection as an excess created by struggle, hate, and spitefulness: its original connection to truth is undone once truth becomes merely an effect—the effect of a falsification what we call the opposition of truth and falsehood"; Foucault on Nietzsche, in "History of Systems of Thought" (in 1977, p. 203).

in the village in terms of benefits to either themselves or their employers. It is best to explain that research is conducted not because "I am interested" or "I want to help," but because "I am working on a university degree." The value of education is widely accepted in rural Thailand, so work that will lead to a higher degree, and consequently to higher-paying positions (or so they assume), makes good sense. The villagers now "understand" the motives of the worker and happily situate him or her accordingly. If the researcher insists on maintaining the claim of selfless motives, the villagers will more likely shun him or her out of a certain distrust of what the real motives might be.

This description may at first seem to confirm the attitude of the intellectual Westerner condescending to the concreteness of the villagers who need concrete selfish motives. But such condescension totally fails to recognize the complexity of the Thai understanding of motives and the reasons to claim them. Indeed, Thais often hide selfless actions under claims of selfish interests, while Westerners are more likely to hide selfish interests under claims of selfless motives. Any visitor to Thailand, no matter how brief or shallow the exploration, is struck by the genuine hospitality and warmth of the Thai people to strangers. The examples of wide-ranging selfless actions abound. Yet, the rhetoric of selfishness is almost always employed.

Thus a Thai story tells of a group of villagers carrying a heavy load along the road. One man, older and smaller than the others, is especially struggling with his share. A young man, seeing the situation, steps in to help the old man, but in so doing says, "*auw boon*"—literally, "I want the merit"—which is to say he claims to be stepping in because he sees an opportunity to gain karmic merit. By claiming totally selfish motives, he spares the old man both the embarrassment at his inability to fulfill his task and any requirement of reciprocity that would be incurred. Because the young man is "receiving" the merit, the reciprocity has already been fulfilled. Yet all involved understand that he was responding to the needs of the older man; he has done so in a way considered appropriate in the Thai episteme.

The questions of interpretation and representation raised by consideration of Thai notions of selfishness recall similarly contrasting and sometimes conflicting worldviews in notions of rights talk. The classic pluralism normally associated with human rights, rights talk, or basic needs discourse is distinct from the pluralism tied to the postmodern critiques that question the extent to which coded orders of meaning are interpenetrable, trespassing, in constant transition, and in open negotiation. This postmodern notion, which takes into account how specific cultural contexts and histories penetrate some ideologies while perpetuating others, displaces the understanding of pluralism that reigned in the project of modernity. That earlier, smorgasbord view of value neutrality tolerated the coexistence of distinct judicial orders in shared jurisdictions (what anthropologists call "legal pluralism") and the structures of colonial administration that juxtaposed indigenous labor forces, nationalized (native) civil service, and colonial (European) administration. One might say that the older regime of separate but equal (interpretations) is giving way to an uneasy intermingling. Yet an intellectual kind of busing, rather than just the racial and class kind, will still be needed.

To those who directly engage in organizing efforts to empower individuals and groups of people previously disenfranchised, the relations with external sources of power and finance are always problematic. From the politicized viewpoint of power relations, the dynamic between development goals and charity efforts usually mirrors the struggle between empowerment and subjugation. In the practical terms of everyday work, however, such pure distinctions are not always possible. As those in need scramble for basic resources necessary for individual and group survival, they have little luxury to attend to the intentions of the donor. But those who are striving to sustain organized action cannot so easily ignore the relationship with sources of financing and the expectations that are always attached to aid.

Most project-oriented groups that seek to enter into the terrain of administrative discourse, which is to say move beyond the discrete actions of a few individuals into sustained programs supportive of collective action, depend on external funding and resources in the beginning; many depend on outside help for an extended time. Groups that have long been disenfranchised or otherwise excluded usually require some type of external catalyst to assist their efforts at self-help. The particular type of assistance that might be needed in specific circumstances may vary widely. The demands and expectations that come attached to external support also vary widely–but, in some form, they are always present. The demands may be linked to visible status and perceived merit, or they may be in the terms of goals and objectives achieved favored by foreign donors. The point here, however, is that external agents, under whatever name (change agent, animateur, catalyst, etc.), are often crucial elements in disrupting current practices, introducing notions of alternative practices, or sustaining efforts at new practices.

Such outsiders, alone, cannot effect anything lasting. That is the domain of those directly involved. Nevertheless, the outsider may see forms and processes that escape those who are too close, too directly affected by their everyday manifestations. By impertinently calling attention to exclusion, oppression, or processes that maintain disenfranchisement, the outsiders bring to light assumptions well-known yet left unquestioned. The very act of this calling into question often suggests that other possibilities exist: "Even the thought of a possibility can shake us and transform us; it is not merely sensations or particular expectations that do that! Note how effective the possibility of eternal damnation was!" [10]

Indeed, the leaders of the Deaf Thai movement have often acknowledged the crucial role of the catalytic ideas of outsiders in their initial efforts to create a national association. They took great pains, as the organization grew, that it would be fully controlled by Deaf Thais, but they often referred to both financial and technical support from the outsiders as crucial ingredients in turning simple desires into working programs and activities. Those of us who made up the particular "outsiders" in this project spent many late nights across the kitchen table examining our mutual concerns about "boundaries" that might be or were being overstepped. The outsiders were

10. Friedrich Nietzsche, quoted in Heidegger 1979, p. 129.

foreigners—hearing, wealthy, and privileged, at least in comparison to the native Deaf Thais with whom we were working. Compared even to emerging middle-class Thais, we were certainly neither wealthy nor particularly privileged.[11] But though these assessments were clearly relative, they were nonetheless valid.

Sources for financial and technical resources, particularly funding sources that are also empathetic to poor, dispossessed, disenfranchised, or otherwise disadvantaged groups, are quite limited. The competition that is fostered, both by the need of the potential recipients and, more purposefully, by the donor groups themselves as they compete with their foundation peers for prestige in their grant portfolios, mirrors the degradation of the value of grassroots programs as they accept the tainted money of the elites: the donors and recipients are caught in a Hegelian master-slave dynamic. The competition is also destructive of the networking efforts of the small nonprofits that prepare and manage grants and provide technical expertise. They—referring to any of the above: donor, nonprofit, or indigenous group—cannot risk sharing information that may lessen their own chances for the limited benefits available, whether in the material of funding or in the semiotics of prestige.

These, however, are not the only constraints suffered by those trying to create collective notions of self-identity and "community." The dynamics of "self-help" efforts by young Deaf adults occur on playing fields already delimited. The practices that naturalize the ground rules of these delimited playing fields begin with a diagnosis. The particular diagnosis occurs in the preschool.

Cultural Triage: Preschool "Failures"

What might a deaf child begin to understand about the world he or she is growing into when, by dominant Hearing norms, he or she is

11. In the descriptions of early efforts, the "we" refers primarily to Charles Reilly and myself. As the director of the foundation providing the grant support, I also brought a range of technical consultants to Thailand specifically for this project, as well as for others. Many of those engaged in other projects became active in advising the NADT, simply because the project and the people involved were so dynamic and so interesting.

already a second-round loser, formally labeled a "failure," when only six years old? Will that child consider it to be, after all, a "hearing" world and gather that strength of inner inspiration needed for the heroic endeavor to acquire the competence now held out as required for basic membership? Or, rather, might the deaf child get the idea that this so-called hearing world is simply uninterested in anyone whose difference might suggest that certain choices had already been made—and forgotten?

A child only just out of preschool does not have the option of presenting objections strong enough to renegotiate rules of societal membership. Already rejected by two systems dedicated to the production of acceptable identities, simply because of a difference that interferes with their ground rules that set how teaching and individual communications will take place, the deaf child, with so few backup support mechanisms either personal or familial, is by definition effectively excluded from any meaningful participation. While the particular circumstances I will describe occur in Thailand, they commonly take place in educational systems throughout the world. Call it "marginalization by preschool."

How can this happen? (And why are good preschools for deaf children so crucial?) A curious phenomenon seems to occur when official efforts are made to establish special preschools for deaf children. The deaf children selected are generally identified as failures from regular school entry groups, or they are similarly selected out as teachers give up on further efforts to communicate with—or control—the different child. After gathering these "problem" children to form a special class of the "deaf," children identified by their hearing loss, an odd shift takes place. Rather than accepting what all the children do have in common, nearly all efforts are focused on discovering which children, in fact, "don't belong"—which demonstrate any residual hearing. These children, the ones who can almost hear, are then given nearly all the instructional attention. The defining characteristic that brought the children into the class—that they did not hear—becomes grounds for further exclusion.

Typically, all "teaching" efforts are focused on the residual hearing of those children more accurately called "hard of hearing" or "hearing impaired." Those children who are actually deaf are ignored after failing this further test. Those children whose residual hearing enables them to exhibit some speech skills are particularly prized and receive special attention. They are labeled as "successful," while those for whom the special class was originally designed, the children who are deaf, are (again) labeled as "failures," a labeling that reproduces and reinforces the negative stigma.

After the significance of this early label is fully appreciated by both children and parents, these children are relegated, if they are lucky, to the official schools for the deaf as "failures" of the preschool program. Nothing could be more destructive (except not to be given the chance to attend these schools). This segregation in the name of special attention serves to reinforce only the most negative stereotypes of the disability, while attending to few, if any, of the needs of the deaf child. This is especially so as few schools for the deaf have administrators who are Deaf or have more than a token number of teachers who are Deaf.

Preschool triage based on the oral-centric model of the body presumes an "either/or" approach to language. Either the children can be "taught" to be hearing, or, as failures, they can gesture to one another. In the final stage of triage, as the last "survivors" of hearingness that might yet "succeed" in the hearing world are sought, the "either/or" restriction is converted into a question of "which first?" As one high-ranking Thai official said, "Sign language is easy. They can learn it anytime. Better to try speech first to see who can." The phrasing has little effect on the bureaucratic apparatus and its policy choices. The question "which first?" almost always assumes the same answer: voice/hearing. Always the answer is determined by what is convenient for bureaucrats, teachers, and parents, not by the interests of the deaf children. Whatever is chosen as "first" further enacts a delay, a silencing, or an exclusion of the "second."

Since the issue is access to language, asking "which first?" denies access to one modality by implying that such access must be detrimental to the privileged choice—to speech as language. This remains a central claim of oral-only and oral-centric policies for the deaf. Access to both modalities seems too inconvenient for consideration. Common sense, as well as the evidence of research, directly counters such an assumption. It is curious, but terribly oppressive, that only in deaf education is access to more than one language still considered detrimental and formally discouraged. This idea that contact with foreign languages and ideas is potentially "contaminating" was discarded by most educators earlier this century,[12] yet it persists in the management of deaf education. Consequently, sign language is recognized less as a viable option than as the simple and final "safety net" or "basket" into which the children who fail in becoming "talking-children-who-don't-hear" may later fall. Now, with the shift from "either/or" to "which first," the policy might appear to reflect a softer and gentler approach, with less rigid procedures and labels than in the past, but the goals and the general results remain the same.

Currently, various "total communication" techniques are tossed in the general direction of deaf children in school. Most often, these methods are reduced to the teacher writing on the blackboard and the children copying. In the Thai schools for the deaf, "copy from the blackboard" exercises are quite popular, as they give like-minded teachers ample free time to gossip over tea or coffee. Should communication occur in the classroom, it is almost always of a one-way nature (teacher at child).

Actual conversations between students and teachers are rare. Few teachers bother to observe the emerging grammatical usages in the signing of the children assigned to them. Most simply note that the form differs from the written grammar sequences that they wish the children to learn. Thus the children continue to exhibit their "inability to learn." Most communication between teacher and child, be it direct or indirect, is about discipline. Rarely is it about content or ideas. Deaf teachers would more likely attune to the de-

12. Exceptions remaining include certain fundamental religious groups and fringe "English-Only" movements. Each of these movements frames the issues as ones of purity and defilement by others.

veloping grammatical skills of the children and build them to that point at which "metalanguage"[13] could be understood. At that point, the deaf children can begin their understanding of their first "foreign" language, the written form of the national language—in this case, written Thai.

Hearing teachers—usually those who have good communication skills yet are not particularly fluent in sign—are the ones who promote the idea that sign is a simple skill and can be postponed until other options have proven the children "failures." This misrepresentation suits the teachers quite well, as it perpetuates the habit of blaming the victims for not becoming better-educated children. As the children are already karmically marked as failures at birth, their continued failure is, to a real extent, expected. This is not a conscious ploy that bad teachers have undertaken with some hope of personal gain; rather, it is a strategy for coping with their generally poor training and worse results in teaching. Whatever the rationale, it is a powerful influence, whether those affected are conscious of it or not. The economics of merit accumulation legitimate the conclusion.

This designation of failure is further reproduced in educational reporting about the achievements of deaf children throughout their school years. Both officials and teachers, for example, often refer to deaf school children as "learning impaired," because they have records of poor achievement. Under the circumstances, a more accurate label for these children is "instructionally impaired." While the limitations on learning for deaf children may be said to begin from what I have called marginalization by preschool, the low expectations are reproduced in a self-fulfilling manner, from the status marker of their affliction through each level of educational experience.

The negative marking of the child thus becomes inescapable. Having been deprived of early access to sign language in the course of their "failures" in oral education, many deaf adults suffer the next stigma of "signing like a hearing person" when they later attempt to

---

13. Language used to talk about language and, here, about the rules for writing the spoken languages they do not hear.

enter into a Deaf social community. Because they learned the language late in life, their articulation skills mark them as "nonnative." Their legitimacy as members of the Deaf community—even when they are marked as "oral failures"—is compromised. They lack the social competence, in this case the fluency, required of the native. They are marginalized yet again.

Let us contrast, if you will, education for the blind. Here, education focuses on two sensory channels: hearing and touch. Since blind children hear, lessons are provided by verbal instruction. Reading, for the fortunate few, is learned through touch via the code to written language known as Braille. Hence, education focuses on those sensory channels that are available to the blind schoolchild. Oddly, deaf education also focuses on the same sensory channels: hearing and touch. For the majority of the deaf child's school years, enormous attention will be given to "residual hearing," auditory training, and other methods of speech therapy. For those who are too profoundly deaf to make use of hearing aids, efforts are made to teach them to "feel" sound vibrations. Musical instruments are popular auditory equipment. Typing is yet another major focus of tactile skill, which promotes hand-eye coordination, not literacy. Hence, while the sensory impairments are totally different, the educational approach relies on the same senses. Rather than shining bright lights into blind eyes and stuffing larger loudspeakers into deaf ears, educators should focus on the sensory channels open to learning. Yet, the obsessions of the hearing with the sound of their own voice [14] dictate that deaf children continue to be poorly served in education, and deaf adults in other social services.

Like other colonizers before them, educators often refuse to see evidence contrary to their expectations. As noted earlier, the sign language research at the National Association of the Deaf in Thailand, and the Thai Sign Language dictionaries that resulted, explored the sophistication of the native Thai Sign Language. This work confirmed other recent research in and by native signing com-

---

14. The cultural coding draws from RCA Victor's trademark, "His Master's Voice" / ("arf, arf").

munities around the world. The linguistic richness of sign is much deeper than had been (or is still) suspected by the majority of hearing educators. Most hearing educators, of deaf Thai children in this case, know only the public world of the schoolchild. To them, the simple level of sign language required merely to gain control and maintain obedience within the classroom, as well as to invoke a ritualistic bureaucracy, confirms their belief and "knowledge" that sign language is a simplistic form of communication, a mere subset of a language, by which a lesser-born form of human is indulged or "provided for." Such assumptions "prove" themselves true, in the practices of deaf education and in the broader social practices that sustain them, in spite of abundant evidence to the contrary available in the public domain created by deaf people themselves. This domain, however, is small and passes unnoticed in the late-modern urban swirl.

Today we are witnessing the first generation of hearing children of Deaf Thais who are learning the sign language of their parents. In the past, Deaf Thais were rarely allowed to marry. The few deaf couples who had children usually lost control over raising them to the extended family. Certainly this new generation of children exhibit no harm from "exposure" to sign language from the earliest ages, a fear most often used by hearing grandparents to deny their deaf children access to their own offspring. For these children, as for their hearing peers, public performance and achievements are somewhat tied to their parents' economic status, which determines their opportunities for education and social advancement. A few Deaf Thai parents have been able to provide a rich and interactive environment in supportive, extended families. Some of their children are high achievers at this early stage of life.

However, hearing children who actually grow up with active and direct relations with their deaf parents in Thailand are almost exclusively those in poorer, working-class circumstances. This status puts them at a disadvantage regarding the all-important contacts and family ties that Thais require for access to higher education and employment. Thus, while we see a handful of bright, articulate, and sign/speech bilingual children emerging within the urban Deaf Thai setting, the hope they embody may not necessarily bring any tangible returns for this generation. While the first native interpreters solidly rooted both culturally and linguistically in the Deaf Thai community could and might come from among these children, their limited options for higher education and their lack of connections might bar access to the few opportunities for employment that do appear. As interpreters are needed by mass media, those hired are freelancing school officials who have the minimal signing skills needed to fool the hearing television executives.

An example: one of the most talented of these young interpreters, a hearing sister of a TSL dictionary research team member, had signing skills good enough to pass as a Deaf person in large gatherings of Deaf Thais. Her skills for translating spoken Thai into TSL were also good. However, her interpreting of TSL into spoken Thai was problematic as she lacked the formal schooling necessary to produce the vocabulary nuances of educated Thais. And, of course, she had no familiarity with the class-bound formalities of elite rhetorical practices. Which is to say she signed wonderfully but signaled her class and educational background when speaking. Thai public culture is very conscious of such status-marking codes. Thus, to help her training she was given entrance and tuition fees for college over several years, as well as teamed with our other hearing Thai interpreter, whose mix of signing and cultural skills was just the reverse. She is currently doing freelance interpreting and living at home. And these are the options of hearing members of the "community."

"A Little Hearing Can Be Made to Go a Long Way"

Popular media often reflect, or attempt to reflect, dominant values. Nowhere is this more evident than in Sunday feature stories that are tagged "human interest." One such offering was found in the *Bangkok Post* on 8 December 1991. Saowarop Panyacheewin's feature section cover story was entitled, "A Little Hearing Can Be Made to Go a Long Way." This article could have appeared in any urban newspaper anywhere,[15] as it represents a popular view of deafness or hearing impairment that has spread globally. It is the usual story of piety, sacrifice, and the dedication needed to overcome great odds. While the achievements are small, they are ennobled by the efforts necessary to achieve them. The story revolves around several mothers, their hearing-impaired children, and the headmistress of a demonstration day school (nonresidential) run by a major teacher-training college. There are no grades and advancement is exclusively pegged to speech production. They "have to understand this is a speaking world and that they must speak in order to communicate."

This article and its language are filled with unconscious irony. Certainly the call to teach hearing-impaired children is a noble one. Nevertheless, the self-ennobling statements of the experts quoted in this article explicitly deny differences in individual children. As the headmistress says, "Everyone wants to be normal. These children, too. They don't want to be different, or even look different. That's why some of them don't put on hearing aids when walking in the street. They are ashamed to sign. It's better for them to speak, even unintelligibly." Even unintelligibly! A stunning claim. A more accurate representation of the goals of mainstreaming could not be devised. Better these children become little more than frustrated parrots than admit or look at their difference. Better they pass unnoticed than be seen at all. Actually, hearing-impaired children take off their hearing aids because they often fit poorly, amplify noise to painful levels, and do remarkably little to reproduce "normal" hearing.

The belief that with discipline and faith, two virtues stressed in the article, all hearing-impaired children will learn to talk is deeply misguided. The headmistress stresses, "With proper training and lots of patience, I believe all hearing-impaired children will finally be able to talk. It's just a matter of time." But the obsession with reproducing speech, even if unintelligible, is at the direct expense of

15. Indeed, a story along this familiar narrative vein appeared in a Sunday *Honolulu Advertiser/Star-Bulletin*, "'Disabled' Is a No-no Word," by Esme M. Infante (26 April 1992).

intellectual and social development. Most commonly, it produces children with extremely limited vocabulary who are intelligible only to their speech therapist. Better to recognize that all children are different than seek to force all children to meet an ideal of "normal" (impartially average). Nevertheless, this school, like so many that commit themselves to the denial of difference in children, insists that focusing on speech, even unintelligible speech, will produce the normal children the parents so desperately want.

The article is filled with the oldest of dead platitudes, such as the claim of how difficult it is to teach deaf children. "Who wants to teach hearing-impaired children? The job demands a tremendous amount of sacrifice and perseverance, much more than teaching ordinary children." The statement subtly insinuates that any failure of the children is either the fault of the children themselves or is caused by lack of "patience," "discipline," or "practice" at home. The teachers are not responsible for the failure of their students. If the children don't become normal, the reason must be the parents' or the child's inherent limitations. The reporter is at pains to point this out: "Patience is the key word. The fact they can't hear makes it difficult for them to understand the meaning of words. To teach them one word, it might take 10 times longer than for a hearing child. 'Another important factor we always point out is parents' expectations,' Headmistress Orn-anong went on, saying, 'It's natural that every parent wants his child to achieve academic excellence. We remind them to consider the reality, possibility and suitability in all aspects.'"

While forbearance and discipline are called for, failure is predicted and is, predictably, achieved. The mother around whom the story centers admits that she quit her job to focus on the challenge of teaching speech to her deaf son. She talks about her feelings of discouragement but draws strength from the other parents who are also part of the program. The article concludes: "But whenever she's in despair, sharing the experience with other parents is often helpful. The flattened heart is then inflated with hope again. [Headmistress] Orn-anong's words always ring in her ears—given time, every child who can make sound, can talk."

The heart reinflated with such hopes will be repeatedly punctured by the false promise of the school headmistress that hides a horrible lie. It condemns the parent to eternal guilt when the child does not fulfill expectations, and it denies the deaf child the most appropriate vehicle for his her or intellectual and social development.

Better Dorms and Gardens

Ceremony and display are significant features of social life in Thailand. Virtually all events, and certainly all public events, are marked by distinct opening and closing rituals. There is a rich Barthesean range of imagery on display within the ritualistic presentations of Thai culture. The conduct of institutional life also enacts these formal codes.

Because of my professional position in Thailand for over ten years, I have had extensive access to senior officials of programs relating to education and schools throughout rural Thailand, and I have had many opportunities myself to observe the country's culture of education. During that time, the schools for the deaf were not a particular sphere of my work. I visited all of the schools at one time or another, a few on a regular basis. I loved to play with the smaller children. We had great conversations, but I was primarily on the lookout for those ready to graduate who might be possible candidates for apprenticeships in the adult organization. My comments on Deaf Thai school experiences have been greatly enriched by insights that Charles Reilly has shared. His field research in the schools demonstrates both the extent and the significance of the education that occurs in spite of the "education." The anecdotal material that accents this section draws heavily from my discussions with Reilly during his 1991 research in the Tak School for the Deaf, academic work that followed five years of our collaboration in community organizing. I fully acknowledge the importance of his work within the schools to mine here, particularly his study of self-education processes among deaf schoolchildren. The political, ironic, or even occasionally sardonic perspectives about what such evidence might mean within the framework of the surveilled body are entirely my own responsibility.

A brief overview of the bureaucratic structure of the Thai educational system is in order here.[16] The Department of General Education, part of the Royal Thai Government (RTG) Ministry of Education, is responsible for welfare schools, special schools for the handicapped, and education of hill-tribe minorities. The special institutions and the welfare schools are under the authority of the Division of Special Education in the Department of General Education. This division may soon be upgraded to the status of a department within the Ministry of Education. The six mainstreaming programs, all currently located in Bangkok, are under the jurisdiction of the Office of National Primary Education Commission, which handles regular schooling. The Ministry of Public Welfare cares for multihandicapped and abandoned disabled children. On the usual bureaucratic playing fields, these three state entities each seek to define both their mandates and the terms by which the objects of their ministrations, the disabled people themselves, are to be understood. Each of them determines the status of disabled people as distinct "problems" to be managed, although how this problem is to be managed, meaning by what administrative categories and procedures, is peculiar to each agency. Such peculiarities have little to do with the needs or interests of the target groups and everything to do with justifying institutional authority and prerogatives.

The policies toward the education of children from the ethnic hill tribes that populate the border areas of the northern and northeastern regions reflect the shifting management-by-definition of social otherness. The children from these linguistically and ethnically distinct minorities were long referred to as simply being of the "hill tribes." Yet over the past decade the category has shifted, reflecting the changes in national identity policy. Their assigned official iden-

16. For further details on the bureaucratic structure, see Reilly and Suvannus, in press.

tity went first from "Hilltribe" to "Thai Hilltribe." Then it shifted to "Thai people of the Hills." It then went to "Disadvantaged Thais"—that is to say, what disappeared was an ethnicity. Accompanying these changes was a language policy of not teaching the children any of their mother tongue; the notion that they might have any other language than Thai is ignored. It is important to note here that *Thai* refers only to the Central Thai dialect. Thais who speak, for example, either the Northeastern or Southern dialects have long been accustomed to social discrimination on that account. Hill-tribe ethnicity, however, much like Deaf ethnicity, faces obliteration.

Curiously, the schools for these erstwhile hill-tribe children, now "disadvantaged Thais," are administered by the Division of Special Education. They receive only the truncated curriculum, reduced from the national standards, that disabled and welfare school students receive.[17] Thus even as they are stigmatized by being labeled socially inferior, that social inferiority is materially reproduced in the substandard education they are offered, while at the same time the very source of that identity is denied. The mechanism is similar to that in the policy toward deafness, which functions in the same manner as earlier American policies that infantilized women, Blacks, and Native Americans by placing them into the same categories as children and mental incompetents.

Objectives and policies for educational services to disabled children are presented in three documents: National Scheme of Education Buddhist Era Year 2520 (1977), National Curriculum for Elementary Education B.E. 2521 (1978), and Elementary Education Act B.E. 2523 (1980). As part of the seventh five-year national plan of 1991–96, the Ministry of Education has approved a Plan for the Development of Education, Culture, and Religion. There is no central plan common to all governmental work in Thailand, as the five-year plans are sector and ministry specific.[18] The resulting conflict

17. Charles Reilly, conversations with author.

18. The current five-year national plan for 1991–96 is the seventh national plan for Thailand. See Reilly and Suvannus, in press.

สะอาดมาก, เรียบมาก, เรียบร้อย, เหมาะสม,. พร้อมเสร็จ

ท่ามือนี้เป็นรูปแบบของการเน้นของท่ามือข้างบน
แสดงออกโดยการเอนศีรษะและลำตัว

very clean, very smooth, neat, proper, ready

This is an emphatic form of the sign above,
shown by the shifted head and body.

Figure 2. Thai Sign for *riep-roi* (Suwanarat, Wrigley, et al. 1990, p. 62).

and overlap of authority often produce administrative policies described at best as benign neglect. As many as five ministries may
share responsibility for a single area of work. Appropriations for the
education of the deaf come from the Ministry of Education, Ministry of Interior (Department of Public Welfare), Ministry of Public
Health, Office of the Prime Minister, Office of the Royal House-
hold, Bureau of Universities, and Bangkok Metropolitan Authority.

The Thai schools for the deaf, along with the other special
schools, are best approached as large warehouses for children that
also have nice gardens.[19] That the gardens should be vigorously
maintained to increase the beauty of the schools is a prime matter
for attention from the highest levels in the Ministry of Education.
This is proudly proclaimed in the only magazine published by the
Department of General Education, which has a title perhaps best
translated as *Beautiful Gardens, Handsome Schools.* The preoccupation with proper appearances is found throughout many aspects of
Thai social life. The term *riep-roi,* meaning both "proper" and
"complete in preparation," marks a central social value (see fig. 2).

The central manifestation of this obsession is in institutional dis-

19. Hence the title of this section, part of the communal idiom coined at the
East-West Center, which honors the style of Dr. Patricia Masters. Additional thanks
to Dr. Joanna Crocker.

play. More attention is given to the school (and its appearance) than to the deaf children who inhabit it. Some observers have suggested that nearly 60 percent of school hours may be spent in gardening and grounds maintenance by the children. This institutional focus on "appearances," for want of a better word, overshadows all other pedagogical concerns. Thus, as the level of formal (RTG) attention to the schools for the deaf increases, there is both evidence and reason to suggest that the actual quality of education received by the children will *decline*, rather than improve. This is, as I have been demonstrating, exactly as would be expected.[20]

Previously, the schools were "ignored" and what education might or might not have occurred was determined by the circumstances of the particular school, by the occasionally interested teacher, but mainly by the children themselves. As interest—and surveillance—increases, the deaf schools are absorbed into the ritualized regime of national goals of education, and the daily time schedule within deaf schooling is more tightly policed. With less time available for the child-child and younger child–older child interactions whose function is so crucial, particularly in deaf education, students have fewer opportunities to learn; the ever-tightening rules and procedures directly harm their cognitive opportunities. As this increasing attentiveness by the authorities does not seem to extend to the content of the education (except perhaps to find talents that "hearinglike" deaf children can display), the product will most likely be a more docile and polite (and consequently more acceptable) deaf child, but not necessarily a better educated one.

Content, when it does make an appearance, generally falls into the category of "copy this." Deaf children often learn good penmanship, which is to say that "calligraphy" may describe their curriculum better than any list of academic subjects. But while attractive penmanship may be learned, literacy rarely comes with it. In my own observations in the Thai schools, I often found teachers gathered

---

20. See Foucault 1979. Reilly's (1995) ethnography of a Deaf Thai school documents the mechanics of this transition now underway within the Thai educational setting.

คัดลอก
(ข่าวสารไม่ว่าจะเป็นข้อเขียนหรือคำพูด)
จากแหล่งอื่น

เช่น "เขาคัดลอกเอกสารจากแหล่งอื่นทุกหน้า
        ลงในสมุด"

copy from, transfer from, duplicate from

(written information) from another source

Figure 3. Thai Sign for copying (Suwanarat, Wrigley, et al. 1990, p. 605).

over coffee for gossip away from the classrooms, leaving the children to repetitively copy text from the blackboards. While the children may learn the meanings of individual words, it was rare to find a child who actually understood most of what he or she was copying. The children's description of this activity is a sign that depicts a crude transposition from one location to another (see fig. 3). It is a rather accurate portrayal of their education.

This mechanical approach is certainly not new, although it has been long gone from hearing schools. In 1801, *The Complete Description of the Genetic Writing Method for Public Elementary Schools* was published. This early attack on the old cultural technique of imitation, the simple mechanics of copying, attempted to transform it into psychologically motivated, self-initiated activity: "As in most subjects, writing teachers were accustomed to using only the most mechanical teaching techniques and did not have the slightest inkling that writing instruction should be employed as *material for the autonomous development of intelligence and imagination*. . . . Up to now the usual procedure consisted in constraining students to copy and recopy examples until they developed a *mechanical skill* that allowed them *to copy correctly*."[21] Though the "now" of that extract refers to the year 1801, this mechanical procedure, as well as many

21. Quoted in Kittler 1990, pp. 81–82 (emphases in original).

other techniques from that same period, are still in use today in the schools for the deaf.

Deaf children generally create a richer peer society than do "average" (hearing) children.[22] Because the deaf receive so little stimulus from teachers or other external sources, they create these rich worlds themselves. Part of this "richness" has to do with the "loaded" nature of the experiences. In the private world of deaf children, both unenriched and unimpeded by the hearing society around it, the significance attached to meaning production is heightened due to the exclusivity—and scarcity—of its production and its audience. The rural residential deaf school is a "static free" communicative world. There is little input from any external source, be it radio, newspapers, or teachers. This is no idyllic recreation of a bucolic, simpler past, but rather an isolated environment without intellectual nourishment, into which bright and inquisitive children are placed. Most survive, but very few thrive. In chapter 3, the experience of signing itself was seen as "value laden" because of its rarity. In this situation, it is not the language modality that is rare, but the access to any content-laden event, educational or otherwise. Any source of information thus gains value because of its rarity.

Lacking substantive input from the adult world, whether hearing or deaf, deaf children are left to produce a world of their own. From an administrative standpoint, the teachers are all too happy to oblige. The children learn most, it might well be argued, from mimicking the relations they observe among the hearing officials. As the officials put most of their energy into maintaining relations of status, rather than into teaching, the children merely follow their lead. The content of the adults' activities are best described as the daily tactics of petty officialdom. These methods, plus the direct disciplinary tactics applied in the class and dormitory, are the models of control that the children actively copy.

Reilly's fieldwork notes that leaders for lineup and dormitory duties are selected by the school officials. These are the legitimated dominators. The bullying personality is usually rewarded, particu-

22. Charles Reilly, communication with author.

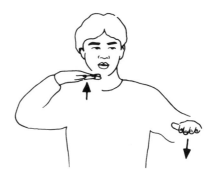

ฉันแก่กว่า/เขาอ่อนกว่า, ฉันอายุมากกว่า/เขาอายุน้อยกว่า
เช่น "ฉันแก่กว่า เขาอายุน้อยกว่า"
แก่กว่า/อ่อนกว่าของความสัมพันธ์ทางสังคมหรือ
"พี่/น้อง" เป็นด้านหนึ่งของหัวข้อที่สำคัญของ
วัฒนธรรมไทย ท่ามือต่อไป 253.3 เป็นท่ามือ
เหมือนกันที่หมายถึงสาระสำคัญอื่นของฐานะ
เช่น จำนวนเงิน
I am elder and he/she is younger, he is younger
and I am elder
"I was elder, he the younger."
The elder/younger, or "Pi/Nong," social relation
is an important facet of Thai culture. The next
sign, 253.3, is the same sign referring to other
elements of status such as amount of money.

Figure 4. Thai Sign for *pii-nong* (Suwanarat, Wrigley, et al. 1990, p. 253).

larly if the other children are kept in line with minimum effort by (or minimum presence of) the instructors. The bullies represent the pecking order of the dominant society and thus, in this limited sense, serve a specific instructive and formative purpose.

In Thai institutions, a particular set of anchor points revolve around relations of rank and status, the first frame being simply of age. These are intimately linked to, and often framed as rooted in, the *pii-nong*, or "elder-younger" relation, which is a crucial marker in Thai personal and cultural relationships (see fig. 4). The relationship called *pii-liung*, or "elders take care of younger," is an extension of the ranked patronage system into the personal sphere and is considered one of the strongest of Thai cultural bonds. Elder students learn to take care of younger as part of the cultural training in self-positioning.

The use of such anchors, like other hermeneutic resting points, depends on the practices onto which they are grafted. They may encourage warm and supporting relations, but they may rigidly reinforce privilege and subordination. In the Tak school, Reilly discovered a young tough, little more than eight years old, assigned total control over the bathing time of the youngest and least-educated boys. This authority was given to him by a deaf student leader appointed by the teachers. The control exercised by this boy within his little domain was both total and tyrannical. As "bath master," he drilled and marched younger boys in a naked and regimented bath— time discipline. In lineups, such as before meals, he likewise held absolute sway over them. In a display of petty arrogance over his own charges, and as further evidence of the splendid isolation of its power, I watched this boy, after first whipping several young boys into a premeal lineup, turn on a teacher who was walking past and, in clear and precise signing, tell him off in no uncertain terms. The teacher, unable to understand sign, gave an indulgent smile to the posturing young martinet and walked on. The boys in the lineup, however, saw this display as only further confirmation of his absolute power over them. In some regards, a world not unlike that portrayed in William Golding's *Lord of the Flies* (1954) is reproduced within institutional confines.

There are also many positive relationships that emerge from within this child-created world. Occasionally, a school-selected leader may coincide with a peer-identified teacher-leader. It would appear, however, that generally those roles are quite distinct. The most important sources for learning and self-awareness are the storytellers, those among the children that Charles Reilly calls "the sign masters." The storytellers are leaders who are not appointed but simply emerge. Children gravitate to them out of their own desires.

The sign masters are the storytellers and comedians produced within each generation of children. Small groups of Thai school-children form friendship packs, which in turn gravitate toward image and role models. Author Christopher Moore describes them as "puan pods," a hybrid term using the Thai word for "friend," *puan*.[23] One such group will be discussed in detail below. The storytellers are the primary providers of narratives and intellectual stimulus for deaf children in rural schools. Rather than offering a passive source of entertainment, such as that from television or video, the storytellers engage their listeners through a direct linguistic narration that is both interactive and personalized.

My own presence as a visitor to these settings was always some-

23. Moore's works include *A Killing Smile* (1990), *A Haunting Smile* (1991), and *Asia Hand* (1992).

thing of an event. Visitors to the more rural schools are rare, and visits by foreigners even rarer. But a visit from a foreigner who signs in their own Thai Sign Language both seems unbelievable and also routinely leads several children to assume and then ask if all foreigners must not then know Thai Sign. Most questions from the younger deaf children, however, are what might be called "reality checks." They have seen either the videos of *RoboCop* and *Terminator* or their embellished recreations by one of the sign masters, and often the most important thing in their lives is to verify if these movies might be "true" or not. I could not help but marvel at the impact of the sign masters as manifested in the imaginative worlds of their young charges, an impact that provides further evidence of the severe paucity of stimulus and input from other sources.[24]

As holds true in other storytelling traditions, styles vary substantially among sign masters. Some take the plots of popular movies and embellish them with dramatics that draw the listeners into the events retold, while others take troubles and experiences from their own lives to talk out lessons and morals to be learned. Some are comedians; some are serious and concerned. These creative reflections by sign masters, children themselves, some of which deeply mirror their social positioning and future prospects, provide among the most significant, if not the only, intellectual stimuli in the deaf child's educational world. Regardless of style, each sign master finds an eager and hungry audience of younger children who hang on every nuance of the stories.

The hunger is real. In that static- and input-free world, the storytellers create through imaginative retellings a rich fabric that is the only intellectual world to which the children have direct access. When children are directly asked why they want to sit with the story masters, why they like the stories of the sign masters, why they are eager to participate in their retellings, the response is invariably a sign that translates as "desire, hunger, crave" (see fig. 5). Manfa Suwanarat, the leader of the Deaf Thai Sign Language research team, frequently spoke of her "hunger" to learn. Even in re-

24. Charles Reilly, communication with author.

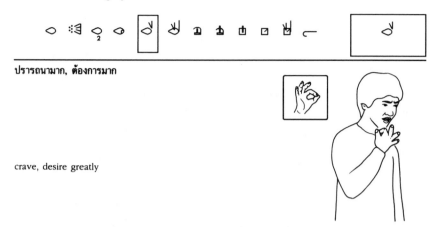

ปรารถนามาก, ต้องการมาก

crave, desire greatly

Figure 5. Literally, this is the "thirst or hunger for narrative" (Suwanarat, Wrigley, et al. 1990, p. 463). This image also includes the handshape radicals that are at the top of each page of the dictionary. These radicals, which indicate the base handshape order, are similar to radicals in Japanese or Chinese language dictionaries.

ferring to social opportunities to meet new people, she often used a compound phrase that I might metaphorically translate as a "hunger to socialize." Reilly has discovered through his research the same sentiment emerging independently among the school children of the Tak school.

The storytellers, or sign masters, seem to play a crucial role in the reproduction of deaf culture. While much of the recent writing by Western Deaf writers seeks to confirm a privileged transmission of cultural traditions within families, the experiences of those in these rural schools suggest that the traditions passed include not simply the content of the stories but, more important, the tradition of storytelling as an art—the tradition of "sign masters" themselves. The heritage of storytelling has resonance across cultures. But Deaf storytellers are unusual because of their emergence among young deaf schoolchildren left to their own devices, the necessary regeneration with each cohort that is distinctive to Deaf cultures, the relative absence of cross-generational or familial narratives, and their long existence unnoticed or ignored by administrative functionaries.

These characteristics of Deaf storytelling are significant for a number of reasons. One is that this tradition, flourishing in unrestricted time spent among signing peers, suggests a richness and diversity that could be actively supported within an institutional setting. The "warehouses" have made possible the conditions of a sign-intensive language environment. But rather than support emergent potentials, the Weberian—and current—approach is to ever increase the management of time and daily schedules through a strict adherence to discipline.

The use of discipline and schedules within schools to foster acceptable and appropriate identities is a modernist invention widely adopted and much refined during the mid-twentieth century. In her study of memory and consensual identity in Japan, Patricia Masters examines formal edicts of educational policy "like the *Kokutai no Hongi* of 1937 which was a manual of patriotic education issued by the Ministry of Education." It is partially "an ethics guide, while in actuality, it was part of an intensive propaganda effort directed at school children. . . . Out of this . . . grew the mentality that called for confession, conversion, re-education and rehabilitation."[25] The mechanics she explores demonstrate fastidious attention to minute detail.

There has been a certain safety in the lack of attention given to the processes that produce the "sign masters" and other aspects of Deaf cultures, as increasing attentiveness by the Hearing caretakers within institutional settings usually decreases the opportunities for these activities of cultural transmission to flourish. Free time and unregulated spaces were the blessings of benign neglect, providing the opportunities for those imaginative tellings to occur. For the caretakers, control simply means filling this free time and space. Yet, in so doing, they offer no new creative options, add no new value. Creative opportunity is replaced with the mechanics of control over the body.

Here again, concern can, and should, be expressed about the possible consequences of divulging such mechanisms of cultural integrity. Making visible these "weapons of the weak," the spaces of strength quietly surviving through an oversight of authority, may

25. Masters 1992, pp. 93–94.

well increase the vulnerability of the weak rather than strengthen them. However, the increasing surveillance most likely is occurring for reasons having far less to do with the "need" to control resistance than with bureaucratic concerns, such as institutional display and improved gardens. The opportunity structures within the larger bureaucratic network have little to do with the opportunities available to those within particular institutions. Consequently, whether these strategies of "cultural resistance" are revealed or not, the evidence suggests that the Deaf would receive little attention of any type. They look ripe to be trampled underfoot, regardless of what is or is not said. Welcome to late modernity. I didn't say I like it; but I describe what I see.

Down and Out in Bangkok, Part Two

As was noted in chapter 1, Deaf "communities" in less wealthy nations are mostly found in urban settings, as rural deaf people migrate in search of both employment prospects and other deaf people with whom to congregate socially. Restricted to the lower rungs of the social and economic spheres through lack of education or employment options, and isolated linguistically from the surrounding dominant culture, they focus their attentions primarily on each other. Thus, village or "small town" attitudes and atmosphere are found even in very large urban settings. The Western notion of "the village" resonates with the romantic notions of cultural purity and of a time and place of simpler virtues. As with many other romantic notions, this one has little to do with life as lived in those villages. Generally in Deaf culture, the city is the village. While the backdrop may appear to be a cosmopolitan modernity, the interests of the deaf villagers are generally each other—who's doing what to whom and with whom. The city is merely a backdrop, the "forest" in which this village is located. However, to borrow a phrase from classic primatology, it is a dark and nasty jungle.

Because of their limited economic options, Deaf people in less wealthy nations rarely can make an independent living. Most rarely rise above dependency on family or local indulgence for their livelihood. Peasant life in agrarian and fishing communities makes little distinction of hearing status, but there the options for fulfillment are circumscribed by birth position. Urban settings, while acting as magnets for deaf people seeking other deaf people, offer only a slightly wider range of options. Most deaf men without family connections are laborers of various types. Women have traditionally had slightly more choices, but the risks are frequently higher. Cooking, sewing, and domestic skills have often allowed deaf women to gain employment outside the home, although stories of exploitation and physical abuse are common. As education has become available to an increasing number of deaf people, employers are still more willing to employ deaf women than men, simply because the women are more likely to be docile in the face of poor communication.

Much can be said about Deaf Thai life and opportunity. The growth of the self-representative organization has occurred at the same time as Thailand's phenomenal growth in both physical size and economy and, more particularly, Bangkok's growth as the country's sole urban node. Tourism has been only one part of this development but has actively fueled the expansion of "local culture" industries. Many offer fertile ground for analysis, but here the boom in the street vendor economy is examined as providing a free market in which deaf people found some form of "equal footing" with their competitors.

Vending from baskets on poles, pushcarts, or small storefronts is part of all trading societies. The tourism industry has built on the traditional, periodic agricultural and holiday festivals to create a daily chorus line of displays piled high with any consumer good that looks to be selling well that season. They vary little from the wares offered in any other tourist destination in the world save in thematic overlays and distinctively tacky colors.

Prior to 1981, vending by deaf people was very unusual in Thailand. Only three or four deaf individuals were visibly engaged in the tourist trade, and these were from families of vendors. The exceptions were two artists who had begun selling their own artworks near a major tourist attraction in central Bangkok. In 1985, a government "cleanup" campaign aimed at clearing the footpaths of vendors and hawkers made a few deaf individuals aware of the money being made in vending. As the overall government campaign backfired, increasing rather than reducing street vending and public support of vendors, deaf people also began to join in the ranks of the vendors.

Bangkok, widely promoted as an exotic destination with more than slightly naughty allure, has seen an active vendor culture of petty capitalism fill the streets in both tourist and local shopping entertainment centers, most particularly amid the nightlife areas surrounding the well-known Patpong Road, which is somewhat erroneously labeled Bangkok's "red light" district.[26] A night bazaar opened down the middle of Patpong Road itself, transforming a tawdry go-go, strip bar, and prostitution district into a tawdry go-go, strip bar, and prostitution district with its own market brazenly displaying counterfeit watches and fake designer clothes. It has proven a huge financial success, if not exactly an aesthetic or cultural improvement.

This addition of the night bazaar to the bar district is only a few years old, but fortunes have been made in that period, both by the "landlords" and by the renters of each parcel of approximately one square meter. Rent for such space can be over $1,000 per month, depending on precise location and arrangements with the local officials. This includes electricity for lighting but no protection from the elements. "The elements" include pimps, pushers, prostitutes, and police, in addition to the acid rain and polluted air. Nevertheless, income is good, and deaf vendors are now a very substantial and visible percentage of the vendors along Patpong and the adjacent streets. These deaf vendors include some of the highest-educated and most well-traveled members of the organized community, as well as hired labor with no formal education at all. Income by a few

26. The naming is erroneous not because go-go joints, strip bars, and prostitution are missing, but because the neighborhood is only the open, sanitized version of what exists in several other areas in the city. It is featured, albeit only briefly, in nearly every government tourism presentation on the country. The image is thus "promoted" by formally disapproving glances accompanied by winks to the bankers and police.

of the vendors on the main Patpong Road, for example, can be in excess of $4,000 per month for multiple stall owners. The average national income is several hundred dollars per month.

The deaf vendors have found a qualified form of equal footing in competing with hearing vendors for the tourist trade. With so many languages flooding the street, establishing clear verbal communication is often a slow and laborious process (particularly over the din of pimps and bar hawkers). Gesture and use of calculators to cut straight to the numbers are simple, effective techniques employed by deaf vendors that now are often emulated by the hearing vendors as they conduct business. They do not fake deafness, which is hard to do for very long, but simply use the same broad gestures—and calculators—to lead their customers' attention toward the products and their prices.

The main issue or story here is the impact this sudden avenue to wealth has had. Key to basic street capitalism is, surprise, capital. The few Deaf Thais with family wealth or other connections to funding dominate, while lowly employees are in the position of serfs or very subservient relations. Several of the most promising graduates of the deaf schools now make their meager livings by peddling tourist trinkets as sales assistants on daily wage.

The upside, if you will, is that, as the first of a generation to have such options, many more Deaf Thais can pay their own way; they need not live back at home or in worse conditions of servitude. More Deaf Thai couples have married in the past decade than in the past known visual (oral) history of the Deaf in Thailand. Two major factors have made this possible: the expanding sign language communities, a result of the organizing efforts that provided crucial opportunities for socializing, and the expanding economy into which the deaf could enter, if not by invitation then at least on terms sufficiently favorable to earn incomes unheard of only a few years earlier.

As the "community" grew in numbers and wealth, it began to contract in its perspectives and articulated concerns. With only a few exceptions, vending on Patpong or in other zones has been a one-way ticket out of community involvement. As the vending phenomenon grew in the late 1980s and early 1990s, it became the sole

activity and concern of the best and the brightest, even of the research and organizing staff. Some were those who had traveled to
numerous other countries as representatives of the community—
those seen as the highest "beneficiaries" of the foreign donors.

Many of the more successful vendors admit that their social interaction skills with foreigners were honed through participation in
activities with the National Association of the Deaf in Thailand
(NADT). Yet today, very few have time to contribute back to that
organization. More than one admits that the unpleasant elements
noted above have a stronger influence than they initially suspected,
and many are not happy with what they see happening to themselves
and to their friends. Bickering, greed, and jealous fights over wholesale prices for tourist art and trinkets have become the acknowledged life of several of the most highly trained researchers, who for
ten years took part in multidonor programs and successful projects.

Such projects included researching and producing the two-
volume dictionary of the Thai Sign Language, as well as presenting
the first World Federation of the Deaf (WFD) Resolution on Sign
Language Rights. This resolution was presented formally to the
United Nations by Manfa Suwanarat. She was presented cited by the
Secretary-General of the United Nations, the only Deaf and only
Asian woman cited in 1989, for her work in the field.[27] Today, the
remaining members of the once world-renowned research team all
work as street vendors and sheepishly admit they have all but forgotten the linguistics training that had made them famous. Other former organizational staff, also now found vending on the streets, say
they miss the camaraderie of the organizing teams, but they need
the income to build their own dreams or, at least, forge some semblance of independence.

There are some nice young families of deaf couples with young
children (all hearing so far) struggling to make ends meet with
everyday heroism in their own fashions. One young woman, one of

27. The award was presented posthumously following her death at 37, in 1989,
from an allergic reaction to misprescribed medication. The final volume of the *Thai
Sign Language Dictionary* is dedicated to her memory.

a pair of deaf twins who had long been among those central to form-ing the NADT, described how she first saw working as a vendor simply in terms of trade or daily labor, but she came to feel a cor-rupting of her spirit from her daily contact with such venality. Her lyric and descriptive telling in Thai Sign made a powerful impression upon me. I fully understood what she was saying, but I was no more able than she to offer any alternative means by which they could support themselves. They were at least fortunate enough to have family that could provide start-up capital for their stall. Thus, while vending has been the first major financial entrance into the economy for many urban deaf, it has not been without ambivalence.

Prior to the explosion of street vending, those organizing among the various Deaf Thai factions either had sufficient wealth to labor without pay or had paid positions. Manfa Suwanarat was one of the rare few with financial independence and dedication to this work. While as a dynamic individual she made a lasting impact, her efforts were possible only because of unusually fortunate family circum-stances. But paid positions were equally unusual; politically, mem-bership dues from a community in which employment was such a rarity could not go toward salaried positions, and in any case they could not have covered salaries. Those funds barely supported a bimonthly newsletter printed on donated materials with donated equipment. Donors provided positions in what became the NADT that made possible organizing activities, but in the process they also created coveted "secure" employment. Jealousy rooted in greed fuels squabbles in all cultures. Among those structurally excluded from society as a whole, with the turf available all the smaller and the experience of achievement all the more rare, those issues are addi-tionally loaded. The security, or the position of perceived relative security, was to be coveted.

The efforts of the newly created NADT, however, have begun to pay off both in tangible terms and in an increased social awareness of deafness. In part because of the high visibility given to deaf social issues, a rapidly improving school system is expanding to include the full high school curriculum, although this is still limited to the Bangkok schools. Additional rural schools are also opening and thus increasing the percentage of deaf Thai children in school over the current 15–20 percent. A new legislative package regarding disabled people, although greatly reduced from what earlier drafts had provided, was recently passed. A wide range of feature stories on individual Deaf people and the broader issues of Deafness have peppered both English and vernacular newspapers and magazines over the past decade. This particular urban cohort of Deaf Thais appears to be enjoying a better life than that attained by any cohort that preceded it.

For most Deaf Thais making ends meet as vendors and laborers, private social events among their Deaf friends provide much-anticipated highlights. Friends gather for birthday dinners on a regular basis, the Thai tradition holding that the birthday celebrant pays the bill. The number of public celebrations are few. The Royal Thai Government hosts a National Handicapped Day, which, although it seems patronizing to many outside observers, remains popular because it offers free food and the opportunity to meet others not seen in a long time. The large residential schools and welfare institutions bring their charges to this event. Beyond this, the occasional wedding, the more frequent funerals, and the annual New Year's parties are the usual high points of the Deaf social calendar in Thailand.

Social events, ranging from parties to funerals, produce ad hoc arenas for both rehearsed and unplanned events. Reading the evidence of these human dynamics comes after the constructions of stories: evidence is not neutral any more than stories are innocent. The members of the particular cast of the scene that follows portray victims, of a type. Yet that type is not an essence, though it is sometimes made to seem so. Behavior can be described as reactions available in specific circumstances, and when the circumstances are themselves "typical," essentialist notions may be further naturalized. What we see below, however, are illustrations of limitations that circumstances impose, not instances revealing inherent damage or essence.

The events of the specific party described can be taken as either typical or exemplary in highlighting certain stereotypical views of deaf people. In part, the view presented is one of victimization and of limited lives.[28] Yet such limitations are caused not by their deafness but by the severely restricted social opportunities that have been available. While the description in part reproduces stereotypes, I hope it also more clearly demonstrates how social forces produce such identities. Separating out the process from the product is rarely done by observers or by the deaf themselves. To those frustrated in so many aspects of emotional and psychological development, anger becomes a constant companion. When anger takes a break, it is replaced by defeatism or nihilism.

This progression could be plainly seen at this particular New Year's party. As part of the activities, an exchange of gifts was organized. One couple brought only one gift for the exchange program. When the exchange of gifts took place late in the evening, the man, by then drunk, became angry that he did not receive an individual gift. He started a fistfight with another deaf man who laughed at his anger. When he was finally subdued, he sank into a depression and sulked in a corner until he passed out.

A more curious event of the party was a "fashion show," which was first of men and then women. Some people had been told to prepare costumes, and several more—mainly in the women's event—were then roped in from the crowd to parade as if on a fashion runway. Each group had costumes aimed at amusing. The "winner" of the men's group was dressed as an infant, complete with a heart appliqué on the seat of his diaper. The infantile male. The women's show was more elaborately staged; it began with the comic hag but quickly moved to vamps in several guises. One was a cat, who pranced and enticed. Another was the French-styled streetwalker, who began her walk with a deep *wai* of obeisance to the audience indicating at once the fabrication and, thus, the validity of the role enacted. A third, the "winner," was Playboy bunny-like, with gift-wrap bows on her breasts and rear. She had clearly caught

28. I must further add that these are not strangers I describe. Most of the people present at this party had been known to me for years, some even as long as a decade. I am well aware of a pathos in my description.

the eye of the leader of the main faction organizing the event, and her win felt predetermined. Several other young women from the audience were also encouraged to parade for the audience. Each one chose to do so in as "seductive" a manner as she could portray. Competition for the attention of the few desired and available men was clearly intense, though most of the men present were not in that category. It seemed to be what was expected.

The major event in the evening was a lottery for donated prizes. Everyone gave an enormous amount of attention to a deliberately elaborate procedure, which cleverly served to turn the main event—the material gain offered by the lottery—from a passive and brief drawing into a time-consuming and totally engrossing activity for all present. Each person drew for a passing win; a dozen winners then drew again, which dropped the contestants to six, who were further reduced to two, who then drew for an actual prize. This procedure was repeated for each of the prizes. As both an outsider and some-one taking part in the event, I observed the lottery process and how it provided a form of entertainment in its own right. Several of the leaders saw it as the best way to get the best "party value" from the few prizes they had to offer. They also knew, however, that most of those present could barely afford the price of the lottery tickets and were deeply ensnared in their desire to win.

Winning took on an increased significance, both personal and so-cial. For example, one prize highly desired was a small television set, and the crowd became very excited in following the chain of win-ners. The final winner was a Deaf man whose pretty and popular wife had committed suicide the previous year. The families were Chinese, the wedding arranged, and the wife had been despondent over the strict rules set by the in-laws with whom they lived. His winning of the television in the lottery was, he emotionally proclaimed in the flush of victory, karmic vindication of his innocence in his wife's death and the end of his ostracism from the broader community. While I was stunned by this declaration, as well as by the sheer power of his emotional outburst, my Deaf Thai friends generally nodded in collective agreement. As in the "rich peer environment" produced in the schools, the available meanings of the lottery win were overtly loaded yet consensually experienced within the community itself. Winning the television signified communal forgiveness of his karmic burden and reentry into the membership of the community.

The fragility of this community, and the significance of that rich peer environment in constructing it, may be further illustrated by considering a peer support group of young deaf women attempting to make their way in urban Bangkok.

A "Place" to Leave

The following is a brief story of a group of young deaf women from rural Thailand who may be seen as curiously mirroring the Deaf community itself under the pressures of urban capitalism. The particular group of young women described here have known each other since they were small children. They had been friends for years, but in the course of one year that collective cohesion totally disintegrated. Petty capitalism, donors, foreign travel, foreign boyfriends: each reproduces an object of jealousy and spite, each experience reinforces an identity as other. The choices that remain are starkly limited.

Meena is a young deaf woman from the northeast of Thailand. When she was six, she was sent to the only residential school for the deaf in all of northeastern Thailand, located several provinces away from her home. In this regard, she was quite fortunate. As noted earlier, the percentage of deaf children attending school remains low. When Meena graduated from the ninth grade, the highest grade available in the schools for the deaf outside of Bangkok even in 1995, she moved to Bangkok to seek work as a seamstress in a factory. She was one of a tight gang of buddies who grew up together within the school. These deaf girls all came to Bangkok after completing school and remained very close over the following six years as they moved among various jobs and living arrangements. They gathered socially, when they weren't already living together, and supported one another in times of need.

Yet after the events of a fairly brief period, only two can be said to be on friendly terms with each other; none feels the friendships will ever be revived. There is no clear and simple reason for what has taken place. The cross-current of cultural pressures can be described individually, but each perspective falls short of a totalizing explanation. Collectively, however, the events illustrate the pressures of urban modernity on the larger Deaf Thai community.

Of the group of former friends, two have been traveling frequently in Europe, supported by foreign Deaf boyfriends. One of these has been very successful in balancing a French and Swedish boyfriend, convincing each that the other is only an acquaintance while extracting financial support from them both. Four of the young women are street vendors, but no longer meet one another as they work their own street vending turf.

Of the vendors, only one has been successful in capturing the attention of a visiting Deaf tourist, although his attention may be fleeting. Still, all but one of the girls agree that this is a prime objective. The exception simply says she is not interested in fighting over boys and has retreated from the others. Given the spread of news over the Deaf networks of Europe and America about the "availability" of young women in Thailand (which is to say that just as there are women "available" in Thailand, so are there Deaf women "available"), doubtless a growing number of prowling bachelors will be arriving. Certainly the number has been increasing over the past several years, and the number of Deaf Thai women leaving with them has also increased.

Meena, who has an older Deaf sister married to a Hearing American, acknowledged she would actually prefer to marry a Deaf Thai, but said she knows that this option is not likely. She told of the return of a lost school-time sweetheart, who lamented that he had newly married another deaf woman, not knowing Meena remained single and having been unable to locate her. He is not only educated but has one of the rare jobs that pays modestly well and is secure. This story both justified her sense of being desirable and also proved that the only truly eligible bachelor was gone.

Recently, Meena met a young European Deaf man who came to Thailand as part of his postsecondary program of study. They were mutually smitten, and the object of his study became Meena. This is the story of many other programs of ethnographic study and the "objects" of their gaze. The couple were engaged within three months and were married a little over six months after they met.

The marriage suffered a rough beginning. According to Meena, because she had succeeded in capturing an eligible foreign bachelor her own age, former friends and acquaintances seemingly raced to discuss how "loose" she must have been in any earlier efforts to attract boys. The new husband was the primary recipient of these comments, which inflamed both his jealousy and insecurity. Prior to their moving to Europe, Meena was already fearful that she would be kept under virtual house arrest because of her husband's jealousy. Friends and family know she does not deserve such treatment. While she expressed fears that she may have chosen unwisely, she still looked on marriage to a foreigner as the best possible hope in life. She framed her attitude as one of forbearance in hope. Escape, even into the unknown, provides hope.[29]

The core observation of each of the young women is that marriage to a Deaf Thai man is the least viable option. While we might feel some sympathy for the deaf young men, the women's reasoning has some logic. Only the deaf boys born into wealthy families have any hope of being able to support a family. There aren't many of them, and making acceptable arrangements for a family is equally out of reach for deaf girls from average backgrounds. While romantic images of a lifelong sweetheart fuel their desires, practicalities outweigh these dreams. Employment options, even for the brightest of the educated deaf young men, are extremely scarce. Social pressures on them to live up to the macho image of Thai males also contribute to their lack of appeal to the women as potential husbands. Many young Deaf Thai men spend what money they might earn, whether as wage labor or as street vendors, on gambling, alcohol, prostitutes, or, at best, on motorcycles.

The picture does not appear much brighter from the perspective of the young deaf men, either. Saving to support a family, even if

29. With the passage of time, it appears that the marriage is doing well and both are happy.

employment makes that possible, seems futile to most of them. The costs of home ownership, setting up a rented house, or even of the wedding ceremony seem out of their reach. Of course, exceptions do exist. There are a small number of young families, more now than ever before, of Deaf Thai couples working to raise their children. However, the total number of these families is very small. Of these, most who either have children or no longer live with parents also face serious financial hardships of which the wider community is well aware. They serve as proof, to the Deaf observers anyway, of the realities of an independent family life as it might be available to them. To most, it does not appear all that appealing.

By contrast, while not every marriage of Deaf Thai women to foreigners has been successful, the majority of them appear to have been. Even some of the deaf women who were bought out from the brothels or bars as wives for foreigners have returned to visit—well dressed, bedecked in jewelry, and seemingly happy. Naturally, this has not passed without notice or comment by other Deaf Thais. Like the move into vending, marriage to foreigners is appealing because it offers the possibility of escape.

Such limitations on life options circumscribe this "community." Just as the triage that takes place in preschool narrows the choices of deaf children, so the options for adult life are limited by discursive definition. The escapes or leakages through the borders serve to make more visible the socially constructed nature of such limitations. Deaf Thai culture, as with other Deaf cultures, has more than one center. Yet, as noted throughout this work, my concern here is not with the cultural center of any Deaf culture but rather with the ambiguity of all borders, including theirs. The circumstances of Deaf life in Thailand, as in other countries, provide little chance for change from within. Those described above are driven to seek their escape from a place that is no "place" for them. In a framework of cultural politics, Deaf people are refugees in hostile territory.

5

Meat Puppetry
Cyborg Appropriations of the Deaf Body

The sovereignties of space and place, mediated only by temporality, are the stuff of telephones, language, and money.
  Money is how I was enabled to raise this topic, but we began from the curious linkages between telephones . . . and deafness.

Time and Money, Sound and Space

This chapter is a departure from the others in this book, yet both its anchors and its linkages have been long in place. I examine issues emerging from SF (science fiction or speculative fiction), most particularly its Romanticist fascination with pure technology. There is a direct relationship between the tropes of this SF terrain and the discursive placement of those who are deaf. The conflation of language with speech, both in institutions devoted to that belief and in emergent technologies that have simply presumed it, is best seen in what could well be called the bitter ironies visited upon those deaf. While exclusion has made some irony inevitable, this conflation has done more than merely silence other potentials. The ironies have a bitter taste, indeed.

Here I take as one of my starting points the apparent glottocentric bias both among the average population and among theorists who assume that sound is central to language or that sound insinuates itself into the essential structure of language—indeed, that knowledge without sound is not possible. The bias is vigorously defended across the terrain of language study. As one researcher bluntly asserts:

165

Visual signals have several obvious limitations which phonetic ones do not have. . . . They have a much lower ceiling as to the number of distinct signals and as to the rate at which these signals can be transmitted. . . . While it is true that a class of concepts can be associated with a class of signals of any medium or make, human language derives its tremendous wealth by having evolved along phonetic lines. . . . [It is] hard to conceive of any other system of bodily signals that could have been evolved that could function adequately as the carrier of man's rich stock of concepts. . . . Man's sounds are a crucial ingredient in the emergence of his language, and should be studied in that perspective.[1]

While research into sign language linguistics has delivered ample evidence to the contrary, it should be noted that in a framework such as that offered above, even thought or mental processes are understood as "inner speech." Written text or other orthographic presentations are separate from speech, but both are secondary to and derivative of spoken language.

A basic distinction will be useful for much of the discussion that follows. On the one hand, spoken language is serial and sequential, consisting of phonemic segments that follow one another. Sign language, on the other and both hands, consists of the five formational parameters of handshape, location, movement, orientation, and the nonmanuals that are produced in space and occur simultaneously. This distinction is, technically, a simplification. Signs in a signed phrase do follow one another in a sequence. Yet while signs do have a durational aspect, they are not conceived of as consisting of segments following one another, as are individual words. Conversely, the sound structure of spoken languages is not exclusively sequential. As Roman Jakobson aptly observed, though "the predominantly sequential character of speech is beyond doubt," it cannot be considered as unidimensionally organized in time. Spoken language is conceived of as a "successive chain of phonemes" but the phonemes themselves are "simultaneous bundles of concurrent distinctive features."[2] Consequently, sign language and spoken language

1. Wang 1974.
2. "On the Relation between Visual and Auditory Signs," in Jakobson 1971, p. 340.

both contain sequential and simultaneous dimensions, but sequence is specifically characteristic of phonemes and their occurrence in and as morphemes and simple words in spoken languages.[3] Finally, this broad distinction is compounded by a general observation about the visual and the auditory: things visual tend to be patterned in space, while those auditory tend to be patterned in time.[4]

We inhabit worlds that are constructed in languages, languages that not only constantly change but also differ both in meaning and modality. As we expand our understanding of what is additionally encompassed by "language," we recognize that sign languages are a fruitful addition to human knowledge and communication practices. Their unique grammatical features are already being appropriated in metaphorical representations of data constructs and information grids, both in the business pages of popular media and in technical journals. The logistics of perception, the deployment of linguistic components in a space that is itself grammaticized, and the optical compressions of visual data fields and their transmission protocols constitute the terrain for a twenty-first-century politics of communication protocols and formats.[5] In this emerging political economy, the resource of sign languages is both mined and denied.

Soon this discussion will temporarily leave its apparent topical focus to politicize and open up a wider terrain of such questions that attendant observations of linguistic registers and communication modalities render possible. Shifts in the hardware of communication technologies, as well as the software of social practices emerging from their use and access, are anchored on the several histories of the Deaf. Thus, I will examine some issues and questions seemingly tangential to the histories of deafness that resonate in terrains far removed, but immediately significant—like the value and security of the money in your ATM.

3. See Klima 1974.
4. See Hirsh and Sherrick 1961
5. See Brunn, Leinbach 1991.

Discontinuities of Modality: Serial Acoustic and Digital Spatial

Sign has to do with visual and spatial forms of grammar. Phonology has to do with the serial sequence of phonemes, sound bits and data bytes. Music has to do with orders of tonality and time. A cybernet has to do with multidimensional representations of imaged meaning and data fields. Cyberspace has been loosely described as "where you are when you're on the telephone."[6] We have hardware that can calculate and software that can render, but we lack spoken metaphors to discuss the depth and range of such "information rich" and "dynamic" data now becoming available. Metaphors that grammaticize vision and space may make possible new ways of understanding such depths of data.

The modality by which we understand "language" so thoroughly entrains the notion of sound that it blocks our access to the broader terrain of spatial language required by complex data reference grids. Our language and communications theories and technologies have been tied to the metal cables along which the serial signals of our knowledge have traveled. Solutions that once overcame limitations often embody new limitations. The telegraph and telephone were based on both a material and a mental technology: that sound traveled in serial sequence, that pulses traveled in waves over a crude material base, directly resembled—and shared the limitations of—our crude understanding of "language," which assumed that sound was its sole vehicle.[7] Much like the primitive alphanumeric stream that first was chiseled onto rock, one chip at a stroke, this understanding was electronically born on the telegraph key. Imageries with significance and meaning were relegated to the rarified world of art interpretation. While semiotic studies explore notions of "the language of art" and "the discourse of representation," such "dis-

---

6. Ronell 1989 , p. xv. The epigraph of this chapter begins by paraphrasing one of Ronell's main points.
7. See Ronell 1989; I am paraphrasing her broader discussion.

course" has always been carefully distinguished from any vehicle of direct communication.

Our notions have been tied not simply to a crude metal base but also to the modality of sound. Text is committed to the spoken language for its own representation and for its referent. Written forms of language in Western cultures have been relentlessly phonemic, yet few of their users have paid attention to the limitations imposed by such technology or questioned the assumptions of its "progress." Dyslexia, most often described as an "impairment of reading abilities," is rarely found in cultures whose writing is not phonemic. The phonemic technological base of our notions of language and meaning has been entirely naturalized, as have been our exclusions of other technologies of representing linguistic phenomenon. It is these exclusions that concern us here, as well as their context. Historically, massive shifts in surrounding social orders are engendered by changes in technical parameters of communication. In particular, the natural assumptions about the time and space in which such exchanges occur, and the physical "registers" on which the information is carried, lead to the domain first of telegraphs and telephones, then of money and of vast networks of data-rich imagery. This is a curious terrain within which a peculiar colonialism has been enacted. The older hardware specifically excludes the idea of visually signed language; the newer will not only use but may later require language forms that grammaticize uses of space—and time.

This is made obvious by the recent history of object-oriented database languages. A computer hacker known as Michael Synergy recently spoke at a hackers' conference called "Forbidden Knowledge in the Technological Era":

Let me tell you a parable. Remember Smalltalk? Smalltalk was created for two reasons: to prove that computation could occur simply by manipulations of objects and communications between objects, and that the process of computation should become visible. Great goals. But the industry couldn't figure out what to do after this was accomplished, it was too big a conceptual leap. It took the concept of a graphical user interface (GUI) to make the concept accessible to the folks at home, and then comes the sudden onslaught and acceptance of object-oriented systems. The concept of "cyberspace" needs the same intermediate step. . . . *Right now, nobody has the faintest clue as to how to deal with data in three dimensions.* You have to walk before you can run.[8]

The history of communication technologies is directly related to the historical production of possible social identities for the deaf. The investment has been enormous, which is why it remains, on the surface anyway, curious. Attention to the newer electronic terrain will make clear certain limitations in our theories of language—and their historical legacies in social and educational policies for "management" of the deaf.

Codes and Standards on the Electronic Frontier

Columbus entered the "New World" in search of gold and riches; the Gold Rush opened the American frontier; so, too, money was at the foundation of the first exploration of cyberspace.[9] Whenever any financial transaction is made, it involves electronic data representing money. Cash, in the postmodern world of credit and tourism, is only for native street vendors, the bar tab, and smugglers. Cash always brings the worst rates in the exchange market. Even black-market use of cash and specie is a localized, submarginal practice. Money is now based on data imagery, rather than the reverse. This reversal in reference, familiar in notions such as "junk bonds" and "fictitious capital formation,"[10] appeared first when money was actually released from its previous base, the traditional "gold stan-

8. Synergy 1991, p. 54.
9. This body of metaphors is now regularly appearing on the business pages of financial journalism; credit for the terminology is generally given to SF writers William Gibson (*Neuromancer* [1984], *Burning Chrome* [1983]) and Bruce Sterling (*Schismatrix* [1985], *Mirrorshades: The Cyberpunk Anthology* [1986]).
10. *Fictitious capital formation* is defined as "capital that has a nominal money value and paper existence, but which at a given moment in time has no backing in terms of real productive activity or physical assets as collateral." For an interesting discussion of the transitions between Fordism and "flexible accumulation" of capital, see Harvey 1989, p. 182.

dard."[11] In a literal sense, there is no longer an acid test for what we represent with this data.

Plans not yet finalized for the newest and future generations of U.S. paper currency include not only the highly publicized standards to combat counterfeit reproduction but also a digitally scannable serial number that will make each individual note, each piece of paper money, traceable. A history of every cash transaction in which an individual paper note passes through an electronic gateway may then be "constructed" from an electronic currency audit trail stored in the computer systems of the federal treasury.

This construction will anchor in the net a new valence, an image that is the inverse of the previous value referent. Money will exist only in its image, yet be imminently traceable—much like identities, as both become increasingly bound. The "value" of the new money is that of control and surveillance and, as such, "represents" the new standard being served.

The most easily available legislative vehicle for justifying currency tracking will be some internally contrived "war"—the official "War on Drugs" will serve quite well for this purpose—in which "laundering dirty money" is presented as a significant "national security" threat, which will require a "get tough" implementation of these new financial controls. Once in place, use of these controls will become routine, even "normal." Matching currency transactions to credit records and to Social Security numbers will be technically simple. Citizens, the IRS will be contacting you.

The tracking of money, or rather of transactions involving the image of monetary values, will be ever more closely matched with the tracking of demographics, entertainment, consumption habits, and credit histories. Individual identities are merely "profiles," images in the ongoing search for unexploited market niches. The tracking of market and consumer profiles is already a major subindustry, so descriptions found in current SF writing are only barely fictionalized.

11. J.-J. Goux charts a history of the object of valence into three stages: "a fetishized general equivalent, a 'symbolic' general equivalence, and finally the general equivalent as 'sign'" (1990, p. 64). See also Eichengreen 1992.

Through the Demosphere we fly, we men of the Database Maintenance Division, and although the Demosphere belongs to General Communications Inc., it is the schmos of the world who make it—every time a schmo surfs to a different channel, the Demosphere notes that he is bored with program A and more interested, at the moment, in program B. When a schmo's paycheck is delivered over the I-way, the number of the bottom line is plotted in his Profile, and if that schmo got it by telecommuting we know about that too—the length of his coffee breaks and the size of his bladder are an open book to us. When a schmo buys something on the I-way it goes into his Profile, and if it happens to be something that he recently saw advertised there, we call that interesting, and when he used the I-way to phone his friends and family, we Profile Auditors can navigate his social web out to a gazillion fractal iterations, the friends of his friends of his friends of his friends, what they buy and what they watch and if there's a correlation.[12]

Such displacement of basic "standards" of reference is also what is so often found troubling about postmodern statements. Postmodernist terms suggesting various forms of dis-continuity and displacement vary widely, yet are usually similar in sheer eclecticism. However, those whose questions are based on literary theory cannot give up their own "gold standard" of written speech and spoken words. Like the rooting of individualism in certain forms of property rights, which also rest on significant presumptions long forgotten, "communication" requires languages, as data demand protocols, and these currently presume serial-sequential understandings of what "language" must and may only be.

The addition of visual imagery to our representations of relational information has evoked and is evoking massive changes in our possible understandings of place, belonging, and community.[13] Similarly, the linguistics of vision and the grammars of the spatially contingent movements in signing disrupt many previously unques-

12. Stephenson 1994, p. 95.
13. "But now we're talking about that dislocation that occurs when an entire society looks up and finds that it doesn't know where it is, and it doesn't know how anything works anymore, and doesn't know how to deal with the reality that most of the standard, nurturing concepts that have managed to provide for us since the Neolithic Age—things like place and embodiment and community—are basically suddenly gone" (John Barlow, quoted in Gans and Sirius 1991, p. 47).

tioned parameters of language, inducing a new disembodiment, a "not-thereness" in the terrain of meanings. The loss of "place" mirrors the lost certainty in meanings. This seriously disrupts notions of "text" and "textual boundaries," to say the least.

Other visual terrains, particularly those considered consensual, further this disruption. Computer animation and fractally generated graphics can create a sensory environment as compelling and complicated as any conventional narrative that might be set within it. The technology so effectively portrayed by cyberpunk fiction has the affective power to constitute a story in its own right, an inherent narrative of technology, rather than simply using technology to tell a conventional narrative in visual media.

Consider the work now being done by mathematicians, such as Michael Barnsley at the Georgia Institute of Technology, on affine transformations (equations in fractal geometry) capable of generating virtually any target image. This research suggests that "it may even be possible to convey a movie from one computer to another simply by sending a chain of formulas down a telephone line." More than simply "video-on-demand," such a movie would be qualitatively more detailed than any possible cinematographic or video depiction of existing reality, as it would allow the viewer the unparalleled sense of flying into the picture, examining its components from every conceivable angle, even of predicting and exploring the information hidden beneath its surfaces.[14]

A recently announced format standard for exchanging dynamic data in integrated multimedia is called "Movie." This represents yet another example of what is meant by data that cross the terrain of print and video, fact and fiction, with imagery that is both dense and dynamic. Data as Movie, Movie as data. As noted above, images of money and identity are also becoming increasingly dense and dynamic, but they are no less "movies."

14. "Such a film would be hyperreal, but could be made to do impossible things, like showing a punked-out John Wayne on a pogo stick, . . . or the Beaver in mirrorshades, Ward and June in drag. Would not such a representation be inherently science fictional, the essence of cyberpunk? And won't it be fun?" (Landon 1989, p. 145).

The shift in site of linguistic meaning production to another (or to an additional) sensory modality is akin to the crossover in bandwidth that occurred with the transition between radio and television (visual added to sound-only)[15] and that will occur with the transition from video decks to the HDTV goggles–digital datasuit–based experiences of hyperpresence.[16] The epistemological shifts induced by the construction of media- and image-based "reality reference standards" require new forms of normalization. These processes are not unlike the "naturalization" that occurs in identity formation.[17]

Nor are they very different from the shifts that economic investments require for their production of "natural" social standards. Barriers to specific spatial distributions can be reduced only through the production of other particular spaces (railways, highways, airports, satellite networks, etc.). Yet, as David Harvey has observed,

> a spatial rationalization of production, circulation, and consumptions at one point in time may not be suited to the further accumulations of capital at a later point in time. The production, restructuring, and growth of spatial organization is a highly problematic and very expensive affair, held back by vast investments in physical infrastructures that cannot be moved, and social infrastructures that are always slow to change. . . . The definitions of "efficient spatial organization" and of "socially necessary turnover time" are fundamental norms against which the search for profit is measured. And both are subject to change.[18]

Massive investments are fueling exactly such a shift. A recent estimate suggests that investment in fiber optic and ISDN[19] networks will surpass—in less than ten years—the total global investment in previous analog networks in the 115 years since the invention of the telephone. Like the investments charted by Harvey, the ownership

15. Or its reverse, the addition of sound to silent films: same bandwidth, different manifestation.

16. Digital datasuits, or body suits for electronic interfaces, bring a new meaning to leisure wear. Call it "leisureware."

17. See Anderson 1983, p. 133.

18. Harvey 1989, p. 229.

19. ISDN, Integrated Services Digital Network, refers to telephone networks that use digital rather than audio signals. The long gestation period for the technology has led to jests on the name, including "Innovations Subscribers Don't Need" and "It Still Does Nothing."

and distribution of these investments will shape financial fortunes and political realities based on new forms of capital accumulation. Who these owners are and where they are situated will no longer be of significance.

Claims to being rooted in a particular time and place were crucial to the older terrains. This is as true of the industrial capitalist terrain described by Harvey as of that in Todorov's representation of "otherness" in his *Conquest of America* (1984), discussed in chapter 2. A clear place existed, making possible a distinction between interiority and exteriority. This certainty has been suspended: These claims literally have no place in the Net.

Consider the phrase "beyond a reasonable doubt." Evidence is no longer anchored in perceived reality: "Today, no witness testimony is valid. Sound recordings are manufacturable, photos are manufacturable, video is manufacturable. A jury isn't a judicial process, it's the new audience."[20] The juridical terrain becomes equally bound and created by the event of "authentic reenactments." *America's Favorite Home Videos* as due process. Among media executives, the "yellow journalism" style of sensationalist broadcast entertainment is called "reality programming." But on behalf of whose "reality," of whose house epistemology?

Digital Boundaries and Freedom of Code/Speech

One of the difficulties noticed by both critics and proponents of literary theories is that calling into question any set of hermeneutical anchors necessarily demands a reliance on some other set (presumably but not always different) of hermeneutic anchors. While this book is produced primarily for those inside the literary zone, the metaphors of many of its disrupting terms and questions are drawn from the argot of cyberpunk and computer hacking. In contrast, the "techno-hippies," who, as a class, are more easily understood within the genre of hi-tech "mountain men,"[21] remain rooted in print literate, early TV epistemologies and abide by the sixties ethos best

20. Synergy 1991, p. 53.
21. "Men," because hackers are predominantly young, undersocialized males.

expressed by Crosby, Stills, Nash, and Young in a song whose refrain nearly every baby boomer can still hum: "You, who are on the road, must have a code, that you can live by." Although "code" here has a range of new possible meanings, techno-hippies are pretty faithful to the original.

But the "cyberpunk" is a streetwise, net-running digital skateboarder far more technically competent and far less attached to chemically romanticized sentimentality. Attitude is key, including a particular disdain for the incompetence of authority. As Julian Dibbell remarked in the *Village Voice* about a recent seizure by FBI agents of tapes from a possible "computer criminal," "the evidence fell into four categories: salsa, merengue, house and lambada."[22] Fueled by local music and video cultures, such as industrial HM, Balearic Beats, or acid house, and by all-night, Ecstasy-driven "raves," the cybernaut is committed to "standards" of technical elegance—and to an uninhibited exploration of the vast global networks of information systems.

Advances in equipment are enabling enormous commercial and security ventures to connect informational data resources. Telephones and attendant satellite networks open up avenues of access to such projects through porous boundaries,[23] which are tightly policed for purposes often labeled private or "classified." Others exist simply for the administration of populations: "public security," if you will. Gaining access to these avenues/boundaries, if only for exploratory purposes, is the primary goal of the net runner. So "hackers" understand their own activity. The implication of malicious intent in the term has been largely supplied by security industries attached to corporate interests.

Nevertheless, when damage is concerned, intentions matter as little in cyberspace as elsewhere. A highly publicized incident was the case of the "Internet worm" virus, which made its presence

22. Dibbell is quoted in Branwyn 1991, p. 68.
23. This play of metaphors is deliberate. "Avenues" refers to notions of public access via streets and highways. "Boundaries" evokes borders and immigration restrictions.

known on 2 November 1988 when thousands of computers around the United States slowed to virtual standstill. All were part of the Internet network connecting universities, companies, and the military. Security experts attempted to paint the source as a terrorist; one source went so far as to suggest an "Abu Nidal at the keyboard," and another offered a dark psychological portrait of "an Oedipus Techs." [24] The picture that later emerged was of a typical hacker, a graduate student in computer sciences at Cornell, curiously exploring a vast network but simply botching the job. [25] As John Barlow, of the Electronic Frontier Foundation, explained, "Robert T. Morris, Jr. [creator of the Internet worm] wanted to map the net. The Morris worm was like an explorer. It was going to go around to every node on the net and report back in and tell you just how big this sucker was. Which is something that nobody knows, right? It's a cool thing to do. Somebody ought to do it. Trouble is, he screwed up. His worm wasn't well-written, so the effect was viral rather than exploratory." [26]

The Internet virus was the work of a specific agent, although clearly not the "terrorist" that security forces so dearly desired. Yet the need to present threats as imminent, even when no such actual threat can be found, serves as its own justification. Another case is the famous AT&T system crash, that one-day, systemwide shutdown (unrelated to the Internet virus) that threw panic into the hearts of corporate America and glee into the hearts of security experts everywhere. While this crash is now known to have been created strictly internally, the interests of the collective security systems quickly coalesced in presentations on the dangers posed to network security by potential data intruders. Yet the incident's real significance was that it clearly demonstrated how a locally induced failure in one sub-

24. Schwartz 1991. The not-so-typical detail is that the hacker's father was also head of computer security research at the U.S. National Security Agency. Hence, the set-up of the son-of-hacker punch line of "Oedipus Techs."

25. A criminal conviction, however, was upheld by the Supreme Court on 7 October 1991. It remains the only conviction under the federal Computer Fraud and Abuse Act of 1986 (*Bangkok Post*, 9 October 1991).

26. Quoted in Gans and Sirius 1991, p. 48.

system, sufficiently strategic, can indeed shut down an entire system. This induced a security anxiety of enormous proportions.[27]

Media critic Michael Synergy offers a critical view of the event and its significance:

> The chain of events looks something like this: a telephone switching center shut itself down, taking a lot of other switching centers with it. For hours it stopped telephone service, costing an immense amount of money. There was a bug in the revised code running the switch, a bug that was just waiting to go off and cause this problem. Now the phone companies acknowledge the bug is their fault, but they also believe that the original switch may have had some help shutting down. There is no audit trail to use as evidence, so that's pure speculation on their part. So they got scared because they finally realized that what I've been telling people for years is true—one person can shut down the whole phone system. So they call the stormtroopers at the Secret Service and get them all rabid, and the rest is history. Except that on the phone company's part, it's not history, but histrionics. They were scared not by the actions of a real person or group, but by the implications of their own sudden realization.[28]

This anxiety demanded action, and the security concerns delivered quickly. In May 1990,

> shotgun-wielding U.S. Secret Service agents raided the homes of some 30 teenaged hackers in 14 U.S. cities, dragging teenagers in Anthrax T-shirts out of bed and seizing computers, boomboxes and comic books by the thousands. The hackers were charged not with tampering but with "electronic trespass"—breaking into computers and wandering around.
>
> "It's not what they've done but what they might do by going where they don't belong," an FBI spokesman explained. "We're sending these kids a message: You aren't cute."[29]

This spate of criminal crackdowns on young hackers joyriding on the data stream with souped-up clone CPUs and high-speed

---

27. This anxiety still stands. In October 1991, a news wire story warned of further "intruders" into the Internet system. The intruders were said to be equipped with "a password cracking program" ("Intruder Enters Worldwide Computer Network," *The Nation* (Bangkok), 8 October 1991).

28. Synergy 1991, p. 52.

29. Lynda Edwards, "The Samurai Hackers," *Bangkok Post*, 8 September 1991.

modems, resulting in heavy criminal charges far in excess of their
"crime," was sufficiently worrisome that leaders among the successful software publishers established the Electronic Frontier Foundation. This public advocacy group supports the reexamination of current constitutional interpretations of data, access, and privacy, now
posed as questions of "digital freedom of speech." As one spokesperson noted, "Trying to impose a million-dollar fine and thirty
years in jail on them just because they've trespassed digitally rather
than physically is completely out of scale." [30]

Among both advocates and critics this fertile mixing of metaphors
is rampant. Notions of free speech are crossed with those of rights
talk and private property, which are further mixed with metaphors
of the open roads and highways. Thus Hewlett-Packard, in a 1991
series of corporate "public service" ads entitled "The Open Road
to Open Systems," [31] explicitly exploits the metaphor of roads and
highways to market their "Open Systems" equipment by claiming
that " 'Open Systems' is to IT (information technology) what highways are to cars." The copy is informal, even chatty, as it implores,
"But, for the time being, let's think of Open Systems as something
like the 'highway code' of computing." With that introduction, the
copy delineates a terrain that must be given order, just as had been
demanded by the early automotive industry. It insists, "we also need
standard traffic lights and standard driving regulations, or else there
would be complete chaos." The metaphor turned simile is heavily
mined to justify its own use. With a passing nod to publicly built
highways, a story is told of cars and trucks and petroleum. The moral
seems to be clear: We're all equal at the pump. While we celebrate
variety in our vehicles, the sources of petrol are "standard," the basic
interface of pedals and levers by which we operate the vehicles is
"standard," the power source of engines is "standard," with varia-

---

30. The founders are quick to make clear that the Electronic Frontier Foundation is "not a cracker defense fund." Quoted in Kapor and Barlow 1991, p. 48.

31. "The Open Road to Open Systems," advertisement for Hewlett-Packard
(Thailand), *Bangkok Post*, 25 September 1991. The text, quoted extensively here, is
accompanied by a graphic of a large, busy interchange on a high-speed freeway to
firmly anchor the metaphor.

tions in style and functionality, often described as class and types of performance. Contrasts are drawn between trucks and mopeds, between sport cars, Rolls Royces, and tractors.

But "Without our 'rules of the road,' we would have various problems." Suddenly, what began as a claim of access, lauding new freedoms of movement built from old normative values, is seen as deriving from and requiring a call for law and order. While the phrase does not yet appear, it is clearly implied in the call for strict observance of "standards." Without such standards, dire consequences are imminent. Highways and frontiers invoke the pious virtues of patriotic and dutiful nation building on yet another undeveloped territory, the future. But on the old frontier, as well as in the terrain of language, unruly outlaws are portrayed as the greatest threat to the common good. The homesteaders will only be safe on the new electronic frontier under the badge and flag of familiar codes and standards. The wagons may be pulled into a circle at Fort Matrix, but we've clearly been told who the good guys are. The promise of a new and better life for everyone lies glistening at the end of that rainbow. A frontier saga, mixed with the blessings of industrial production, is the vehicle for a recycled morality play: "And so it is with Information Technology. Just as basic standards for cars, the road system and highway code provide an infrastructure for driving, so Open Systems provides an infrastructure for computing, establishing the rules of the road which not only control the traffic flow of data but create enormous benefits for users." Not to mention the company. In the concluding segment, appropriately labeled "The Bottom Line," the tone is eager: "With the establishment of Open Systems, the use of computers will spread even further, creating vast global networks of services and information, linked together in a single, integrated system—like a network of highways."

The copywriters are essentially clear in expressing what is at stake, but the major topics and questions they leave untouched include operating systems, data densities, formats, and protocols—and the vast amounts of money at stake. Nor does this ad allow much room for questions of access, which are also very much about money.

Clearly, the technoid side of the street has its own share of shib-boleths. (Since *shibboleth* was a spoken password of identity,[32] this is no misnomer.) As suggested earlier, "code" has a range of newly available meanings. In addition to caricatures of pious moral trap-pings, as in fictitious Old West codes of ethics, the word can refer to protocol code for data exchange, to righteous code circuitry, to code-jamming rap and hip-hop, to a framework within which a problematic or master discourse is constructed, or to a line of pro-gramming and trade software, or tradeware. The code that is more important, or shall we say "foregrounded," for today's net-running cybernaut may have more to do with technical elegance or eluding detection than with any notion of restraint and moral identification with "standards" of the presumed order.[33]

Nevertheless, the base code of capitalism, which somehow is ei-ther above the carnage or cynically beyond reach or redemption, re-mains. Should a righteous cybernaut craft an elegant piece of soft-ware, preferably a convenient utility virus or productivity tool with a sophisticated execution, sexy interface, and catchy name, he or she should get rich from its sale and be protected in copyright and dis-tribution deals. Just as surfing presumes an ocean, digital surfing presumes an electronic grid of capitalist economic and security data exchange on which to ride. It seeks to explore, expose, exploit, and escape, yet it depends on that which it hates. One writer calls the relationship "revolutionary parasitism."[34]

32. Literally "a stream," the word takes its symbolic meaning from its use as a test of pronunciation to distinguish friend from foe in the war between Jephtha and his armies and the Ephraimites; see Judges 12.

33. This ethos runs deep among techies of several generations. Robert Morris Sr., head of computer security research for the U.S. National Security Agency and the father of the Cornell hacker who inadvertently created the Internet worm, was said to have commented only that his son's work was "sloppy." This technical put-down is the ultimate disgrace for hackers. No other, traditionally mor-alizing, judgments were reported.

34. Musician and SF writer John Shirley (the phrase was used in the title of a 1989 *Mondo 2000* interview; see Milhon 1989). This is similar to what was formerly known as "guerillas in the bureaucracy."

Working for the Stupids: Digital Young Guns

Getting paid for digital surf time requires a computer hacker to be hired by those who control the networks or by those seeking to hire a digital private eye, a Sam Spade of the information age.[35] These Have-Deck-Will-Access paladins, whom we might call Digital Young Guns, prefer to consider themselves "samurai hackers." The Japanese imagery has been borrowed from the former MBA cult manual, Miyamoto Musashi's *Book of Five Rings*, a sixteenth-century handbook of samurai warfare.[36] It promotes the ethos of penniless warriors trained in exotic weaponry who earn status as mercenaries for minor princes—while viewing them with contempt and disdain. This rarified vision of righteous outlaw elites prosecuting the squabbles of petty nobles fails to mention the peasants who suffered underfoot. The same may be said of the technological peasantry of today: while they are no longer physically available for rape and pillage, their accounts are.

The samurai hackers are building a niche in the current corporate world in electronic countersurveillance and theft. They are hired by white-collar professionals at ad agencies, investment houses, law firms, and security agencies who want to steal or gain access to co-workers' or competitors' ideas, pillage marketing strategies, or review or change evaluations or managerial records. But like the samurai warriors of old, the samurai hackers have little respect for those who hire them. Once called "suits," they are now known as "the stupids": " 'Hey, they really are stupid,' one hacker insists. 'I know! I've scoped their PCs, read their E-Mail, listened to their voicemail. They say stupid things, laugh at stupid jokes. The things they want

35. "What Fred really liked was the challenge of the chase, and he had often regretted that you couldn't make a living in this culture as a sort of private eye of learning, a Sam Spade of the information age, sitting in your nondescript office, a fifth of bourbon on your desk alongside your Magnum .357 and your modem, waiting for a grieving blonde widow to walk through the door and ask you about the connection between the sistrum and the Isis cult" (Hart 1990, p. 111).

36. See Musashi 1982.

are stupid. The people they like are stupid. But they have money—
and I need something to do.'"[37]

The hiring of young hackers, most from lower- and working-class
backgrounds, for corporate or metacorporate espionage is a staple
in cyberpunk narratives. Like their corporate counterparts, the literary cyberpunks are technically talented, economically disenfranchised, and politically disaffected. The usual conditions of work are
cheap hotel rooms with direct phone lines. Perks include pizza and
caffeine-based fluids. They live and breathe the technical specifica-
tions, they need the work, and the stupids have the money.

At twenty-two, he'd been a cowboy, a rustler, one of the best in the
Sprawl. He'd operated on an almost permanent adrenaline high, a by-
product of youth and proficiency, jacked into a custom cyberspace deck
that projected his disembodied consciousness into the consensual hallucination that was the matrix. A thief, he'd worked for other, wealthier
thieves, employers who provided the exotic software required to penetrate
the bright walls of corporate systems, opening windows into rich fields
of data.[38]

[The matrix was] mankind's extended electronic nervous system, . . . a
monochrome nonspace where the only stars are dense concentrations of
information, and high above it all burn corporate galaxies and the cold
spiral arms of military systems.[39]

This concept of a consensual basis of reality, and a consensual nature of network systems, is key to the cybernetic construct. Applying
the property-rooted notion of privacy to electronic systems is directly opposed to a hacker ideal of free access and consensuality. This
returns again to the issues of matrix fragility, access rights, and the
money in your ATM account. This "consensual hallucination" is
also crucial in constructing a metaphorical base for information. An
irony of the cyberpunk argot is its clear recognition that corporate
and military processing systems enforce security and police identity.
Whether using metaphors of the frontier, of ancient samurai war-

37. Edwards, op. cit.
38. Gibson 1984, p. 5.
39. Gibson 1983, p. 170.

riors, of neurobiological systems, or of fractally generated info-glyphs, this idiom is both oppositional and seeking a consensuality. It is the familiar paradox of politics and identity.

The enormous investment in infrastructure creates and sustains a virtual electronic reality. The disaffected within this reality create further subcultures that exhibit many of the same tendencies as minority communities bound up in policing the purity of their own newly defined communalism. There is no illusion of unity, of a more equitable world here. The technologically backward areas, such as those restricted to narrow bandwidth phone lines of ancient copper, will be further excluded from the information and financial grids. Deposits will still be accepted by mail, but the deficit payments (or debt servicing) will ensure that the accounts are always in the red.

In part, the irony of this further division between the global haves and those forever excluded "off-line" is underscored by the construction of hackers as "intruders" into the global network.[40] This forms part of the discursive economy that marks out the members, and "landed nobility," of this private club and rationalizes its need and maintenance of a disaffected technical elite. The genre of "cyberpunk," which gives us the richest metaphorical base from which to grasp the expanse of a data-referenced universe, rises from the disaffected but technically talented who stand opposed to the technological success of communications and security/surveillance. The "cyberpreppie" materials are not being released—for security reasons, no doubt.

Cyberpunk Literature Has No Future

Though cyberpunk literature may not already be familiar, it is also a literary moment already past. As cyberspace is not the topic of this work, but only an example of a terrain both anchored in and questioned from a historical geology of deafness,[41] its early departure is

40. "Intruder Enters Worldwide Computer Network," op. cit.
41. Does an intellectual "geology" follow only the calcified veins of the archaeological body of knowledge rather than engage the "meat" of a genealogy?

not particularly tragic for our purposes. The narratives, based on their own quests for purity, were generally simple, and their call to disaffection relied on the eros of technical sophistication. But from the perspective of a cybernaut, why bother reading it when you can be making it? From this perspective, cyberpunk literature appears as a form of oxymoron, already a map without a territory. Which is another way of asking, "What integrity could cyberpunk fiction possibly have in a cyberpunk world?" As a genre, cyberpunk sought more than "to play out a string of antique narratives against a technosleaze backdrop. Its energy, its premium on information density, its unshakable determination to confront the new realities of postmodern culture, all meant that cyberpunk could never settle down in established comfort, over and over offering its readers exotic, but increasingly familiar territory, a comfy national park of the imagination where the neatly numbered conceptual hookups waited patiently for readers to park the campers of their minds."[42]

Moreover, the cyberpunk world makes obvious the obsolescence of cyberfiction. Benoit Mandelbrot's work with fractal geometry both represents and helps drive a new wave of computer imaging that allows visual and spatial representation, generation, and manipulation of images, viewing perspectives, and degrees of realism never before possible. The central concept in Mandelbrot's *Fractal Geometry of Nature* (1982) is that the notion of three simple dimensions is a myth. The result is akin to that of Heisenberg's uncertainty principle in quantum mechanics. Yet, in Heisenberg, indeterminancy is decently submerged in the spaces between (or among) electrons. In Mandelbrot, it is boldly foregrounded. Chaos theory[43] draws heavily on fractal mathematics, the most frequent example being the analysis of the onset of turbulence in water flow or cloud formation. Objectifying this understanding of things requires new

---

This reminds me of the Tibetan treatment of the dead, which is to hack the body into pieces and feed it piece by piece to scavenger birds. They might save the top of a skull of a highly revered monk, or his thigh bone, for adornment and later use as tea bowl and horn, respectively.

42. Landon 1989, pp. 143–45.
43. Gleick 1987; see also Hardison 1989.

languages. It is a world of science as pure fiction, one that cyber-punks celebrate, but one that has left them behind.

Measured in terms of other fiction, perhaps particularly other science fiction, the speed and density (information complexity) of cyberpunk writing is stunning. But, measured against computer imaging and video technique, even dynamite prose reveals that it cannot compete in precisely these ways. Speed, density, and the process of editing assume dimensions in video and computer graphics that are simply beyond the reach of printed prose. Not a new ballpark, really, but a different game entirely—*comparing pixels with phonemes*, were it not for the self-refractive, techno-intensive qualities of cyberpunk writing, the print-denying inevitability of its milieu. Captain James T. Kirk loses no credibility when he dons his granny glasses to read a novel in the umpteenth century, but try to viddy this: after a rough day in cyberspace, Computer Cowboy Case looks forward to nothing quite so much as settling down with a good book. Or put it this way: what integrity could cyberpunk fiction possibly have in a cyberpunk world? For that matter, how long can cyberpunk's profound lens of technological inevitability be turned on everything in our own culture but the *game preserve of fixed text* print? [44]

Writing is the key here, its two high-tech moments, movable type and the steam press, having come respectively in the fifteenth and nineteenth centuries. Images may not provide the pleasures and the challenges of print, but there's no denying that electronic technology can do infinitely more with images and sounds than it can with printed words. Print literature, cyberpunk or otherwise, is being relegated to the "game preserve of fixed text."

The Perceptual Logistics of Identity— at 0.^{000,000,000,000,4} second

If cyberspace is understood as a vast complex of data networks, then those who inhabit these terrains will form notions of identity that are interiorized to and from the activities undertaken within the matrix. [45] A further articulation of such identities is emerging with the

---

44. Landon 1989, p. 143 (emphasis added).
45. The earliest English use of "matrix," a word derived from "mother," was to mean "womb" or "uterus." Its common current use is "that within which, or

ever-deepening structure of these grids and the increasing extent and duration of disembodied interactions that occur in the net. It is also becoming increasingly complex. Using digital forwarding to multiple sites in the Net for capital, image, and actor, flexible forms of accumulation apply both to financial assets and to personal identities. Global structures of electronic financial networks are already sufficiently complex to render somewhat archaic the simple notion of "national economies."

So, too, does the depth of information potentially available from any personal "dossier" render outdated notions of "self-realized" identity. None of the data creating such "personal identity" requires things like place, embodiment or community: these have, in effect, been suddenly deleted.[46] In fact, restrictions against manipulating such data have proven so porous as to make available for finances and identities the functional equivalents of "flag of convenience registries" for transport vessels. Like tankers made Panamanian, layers of identity are conveniently managed as circumstances demand or warrant. Thus appropriation of identity as "persons of color" has proven quite convenient to those nonwhite elites who otherwise have little in common with the social circumstances that gave rise to the term. Digital identities engender a variety of management approaches that include many "flag of convenience" techniques for disguise and evasion. The expansion (but only partial visibility) of "data havens" is an outgrowth of off-shore banking. Identity, like money, is based only on images in the matrix.

With the increasing spread of fiber optic capacities, vast amounts of data are also becoming more immediately accessible. Current research has produced stable pulses as short as four-trillionths of a second: that is, one pulse every $0.^{000,000,000,000,4}$ second. This translates, theoretically, to the ability to transmit the entire contents of the Library of Congress in five minutes. As one might say, that's information at your fingertips. Although the performance level of 0.2

---

within and from which, something originates, takes form, or develops." Thus, "returning to the matrix" has multilayered meanings.

46. See Barlow interview, Gans and Sirius 1991.

Library-of-Congress per minute ("0.2 LOC/min.") is not yet available on your network, it does suggest that physical locations of information or of those accessing it are becoming progressively less important.[47] The notion of location itself is becoming increasingly porous.

As "place" becomes increasingly porous, so too do notions of identity that are closely bound to it. National identity is no longer circumscribed by place, as was demonstrated during the recent so-called Gulf War. More than half of the Kuwaiti economy consists of earnings from foreign capital abroad. This "national economy" was unaffected by the invasion. Kuwait managed to transmit an entire banking system out of the country by faxing its documents to an office in London by midnight of the day Saddam Hussein ordered his troops to invade.[48] Iraq captured the "territory" but not the "economy" of Kuwait. What or where was "Kuwait" in such circumstances? One goal of the vast United States-led military campaign was to deny and disguise this ambiguity.

But the ephemerality of possible identities is nothing compared to that of the grid itself. At this stage, the fragility of the cybernet is vivid. As data density and complexity continue to escalate, backup becomes unviable. Although, as previously noted, the AT&T phone system crash was an internal error, it proves that only one person at one substation can shut down an entire net. Some dataspaces are already so sophisticated that they cannot be represented in any form outside themselves. This makes them highly vulnerable. As hackers often note, if a system allows access to one valid user, then it's possible to break in. "Just like with a room: if it has a door, you can break in."[49] Or, as another popular version has it: If it's on-line, you're a fool to think it's private.

In this brief discussion of system fragility, the cybernet's vulnerability to deliberate attack must be mentioned. An EMP, an electromagnetic pulse, of the kind produced as a by-product of a nuclear

---

47. Bill Gates, chairman of Microsoft, quoted in Swaine 1991, pp. 229–32.
48. UPI wire story, *Bangkok Post*, 13 August 1991.
49. Synergy 1991, p. 54.

explosion or by a tactical device, would erase all electronically based data storage that was inadequately shielded. The banking system is, for the most part, unshielded. However, a massive EMP is far from the most worrisome or likely attack plan. In one credible scenario, a hardcore "worm" could be written to take advantage of networks that hang off of networks, a predominant feature of current global data systems. Such a worm can seed itself into all the component systems, mutating into specific configurations that grab any new resources available on each machine. The worms then bounce back into the main network to replicate. "Considering that the Internet worm crippled so many machines for so long without trying, a few thousand distinct worms would collapse the whole show. Goodbye banks, goodbye telephones, goodbye credit. How much money do you carry around in your wallet? It might be all you have left"[50]— and what is that "value" based on? Saddam clearly used the wrong weapons to invade (the wrong) Kuwait.

Virtual Citizenship Grid Identities and Identity Grids

"Virtual reality" critically shifts notions of self-identity by displacing our previous understanding of the "place" of humans in the universe. In chapter 3, I used the example of the telescope to illustrate how a discovery—in this case, a technology—can change our image of humanity's place in the universe. Virtual reality provides yet another means of mental telescoping.

The experience of "community" or of social "connectedness" may soon exist principally, if not solely, in the context of a datanet. In a curious twist, virtual communities of financial nets, satellite and cable systems, bulletin boards, and SIGS (special interest groups on electronic networks) may soon offer the only "real" experience of connection to place that is readily available to the average citizen. The imagined communities of nineteenth- and twentieth-century nationalisms[51] are being transformed into the imaginary communi-

50. Synergy 1991, p. 54.
51. See Anderson, *Benedict* 1983.

ties of the twenty-first-century information grids. Membership in these new communities, like its predecessors, will depend on a production of a shared consensus, what might be called a mutually agreed-upon reality.

Consensus has been sometimes called that space beyond politics in which politics is suppressed.[52] *Such consensus, like information, will have ever less relationship to a physical place.* Logical location is no longer dependent on physical location.[53] The emotions of community are being transplanted into the electronic network, having been displaced by modernity from the local physical site of living. A mutually agreed-upon reality is not really a place or a space: rather, it is a notional space. Why talk to your neighbor when you have a modem or satellite transponder and a CPU-based "reality engine"? Step into the global electronic community, as one service invites. It is no coincidence that many network operating systems call their base menu structure "Home."

Early participants in deregulated, disembodied forms of communications (short-wave band, CB radio) took on a nom de plume or "handle," a name by which an "identity-in-use" was suggested. Such identities initially drew from registered identification codes (radio operator codes), but later participants used untraceable names suggesting new or different identities. Early such names were appropriated from various pirate, cowboy, and war narratives. As the next generation went on-line into explorations of dataspace, the names chosen reflected the influences of SF rewrites of these same genres. Teenage computer hackers still regularly identify themselves using these overly fanciful names.

The notion of "existentially anchored" experience, generally

52. Michael J. Shapiro, personal communication, 1990.

53. Recently introduced computer network software, called DataClub, is being marketed as "a virtual server" because "you see only one volume icon. DataClub takes shared folders from each participating [computer's] hard disk and displays this combined storage to the user(s) as a single, shared volume. . . . This ability to *separate the logical location* of a folder (where it appears on the DataClub server's file-directory structure) *from its physical location* (the disk on which it actually is stored) is a dramatic first"; see Battelle 1991, p. 232 (emphasis added.) Logical location is no longer dependent on physical location.

known as "personal" experience, is deeply undermined by a technology by which a visual-tactile virtual reality—a personally modifiable fantasy of role-playing scenarios—may be casually produced. Any user can strap into and virtually experience "plug-'n'-play" fantasy machines.[54] Such virtual realities are both consensual and individual, for while they are software driven, they render questionable all other "measures" of order and reality.[55]

Anchoring an artificially induced sensory awareness in a visual- and tactile-rich environment of dynamic data for extended space-(of)-time, whether through goggles and datasuit or biochemicals (generally referred to as simulated stimulation or "sim-stim"), can produce a lingering adverse effect on basic motor control of the "real" body. Those who have experienced virtual reality compare the loss of coordination to the awkwardness of an albatross trying to land after spending so long in the air over the seas that it has forgotten how.

As is typical of notions of postmodern identity, continuity is not an issue; there is no particular concern about linking the identity established when connection with the "real" body is regained ("naturalized") to the identities created or transited in the vast, visualized universe of network data. The constant search for identity markers has made it clear there is no "original" identity in need of preservation. Within the matrix, the question is not "who are the grid runners?" but "in what formats do they appear?" What structures have been borrowed, on lease or loan? To quote Rudy Rucker, "How fast are you? How dense?"[56]

54. The film *Total Recall* (1990), starring Arnold Schwarzenegger, rests on this premise (the film is based on Philip K. Dick's short story "We Can Remember It for You Wholesale").

55. They also raise questions about the desensitizing that occurs after extended experiences of virtual rape, murder, and existential mayhem in personally modifiable "Disney Worlds." Who says it will be all that different to wake up ("jack out"), take out a "real" Uzi, and dust off some shoppers on the plaza mall? This, of course, is the hook that security experts will "kill" for, so to speak.

56. Dr. Rudolf von Bitter Rucker, professor of mathematics and computer science, *aka* Rudy Rucker, whose works include *Mind Tools* (1987), *Spacetime Donuts* (1981), *Software* (1982), *Wetware* (1988), and *The Secret of Life* (1985). He

Outlaw formations of grid-referenced identities, those not yet fully available to surveillance administrations, continue to thrive owing to "leaks" through the security apparatus. However, this security and surveillance apparatus is expanding as increasingly detailed data ("case" histories of legal records, employment, tax, telephone, credit, investment, purchasing, travel, etc.) are gathered from demographic, financial, and tourist "market" information whose complexity and depth are equally increasing. Part response, part product, many of the largest computer and telecommunications corporations retain large security systems firms and consultants who, in turn, have active "revolving door" exchanges with formal governmental and supragovernmental law and security enforcement agencies such as Interpol.[57]

Yet here as elsewhere, those seeking to evade expanding surveillance grids attempt to create new forms of identities and covers for transiting identities. Most of the technically utopian and humanly dystopian literatures that imagine technologically possible futures center the narratives on "fugitives" and other renegade identities within the increasing surveillance net of the same technologies—hitech versions of righteous outlaws. Their stories, in turn, are ultimately moral discourses in support of a "law and order" culture. It is yet another curious bunch of heroes and antiheroes who

---

frames his approach: "Mathematics can be thought of as based on five concepts: Number, Space, Logic, Infinity, and Information. The age of Number was the Middle Ages, with their nitpicking lists of sins and layers of heaven. Space was the Renaissance, with perspective and the printing press spreading copies out. Logic was the Industrial Revolution, with great steam engines chugging away like syllogistic inferences. Infinity was Modern Times, with quantum mechanics and LSD. Now we're starting on Information. The computers are here; the cybernetic revolution is over."

Rucker is also well known for his statement about punk literature: "The real charm of punk is that stupid hippies dislike it as much as do stupid rednecks" (1989, p. 79).

57. This has been particularly evident in the recent spate of highly publicized enforcement actions against "computer crime," usually targeting teenage computer nerds whose most serious "crime" is evasion of phone bills.

populate this disembodied struggle over an idea of freedom of digitized speech.[58] The descriptions of these heroes, and the terrain they inhabit, are metaphorically rich and resonate deeply with Deaf history.

Alexander Graham Bell, the Telephone, and the Missing Ear of the Deaf

The telephone is not one but two—or more. A single telephone is inconceivable. For Alexander Graham Bell (AGB), separation was something to be overcome. In his life, he suffered a number of significant separations, which merged in his relentless search for better methods of communicating with or reproducing what was lost. While several of these losses will be discussed below, the most important of the missing "others" was the ear of his deaf mother. As Avital Ronell notes, "The telephone was borne up by the invaginated structures of a mother's deaf ear."[59] Telephone technology was born from a deaf body, a discovery plundered from the continent of deafness. The body of deafness continues to provide fertile harvests for communications technologies, but the first bumper crop brought the phone. The telephone is another type of tool, "one which sheds the purity of an identity as tool, however, through its engagement with immateriality and by the uses to which it is put: spiritual, technical, intimate, musical, military, schizonoid, bureaucratic, obscene, political. . . . A technical object whose technicity appears to dissolve at the moment of essential con-

58. Because I seek to displace metaphors that are glottocentric, I tie the familiar call for "free speech" more intimately to a notion of "freedom of movement," that free citizens might travel on the highways and byways as they so please. The telephone lines of old, and the satellite links of today, are more easily understood here as streets and roads. Most national governments include both transport (roads) and telecom systems under a Ministry of Communication. But when all the "roads" are declared private, only the "landed" may travel. This also, of course, leaves untouched the question of "who" or "what" is being mobile. The commercial terrain of "intellectual property rights" raises further issues.

59. Ronell 1989, p. 4.

nection.[60] The engagement, even with silence, enters into a conversation with time and space. Cyberspace, as the popular saying goes, is where you are when you're on the telephone.

As Ronell's observations make clear, this sounds a call to understanding speech, incites a rush to answer Heidegger's call to consciousness. It also opens an inquiry into AGB's curious efforts to honor the contract he had signed with his dead brother: that whoever departed life first was to contact the survivor through a medium demonstrably superior to the more traditional channels of spiritualism. AGB occupies a strange conjunction in the histories of communications, of modern representations of nature and the world, and of the Deaf. His invention of the telephone, his role in founding the National Geographic Society (his son-in-law was first president and his grandson is current president and chairman), and his active devotion to promoting his own views on deafness, deaf people, and eugenics result from his own situation as a third-generation elocution teacher, from the attentions of a deaf mother, and from his objectification of his deaf wife. The complex web of interests is further explored by Ronell, who shows that his devising the telephone had little to do with strictly technical concerns.

Alexander Graham Bell never considered the telephone to constitute a mere scientific thing, an object or even a machine that one day would be subsumable under a notion of technological dominion. His partner, Thomas Watson, wrote of the art of telephony and was a spiritualist who conjured ghosts at nightly séances in Salem. He was, for a time, a strong medium. The telephone's genesis, whose rhizomesque shoots still need to be traced, could have taken root in the dead ear Bell carried around with him and into which he spoke. He carried the ear, it transported him, during one summer vacation spent at his parents' home.

Now, the dead ear that was lent to Aleck by the Harvard medical insti-

60. Ibid., p. xv. Ronnell adds:
When you hang up, it does not disappear but goes into remission. This constitutes its Dasein. There is no off switch to the technological. *Remember:* When you're on the telephone, there is always an electronic flow, even when that flow is unmarked. *The Telephone Book* releases the effect of an electronic-libidinal flow using typography to mark the initiation of utterances. To the extent that you are always on call, you have already learned to endure interruption and the
        click. (emphasis and spacing in the original)

tution may have been the other ear of Hamlet's father or more likely, too, of Van Gogh, insofar as ears tend to come in pairs. Or it could have been that of his deaf mother, calling him home. Still, ears rarely are pricked up for stereophonic listening, so that it might be reasonable to assume that one ear suffices for the telephone as well as for the purpose of invention. The ear of the other is not the other ear, the one excluded from the partial headset that seems eternally to await its fitting unity. . . .

. . . In sum, Alexander Graham Bell carried a dead ear to his mother's house that summer. It is the ear of the Other whose identity is manifold. The telephone, whose labor pains were felt in that ear, has already in this limited example of its birthmark so complex a matrix, that the question of its placement as thing, object or machine, scientific, gynecological, or objet d'art still bears upon us. It was conceived with a kind of Frankensteinian pathos, this supplementary organ to a mother's deafness—mother or wife, actually, since Aleck's bride, Mabel Bell, also suffered the hearing impairment. But she came second to the deaf mother, like a second ear joined in the same determination as the first, with which it is paired. In a certain light, we can ask the same question of the Frankenstein monster as we do of the telephone. After all, both inventors—Bell and Victor Frankenstein—were invested in the simulacrum that speaks and hears; both, we might add precipitously, were elaborating works of mourning, memorializing that which is missing, in a certain way trying to make grow the technological flower from an impossible grave site.[61]

Alexander Graham Bell is most remembered as the inventor of the telephone. Throughout the century since its creation, this simple fact is what most who know the name have recalled. It could be a question on a "cultural literacy" exam.

Q: Who was Alexander Graham Bell?
A: Telephone.

Given current promotions of culture and existing standards of education, no further details would be required for a "correct" answer.[62]

In the language of the times, AGB was a man of science who strongly believed in applying natural science to modernize the universal society of man. This was a modern message, one requiring good listeners. He was in the business of teaching speech and listen-

61. Ibid., pp. 192–94.
62. Hirsch 1989, p. 101. The *entire* entry reads: "Bell, Alexander Graham. Alexander Graham Bell invented the telephone in the late 1800s."

ing. He sought that which had been lost, media to conduct messages, access to inner man through that aural canal, a replacement for the deaf mother's ear in a deaf wife's, a replication of his father and lost brother and son in his own grandsons. He is a complex figure. All the evidence indicates that he was a man of strong passions, good intentions, and generous heart. I want to make clear that any critique of AGB or his invention focuses not on his intentions or motivation but rather on significant shifts in the social bond that followed his work. There is no simple vilification here, no grand villain playing his role in a pious origin narrative.

Alexander Bell, self-rechristened as Alexander Graham Bell, was the third generation of Scottish elocution teachers who were speech professionals. He married the deaf daughter of a wealthy man, having taught the deaf children of wealthy men in several cities. In the successive generations of Bells, the names "Alexander" and "Melville" figure prominently. A substantial part of modern communications history rests on attempted communication between these Alexanders and the Melvilles, across and within generations. As AGB's obsession with genetics and eugenics might predict, he would later play his own grandfather.

His own grandfather, another Alexander Bell, turned from the less respectable field of acting to work as a Shakespearean reader, parlaying this into a career of teaching elocution to the children of wealthy families. He was an expert in "pure diction" and author of a popular text known as "Elegant Extracts." His son, Alexander Melville Bell, developed a system known as "Visible Speech," a detailed notation of speech articulation. Through this system, Melville "reduced to a series of printed symbols the anatomical positions which the speaking organs take in uttering sounds."[63] This system, we are told, was used by early missionaries for notation of unknown languages.

The wife of Alexander Melville Bell, Eliza, who was the mother of AGB, lost her hearing as a young adult. This was the impetus for her son's interest in using Visible Speech to teach speech articulation

63. Mackenzie 1928, p. 19.

to deaf children. In spite of her deafness, or as part of the denial that forms such an active part of the Bell histories, Mother Bell still enjoyed playing the piano. One of Bell's biographers notes, "From his musical mother Aleck inherited the acute ear which was one day to pick up the faint 'ping' of a wire accidentally plucked in a Boston attic, and to recognize in it the electric transmission of speech."[64] Thus we learn that AGB "inherited" an acute ear from his deaf mother. As Ronell observes, "This means that the biographer got involved in the family story of denial. Still, it makes sense. Who would be more attuned to the hearing than a deaf mother?"[65] After his discovery of vibrating wires AGB would spend years attempting to match Visible Speech notations to the sounds of a tuning fork in search of that missing ear.

The Melvilles, as well as the Alexanders, played an important role in the Bell family. Alexander Melville Bell had another son, named Melville, who was very close to his brother, AGB. Together they experimented in communications with the spirit world and made the already-mentioned pact that should either of them die, the other would endeavor to make contact with the departed spirit. In 1870 Melville died of tuberculosis at the age of nineteen. Much of AGB's work in the following years on the harmonics of sympathetic vibrations in tuning forks and pinging wires was in search of a medium of communication with the departed Melville that was better than the Ouija board–like methods they had used together. The search continued into his later partnership with Thomas Watson. Watson, who conducted séances in Salem during this period and later sought the assistance of other spiritualists in developing the new telephonic device, spent hours on the line of the telephone in its early years listening to the pop and static of electrical discharge. He hoped that the spirits were speaking.

Alexander Graham Bell married a deaf woman, one of the students of Visible Speech. Mabel (Ma Bell) Hubbard was the child of a very wealthy family. Together they had two daughters. A son,

64. Ibid., p. 21.
65. Ronell 1989, p. 314.

whom AGB named Melville, died in infancy during his absence. The loss, and his absence, evoked guilt. His grandson Melville Bell Grosvenor was AGB's favorite grandchild in his later years and is today president and chairman of the National Geographic Society, which was founded by his father, AGB's son-in-law. "It was with Melville, however, that Bell came closest to playing the role his own grandfather had played with him. . . . Perhaps Melville's name, that of Bell's dead brother, touched a cord of memory in the old man. Melville's shyness might have reminded Bell of his own boyhood."[66]

Ronell, however, sees a more profound significance in this relationship:

AGB was attracted to the name of the child for whom he became his own grandfather again. . . . As his own grandfather and thus father to his father, Aleck could care for the father, look after him, console him over his loss but also offer himself as the other, the departed brother. . . . The story of Aleck and Melville was to be eternally repeating, Aleck to Melville, Aleck as Melville, his grandfather and himself, all shareholders in the Melville corporation. . . . [W]e can say that Alexander Graham Bell could not tolerate separation. The name of the abyssal catastrophe from which the telephone was cast out, as its monument, was Melville, to whose departure Aleck launched a massively distributed sign of no. The departure of the other, his incommunicability, was a point of radical resistance. Freely translating "Lazarus, arise!" *Come here, I want you*, poses the demand that Alexander Graham Bell inspired into all telephonics.[67]

The history of Alexander Graham Bell's invention is further enmeshed with other "modern scientific" notions of which he was a highly visible proponent. A brief examinaton of these from several competing perspectives will, at least temporarily, displace the standard pieties of the great man and render visible the restrictions and exclusions to which the conjoined histories have contributed. The story of the telephone, as well as the litigious history of its patent rights claim, is the stuff of easily available legend. To construct a slightly different entry point, suffice it to note here that the fortunes acquired by AGB from his invention were devoted to his particular

66. Bruce 1973, p. 459.
67. Ronell 1989, pp. 407–8.

passions. The later part of his life was dedicated to two primary activities, hobbies neither dissimilar nor disconnected from one another: the social eugenics movement and the selective breeding of sheep to bear twins. His contemporary fame and fortunes, however, were tied to teaching of the deaf to speak.

He established the Alexander Graham Bell Association for the Deaf, which celebrated its centennial in 1990. With the money gained from the French Volta Prize, awarded for his invention of the telephone, he also established the Volta Bureau. Both organizations, which still share the same building on Volta Place, N.W., in the Georgetown section of Washington, D.C., are devoted to the oral speech rehabilitation of the deaf. The concern with speech was but one aspect of his passion. In *On the Formation of a Deaf Variety of the Human Race* (1884),[68] an often-cited monograph published by the American Academy for the Advancement of the Sciences, he presented an eugenicist's argument for isolating of the deaf from each other, a prescient demand for what is today called "mainstreaming." He would later suggest that deaf people should not be allowed to bear children with other deaf people, but he stopped short of demanding that deaf people be barred from marriage.[69]

Several titles by AGB are of direct interest. These include "A Few Thoughts Concerning Eugenics" (1908), "How to Improve the Race" (1914), "Is Race Suicide Possible?" (1920), and "Who shall inherit long life?" (1919). These titles, as well as the journals in which they were published—*National Geographic* and *Journal of Heredity*—are connected with each other, with the telephone, and with the deaf. They are a product of AGB's search to overcome separation and loss, shaped by his notions of language, of communication techniques, and of the party at the other end of the line. "What compels attention at this point is the way the telephone, in the figure and person of Alexander Graham Bell, splitting itself off into the poesy of body parts, conceptually plugs into genetic research and engineering. . . . Precisely because *the telephone*

68. Bell 1884.
69. Bell 1898.

was itself conceived as a prosthetic organ, as supplement and techno-logical double to an anthropomorphic body, it was from the start installed within a concept of organ transplant, *implant*, or genetic remodeling in a way that the Promethean Frankenstein monster al-ready had foreshadowed."[70]

In his later years, after the AGB Foundation and the Volta Bureau were established and actively pursuing the goals he set for them, Alexander Graham Bell devoted a substantial part of his time into breeding sheep—with his sole focus to increase the likelihood of birthing ewes with multiple teats that would, in turn, bear twins. These twins played an important part in his search for the missing other and in his attempt to reproduce what had been lost through separation. While he did produce a substantial number of multiple-nippled, twin-bearing ewes, the project was successful only in those terms: "The mutton was tough, the wool inferior, and a farmer once complained that the local butchers declined to take them even as gifts."[71] He spent thirty years on this project. In 1913, AGB collabo-rated with David Fairchild, his son-in-law and new president of the American Breeders' Association, in renaming the body the Ameri-can Genetic Association. He contributed articles on eugenics and sheep breeding to the association's *Journal of Heredity*.

Alexander Graham Bell's several roles in the histories of the Deaf are complex, but his own statement about the origin of the tele-phone is worth noting in detail:

My original skepticism concerning the possibility of speech reading had one good result: it led me to devise an apparatus that might help the chil-dren[:] . . . a machine to hear for them, a machine that should render visible to the eyes of the deaf the vibrations of the air that affect our ears as sound. . . . It was a failure, but that apparatus, in the process of time, be-came the telephone of today. It did not enable the deaf to see speech as others hear it, but it gave ears to the telegraph, and today we hear in Boston what is spoken in New York and Chicago.[72]

70. Ronell 1989, p. 339 (emphasis added).
71. Mackenzie 1928, p. 281.
72. Mackenzie 1928, pp. 56–57.

Ronell glosses AGB, "Still another way of translating this failure that 'should render visible'—as if a commandment or an ethical imperative were being stated—is that Visible Speech failed Alexander Graham Bell at this crucial time of mourning. The deaf and the departed, linked by the register of the interlingual dead, could not be reached, not yet, and not through a speech conjuring apprehended in terms of its visibility."[73] Nevertheless, this part of Ronell's project is to "situate telephonics within an order of deafness." Quoting Dr. Johnson's overworked and shopworn observation that it is "the most desperate of human calamities," she points out that deafness is represented as providing a focus for "the subject's site in language and the spatialization of acoustical images."[74] Yet Ronell's argument here, while drawing on the imagery of Visible Speech (the Bell family techniques of teaching elocution) and, ultimately, tied to the acoustical notions of text it attempts to disrupt, points to the spatialized uses of visual images in displacing the hermeneutical anchor of written acoustics and Visible Speech. It also seeks to undermine a continued colonization of those most degraded by Johnson's "predicament of deafness" as (re)invoked by the heirs to AGB and the telephone.

There is no doubt as to the telos of AGB's invention: he is clear that it was developed for the missing children known as the deaf—children or siblings fully out of earshot. He wrote that "it is only right that it should be known that the telephone is one of the products of the work of the Horace Mann School for the Deaf, and resulted from my attempts to benefit the children of this school."[75] Oddly enough, the modern offices of the Alexander Graham Bell Association for the Deaf and the Volta Bureau deny this telos. The centennial issue of the *Volta Review*, which was dedicated to AGB as the bureau's founder, contains a highly pious historical sketch of AGB, entitled "The Legacy of Dr. Bell." This article is at pains to

73. Ronell 1989, p. 329.
74. Ibid., pp. 328–29.
75. Mackenzie 1928, p. 57.

insist that the invention of the telephone had no connection with Bell's personal relationship with deafness, either his deaf mother's or his wife's. Referring to Bell's wife, Mabel, the author states: "His help with her speech and association with her father paralleled his work on the harmonic telegraph and the telephone." But even the hagiographic historian of the Volta Bureau cannot fail to observe the telephone's bitter legacy for the deaf. "So it was indeed ironic that Bell, who considered himself primarily a teacher of the deaf, should have invented an instrument which significantly isolated deaf people to such a degree."[76]

Helen Keller has been cited as the embodiment of imprisoning or carceral isolation. Blindness, she said, cut her off from things; deafness cut her off from people. Deaf-blindness is quite different from either blindness or deafness, alone. Helen Keller might also be seen as a member of the Bell corporate marketing department, as suggested by the dedication of her autobiography to AGB:

> To
> Alexander Graham Bell
> Who has taught the deaf to speak and enabled
> the listening ear to hear speech from the
> Atlantic to the Rockies,
> I Dedicate
> This Story of My Life[77]

Yet her allegorized story, like that of the telephone, the *National Geographic*, and Alexander Graham Bell himself, is part of the structure that maintains the dominant perceptions of deafness and deaf people. We can take as an example Helen Keller International, a nongovernmental development organization that provides aid to blindness prevention and rehabilitation programs worldwide. It does not assist deaf-blind children or deaf children. Like other organizations of and for the blind, it usually voices support for programs that suppress sign language in favor of speech training for deaf children.

76. Breunig, 1990, p. 89. H. Latham Breunig was the "first hearing-impaired president of the Bell Association"—elected in 1976, though this organization to promote the deaf was established in 1890.
77. Keller 1905.

When it does promote programs for both blind and deaf children, the focus is on teaching them all to listen and to speak.

Much of the familiar narrative of Helen Keller, as well as AGB's imperative to induce the thingly silent ones to speak, dwells on a notion of inner speech. In the technological history of deafness, this notion is hardly innocent. Indeed, it is an obsession that has been inadequately charted. The link between telephony and the cybernetic matrix is the physical body of deafness—more specifically, the physical body of those who are deaf. The search continues for the technology of inner speech that is the source of this link: the site of language.

Cranial Jacks: The Technology of Inner Speech

"The matrix has its roots in primitive arcade games," said the voice-over, "in early graphics programs and military experimentation with cranial jacks." On the Sony, a two-dimensional space war faded behind a forest of mathematically generated ferns, demonstrating the spacial possibilities of logarithmic spirals; cold blue military footage burned through, lab animals wired into test systems, helmets feeding into fire control circuits of tanks and war planes. "Cyberspace. A consensual hallucination experienced daily by billions of legitimate operators, in every nation, by children being taught mathematical concepts. . . . A graphic representation of data abstracted from the banks of every computer in the human system. Unthinkable complexity. Lines of light ranged in the nonspace of the mind, clusters and constellations of data. Like city lights, receding . . ."

"What's that?" Molly asked, as he flipped the channel selector.

"Kid's show."

—William Gibson, *Neuromancer*

The SF literary metaphors that invoke an existence and identity within a disaggregated yet consensual cyberspace are taken from popular dystopias built around "console cowboys" who use a "cyberspace deck"[78] as their mode or vehicle of access. While imaginary brand names are given to the deck, these are often compounds of Japanese corporate terms that suggest an elegantly black, miniatur-

78. Gibson 1984, p. 5.

ized, and mystified high-end technology. Yet little attention is given to the actual need for the console itself, beyond making visible an enhanced tactile skill, or perhaps providing an expanded interface for the exotic software—"wetware"[79] here being a more appropriate name—necessary for accessing the higher realms of dataspace. The keyboard remains the principal thoroughfare leading from human perception to RAM, a thin alphanumeric stream flowing from our fingertips and into the deck as some pale reflection of the thoughts that produce it, and at a pace absurdly mismatched to the capacities of the CPU poised to drink it in.

Both the "deck" and the relationship with it is often mystified.

> On his lap is just about the bitchingest media processor I have ever seen, and judging from the heavy cables exploding out of the back it looks like he's got it crammed with deadly expansion cards. He's wearing dark shades too, . . . but now I see they aren't shades, they are VR rigs, pretty good ones actually. [He] is also wearing a pair of Datagloves. His hands and fingers are constantly moving. Sometimes he makes typing motions, sometimes he reaches out and grabs imaginary things and moves them around, sometimes he points his index finger and navigates through virtual space, sometimes he *riffs in some kind of sign language*.[80]

Strictly for narrative purposes, the keyboard marks out a space over which fingers might dance or fly, signifying a level of skill and dexterity in addition to the direct neural link to the deck. Newer consoles provide a virtual holographic space in which multi-dimensional relations are interactively communicated, even in some kind of sign language, enhancing the skill and dexterity of the talented cowboy. But both scenarios include the direct console-to-cowboy connection via a neural implant, a brain "socket" or "cranial jack," to bypass all external mediation of "reality."

The implant, most often depicted as a neural hardware socket to the brain and usually located behind an ear, is how the console cow-

---

79. The term is used in a variety of sources, but see Rucker's novel of that title (1988).

80. Stephenson 1994, p. 146 (emphasis added).

boy links to the console—by being "jacked in" via a direct tap into his or her perceptual neurology. The physical modification to provide the implanted socket is also a metaphorical link to a hardwire investment into any broader network matrix. More important, it also signifies a hardwire bypass of any mediation of perception, a particular feature of the disembodied data matrix that is called cyberspace: that is, the direct experience of dataspace.

Neurologists may be loosely divided into "hardware engineers" and "software architects," something like electrical engineers and software designers. In the field of language and cognition studies, such as those undertaken at the Salk Institute, the software camp has undertaken very impressive research into hemispheric neurological activities surrounding language events and activities. These studies demonstrate rather conclusively not only that sign languages occupy the same neurological sites as spoken language, but that sign language use also invokes activities at other neurological sites, including right hemispheric functions of spatial and visual relations. This suggests that early acquisition of a natural sign language might well be advantageous, regardless of hearing status, as a means of increasing use of the cerebral neurological capacity that is otherwise underutilized.[81] It does not, however, indicate that deaf people have "different" brains, which is how one popular author has misinterpreted these research results.[82] Rather, the researchers have interpreted the data to prove that sign languages are language, full stop. Sign languages are not "languagelike," "similar to language," or any other ambivalent descriptor: sign languages are language.

The hardware and software neurologists agree about availability of largely underutilized neurological resources of the human brain, but the hardware camp is working on direct hardwire access into the neural receptors in the human brain. Experimental surgery conducted over the past thirty years has sought exactly such physical "access." This experimental surgery has not been about "cyber-

81. Poizner, Klima, and Bellugi 1987.
82. Sacks 1989.

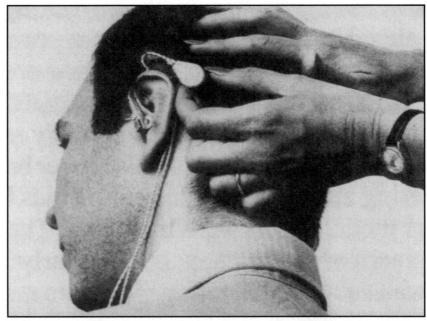

What new colony in the name of communications technology is sited on the body of the Deaf? What "land," what "place," whose body is the site of this exploratory frontier? What "discovery" by a new "Columbus" is reenacted on this new "continent" of language and communication? Is the electronic/cyberspace "frontier" being homesteaded by descendants of the same settlers as those of the telephonic frontier? Did anyone notice any "natives"?

What signification may be read in the "aural-to-neural sensory bypass" of this hardwire receiver/receptacle? What representations are offered? Is it the "miracle of hearing"? What miracle? What hearing?

Figure 6.   The cranial jack. Reprinted with permission from *The Volta Review* 92 (May 1990): 40. Copyright 1990 by the Alexander Graham Bell Association for the Deaf, 3417 Volta Place NW, Washington, DC 20007.

space," but its declared goals have been perhaps even more lofty: the source of speech, and thus language. The site of the experimental surgery has been the frontier of that search—the missing ear of the deaf.

The neural implant socket behind the ear of the cyberpunk cowboy by which he or she jacks in to a hyperreality of unmediated perception has the ring of a fanciful fantasy. But the cranial jack behind the ear is not a fiction. It is an experimental medical technology practiced on deafened adults and now, following U.S. Food and Drug Administration (FDA) approval in 1990, on deaf children. It is called the cochlear implant. The cochlear implant is the prototype for a neurological "plug-'n'-play" socket.

Cochlear Implants: Replanting the Medical Flag on the Body of Deafness

The cochlear implant[83] is a "device that converts sound patterns into patterns of direct electrical stimulation via wires that are surgically implanted near the nerves of hearing, thus bypassing a nonfunctioning inner ear. . . . The performance of cochlear implants varies from individual to individual, sometimes for reasons that cannot yet be explained. Even at their best, the results, though remarkable, are poor compared with normal hearing. Nevertheless, cochlear implants represent an application of developing technologies."[84]

Progress, most particularly in the fields of technology, creates its own demand for application. In this case, a "developing" technology seems much more attractive than an "experimental" one. In fact, one leading manufacturer of cochlear implants goes to great lengths to assure prospective consumers that, because the implants now have FDA approval, the technology is not experimental but "proven." In the same sentence, however, the Cochlear Corporation admits that this FDA approval is for use in specific populations. The company stresses simultaneously the proven performance of the technology and the limited results that are available from the "application of this developing" technology.

The medical literature also documents a substantial number of complications from implantation, although the complications are declared to be "within acceptable limits." While the small size of

83. The purpose of this discussion is not to examine technical pros and cons of implant devices, but to examine the role they play in the broader discursive economy of deafness and communication technologies.

84. Boothroyd 1990, p. 77.

more recent implants seems to be lessening the chance of major complications, the primary factor seemed to be the surgeon's experience with performing such operations.[85] Such varying degrees of experience might seem to correlate as well with an "experimental" as with a "developing" technology.

A careful reading of both the medical and marketing literature reveals a wide range of caveats and reservations. The "implant will not produce or restore normal hearing." While "virtually all adult recipients can recognize different environmental sounds," some show an "improved ability to recognize speech with lipreading. . . . A few can even understand speech through the implant alone— without lipreading."[86]

Careful pains are taken to place the responsibility for success directly onto the implant recipient. The implant maker goes on to note that "there are no tests to predict the level of benefit a particular individual will receive." An evaluation is also undertaken "to ensure that the individual and the family have realistic expectations." Observing that the sounds that are perceived by the implant recipient differ from those of "normal" hearing, the implant vendor stresses: "Recipients must learn to interpret the new sounds. It may take time and experience to achieve maximum benefit from the implant." The therapeutic relationship continues: the recipient is the sole variable, while the technology is a given.

In theory, the implant bypasses the damaged cochlea and stimulates the auditory nerve fibers directly. Implants differ in terms of electrode array, number of channels, and processing scheme. However, a detailed description of one device can serve for all:

The implanted part of the cochlear prosthesis system consists of a 22-band introcochlear electrode array and a receiver/stimulator. The receiver/stimulator produces a biphasic charge-balanced current pulse which can vary in amplitude from 20 μA to 1.5 mA and in pulse width from 10 to 400 μsec per phase. The electrode array consists of platinum foil bands spaced along a tapering Silastic carrier approximately 0.5 mm in diameter.

85. R. Webb, et al. 1991, p. 131.
86. *Issues and Answers* (1991), product pamphlet by the Cochlear Corporation, Englewood, Colo.

The electrode bands are connected to the receiver/stimulator by Teflon insulated platinum/iridium wires. The receiver/stimulator consists of the stimulating electronics in a titanium capsule, a receiving coil and a rare earth magnet for holding the external coil in position. The entire implant is encased in medical grade Silastic.[87]

One cannot help but notice the emphasis on exotic, high-technology materials used in the construction and operation of the prosthesis, perfectly in keeping with the SF hopes for its use; they include platinum foil, Teflon-insulated platinum/iridium wires, a titanium capsule, a rare earth magnet, and medical grade Silastic. The SF descriptions of cranial jacks are no more vivid than this, even given the license of "fiction." These clinical details also serve to provide both proof and assurance that no effort will be spared and no cost will be too great to bring speech to the afflicted speechless. Indeed, the cost of an implant is generally in excess of $25,000.[88]

But the use of these devices is not without some controversy. "The use of cochlear implants with adults is generally accepted by scientists and clinicians even though controversy exists on issues involving candidacy, device characteristics, assessment, and rehabilitation procedures."[89] The "controversy" has primarily centered around use of these experimental devices on profoundly deaf children. Implant manufacturers, and nearly all researchers, agree that the outcomes of cochlear implant use by congenitally deaf persons fall far below the results achieved by those who have lost hearing late in life. Yet the desire of both parents and medical professionals to deny deafness makes the alluring promises of cochlear implants hard to resist. As already noted, cochlear implants have recently been approved by the U.S. FDA for experimental implant surgery on profoundly deaf children. The technical paper cited above closes with a "hopeful" statement: "Results for a small number of children are encouraging and it appears that it may be possible to have a substan-

87. Dowell, R. C. and G. M. Clark. "Clinical Results for Profoundly Deaf Patients Using the 22-Electrode Cochlear Prosthesis," paper delivered to the Tenth World Congress of the World Federation of the Deaf, Helsinki, 20–28 July 1987.

88. *Issues and Answers* (1991).

89. Osberger 1990, p. 40.

tial impact on the *management* of profoundly deaf children with the careful application of the cochlear prosthesis."[90] The World Federation of the Deaf, after some years of indecision on the subject, has issued a resolution strongly condemning use of the implants on deaf children.

As has often been the case in colonial appropriation and use of native bodies, the acts of naming and labeling do much to distract attention away from obvious exploitation even as they point to the new regime being sought. A current high-end model implant is known as the "Nucleus multichannel implant speech processor." Notice that this device to artificially stimulate the auditory (hearing) nerves is called a "speech processor." The use of this phrase is more than just disingenuous, as it demonstrates the technical commitment to the production of "inner speech" and the requisite linkage of speech to language.

Improved performance of intracochlear implants is by no means the final goal. A "1991 Discover Award," announced by *Discover* magazine in December 1991, was presented to the director of auditory implant research at the House Ear Institute in Los Angeles for development of the Auditory Brainstem Implant. Discussions of brain stem implants begin by targeting the same carefully limited population. The article announcing the award notes that "many people considered deaf retain a rudimentary sense of hearing that allows them some responsiveness to the auditory environment,"[91] alerting the reader that only the most rudimentary level of auditory-like perception is at stake.

So who is the market for such a device? Those who have a "rare form of neural tumor," which requires surgeons to cut the nerves that pass auditory information to the brain, causing an absolute deafness. The brain stem implant promises to "restore some environmental hearing." Similar in basic design to the cochlear implant, the brain stem implant bypasses the cochlea to attach electrodes di-

90. Dowell and Clark, op. cit. (emphasis added).
91. "Talking to the Brain," 1991, p. 74.

rectly to the neural stem. Of thirteen volunteers who received this implant, eleven regained "environmental hearing *and one can even understand limited amounts of human speech*."[92] We do not learn what happened to the other two, or what "environmental hearing" really means, or just how limited was the speech perception of the "success" case. The Discover Awards panel called the results "astounding." The FDA has awarded a "new product development" grant to this project.

The goal of a direct neural connection, a cranial jack, into the "source" of language seems one step closer.

In Hopes of Language Deferred: Oral Technologies

Promises, like notions of development, are based on deferments. The ethic of deferring, the need to sacrifice immediate needs for the possibilities held out for the greater good, is also implicated in the language options made available to children who are deaf. The "which first" and "either/or" construction of options, as I have argued, provide no genuine choice at all, but simply further defer the acknowledgment of difference. The acquisition of a mother language is deferred in deference to the ideal of speech.

Deference and *deferral* are quite distinct in meaning, but the words do conjoin in certain practices of power—and in the language options available for children who are deaf. Standard modern dictionaries have two separate and distinct entries for *defer*. Though their spelling merged in Middle English, they are from different Latin verbs and carry different meanings:

defer[a]: -ferred, -ferring, -fers. To put off until a future time; postpone; "against my wishes I deferred writing to you until now" (Emily Dickinson). . . . To procrastinate; delay.

defer[b]: -ferred, -ferring, -fers. To comply with or submit to the opinion or decision of another; be deferential.

deference: 1. Submission or courteous yielding to the opinion, wishes,

92. Ibid.(italics added).

or judgment of another: "Reason is to practice some vague and unassignable amount of deference to instinct," (John Stuart Mill). 2. Courteous respect.[93]

The meanings have similar roots: to put off from, to distance, to render away. But their modern application belies these roots. Post-colonialism is deeply engaged both with deference and with that which must be deferred in the name of greater hopes.[94] So is the management of deafness. The swirling uncertainties of location in the data matrix, while seemingly distant, are tightly bound to the medical explorations conducted on the bodies of the deaf—and on the Body of Deafness—in search of the origins and location of speech. Yet, in fact, the subjective anchors no longer matter, as they become driven by their own imperatives, coded by both deference and deferral.

Technical and medical options aimed at reproducing speech and hearing are products of deferring. Technologies, be they tactile aids, implants, manual codes, or any technical mediation (including mainstreaming) all promise great potential, but that potential can only be realized after further "development." What is actually delivered, along with promises and pious exhortations, is but a small part of what was promised. But the promises justify the enormous attention and further funding that the technique, its hardware, or its practices require. This attention, in the meantime, effectively precludes other topics—and modalities—from being explored and funded.

This partially explains why the diminished curriculum is so crucial to managing certain types of difference. In the case of Thailand, we saw that hill-tribe and welfare school children are taught a reduced subset of the regular curriculum, as are disabled children. Poor performance by the different child is expected and reproduced by further reductions in content. Here we recognize both deference and

93. *American Heritage Dictionary of the English Language*, new college ed. (1981). Note that *deference* is used to refer only to submission, not to postponement as well. (Derrida coined *différance* in part to fill this void.)

94. See also Krishna 1992.

deferment to the promises that program advances and new technologies will abolish the difference. The so-called tragedy of difference makes available codes of perseverance in the overcoming of hardships and handicaps, codes that support the harmonizing justifications for forging ahead with the research and technical development the tragedy demands.

The ethic of deferring requires both submitting to the will of the generalized good and accepting postponements accompanied by promises that forbearance and perseverance will yet deliver such good to all. This issue obviously is not confined to the deaf alone. Perhaps, however, this examination of the deaf and the vigilance with which this category is maintained has illuminated the process by which many such connections have come to feel so, well, normal. The common good is good for some, but rarely for the common people. Indeed, one of the key observations of postcoloniality is that marginality is marginal only in relation to something else; accepting the binary relation is a necessary precondition of its existence.

This discussion of deferring allows a last ironic glance at the hardware industries that have sprung up to capitalize on the raw resource of deaf ears. It is a lucrative economy, one sustained by denial and trade in those recognitions that are acceptable. As the common joke in Deaf circles goes, "sign language will never be popular because no one can get rich off of it." In communications technologies, deafness is implicated with desire. It is a desire of communication bound to the sound of the Word. The desire for that which has seemingly been lost will be fulfilled, and all of life's needs met: this is the promise of consumer culture and its products. If denial of the difference is one side of the equation, and deferral of fulfillment is part of the faith necessary in the help itself, then certainly some product being made right now that will provide the best possible solution is the other side.

It will be useful to examine some of the specific devices that now promise to do the hitherto impossible—to induce the thingly silent ones to hear and thus to speak. Just what does it take to convince parents to defer access to language for their deaf child, to make them accept that only one kind of language may be made available? This meaning of deafness is failure, a damage in the child that must be overcome. The problem may be located in a world that doesn't accept damaged children, but the solution must be situated in and on the child. It is the child, not the world rejecting the child, that is broken. Thus a solution means more than just a metaphorical "fix." It demands a "real" fix of modern science and technology. The industries of fixing broken children are located on a very profitable entrepreneurial field. The language by which this profitable terrain is maintained, and in which the requirements for such "solutions" are explained to the paying customers, has its own fascination. It is a language rich in bitter ironies.

The abstracts of papers delivered to the 1990 Centennial Convention of the Alexander Graham Bell Association for the Deaf on the use of neural implants in deaf children offer an interesting sample of how issues are framed by the proponents of speech-only approaches to the deaf experience.

One speaker explains his project, "Targeted performance includes speech production . . . with special emphasis on the development of *meaningful auditory integration abilities.*" [95] "Auditory integration abilities" means not simply coping strategies but includes the more important ability to pass as hearing. This resonates powerfully with the realm of race, where passing is also a highly contested issue. Is the desired result of a "normal hearing and talking child" so rarely achieved that it becomes necessary to hide even the desire under clumsy technoid terms? Possibly, but a simple "yes" is not yet adequate. Because of the dismal results of oralism as an educational strategy, the technical terms are heavily invested in the denial of deafness itself. One staff member of the Alexander Graham Bell As-

95. A. Robbins, "Maximizing Performance in Children with Cochlear Implants and Tactile Aids," paper delivered to the Centennial Convention of the Alexander Graham Bell Association for the Deaf, Washington, D.C., 24–28 July 1990 (emphasis added). All quotations pertaining to papers given at this conference are taken from the program for the Washington, D.C., convention.

sociation for the Deaf has been quoted as saying, "They can't hear, but they catch on. Some say there's no such thing as a deaf child. Not if it's done right."[96] *Surgery is part of doing it right*:

Another conference paper is described: "The Pro-Social Behavior Program, in conjunction with the Verbotonal Approach, provides hearing-impaired students a unique opportunity *to develop internal language* and interactions skills necessary for productive living and communication."[97] Here we see in action the mandate to interiorize that which cannot be directly experienced. Its corollaries—a dedication to internal speech and the identification of normality with hearing—are unquestioned. The sole purpose of education is to develop those skills needed to make any encounter with a hearing person a therapeutic one.

Indeed, the oldest oral school for the deaf in the United States may exemplify this philosophy. "Ideally, the Clarke School expects that all their graduates will associate exclusively with the hearing. In addition to their historic hope of improving the gene pool, these associations are seen as providing deaf adults with continuous opportunities for practicing their oral skills, thus turning friendships between deaf and hearing into permanent speech therapy situations."[98] This goal is central to the social ideology of oralism and mainstreaming. It does not matter whether oral schools produce a large number of verbal conversationalists, as long as they produce deaf children who are quiet, stationary, inconspicuous, and acceptable to the hearing.

It may be worth noting again some of the ties between the Alexander Graham Bell Association, the Volta Bureau, and other strategic bodies: "The chairman of the board of American Telephone and Telegraph (AT&T) traditionally sits on the board of the Bell Association. J. Edgar Hoover of the FBI was a member for years. The

96. Neisser 1983, p. 32
97. S. Eberhardt, "Internalizing Pro-Social Behaviors through Speech and Language Instructions," paper delivered to the Centennial Convention of the AGB Association for the Deaf (emphasis added).
98. Neisser 1983, p. 128.

mission of the Association is to assure that deaf children become true Americans, patriotic and English-speaking."[99]

Let us return to the Centennial Convention, where the Japanese, never to be outdone in technical devices, introduced a computer-based speech therapy system under the Matsushita-Panasonic label. Both the name and description recall the console cowboy's cyber-deck. "A unique feature is the palatograph, which records tongue-palate contact by means of an 'artificial palate' that contains 63 tiny sensors. When tongue-palate contact occurs during the production of certain speech sounds, dots (which correspond to the individual sensors) light up on the monitor. This enables the student to 'see' sounds that are not visible through speechreading."[100]

We are accustomed to being amused by translated manuals for Japanese VCRs; here, desperately funny ironies emerge from the text. An erotic connection is established between vision and desire through the oral sensation of tongue-palate feedback that triggers an electronic visual display of sound and meaning. The erotic desire for oral gratification may seem to be evoking technically assisted masturbation in this example, but those subjected to such devices have described them as sadomasochistic. In any case, it is difficult to imagine deaf people lugging about their own "palatographs" to stick into the mouths of hearing people they want or need to understand. This too is almost erotic in its own fashion.

Another paper was entitled, "Pay Attention! Deafness and Attention Deficit Disorder in Children."[101] Obviously, when a deaf child doesn't adequately "listen" to the speaking teacher, then the child must be the source of a new "disorder"; hence the added problem to solve—Attention Deficit Disorder. The point is made that medications also "prove effective" in treating this "disorder" of inatten-

99. Ibid., p. 31.

100. K. Youdelman, H. Levitt, N. Murata, Y. Yamada, J. Head, and N. McGarr, "Matsushita-Panasonic Speech Training System," paper delivered to the Centennial Convention of the AGB Association for the Deaf.

101. P. Fletcher, "Pay Attention! Deafness and Attention Deficit Disorder in Children," paper delivered to the Centennial Convention of the AGB Association for the Deaf.

tive children. Drugging uncooperative school children is not a new idea, but the reason given for this old approach to the management of difference is novel.

Together with the new hardware, these newly discovered "disorders," such as the failure of a deaf child to "listen," are placed into a management framework. This has been a particularly useful framing for those techniques—pedagogical, pharmacological, or surgical—that might justify behavior modifications. One paper on implants observed, "A merging of the medical and educational communities has become a necessity."[102] There are some, such as Michel Foucault, who have persuasively argued that this occurred long ago. The argument here, however, is that this merger is nowhere more clearly seen than in education, often referred to in this literature as "management," of (but certainly not by) the deaf.

The possible impression that only the purveyors of commercial hearing aids are implicated in this merger should be corrected by an article in a recent newsletter of a major U.S. university. The article is entitled, "Lab Studies Devices that 'Feel' Sound,"[103] and from start to finish it unintentionally provides a richly ironic caricature of the field. The article begins with a consciously balanced tone, observing that sign language is reasonable but suggesting that its use restricts deaf people to a ghettolike community of those who know a sign language. The conclusion that "it's a hearing world" is presumed as natural.

The objective tone is then applied to a similar discussion of the problems of relying on lipreading alone. It is difficult and even the best miss many parts of a conversation. Given these premises—that speech and hearing are "normal" and that deaf people need assistance beyond lipreading—it is obvious that something based on sound sensations and hearing science is called for to supplement lipreading. The new technology is explained: "One of the devices has seven little vibrators on it, arranged in a line. Low frequency, or low

102. J. L. Bader, "The Role of Educator on a Cochlear Implant Team," paper delivered to the Centennial Convention of the AGB Association for the Deaf.

103. "Lab Studies Devices That 'Feel' Sound," 1992, p. 3.

pitch, components of the speech stimulate vibrators at one end, high frequency components of the speech stimulate vibrators at the other end and medium frequencies stimulate ones in the middle" (p. 3). One then learns that environmental sounds can be better distinguished: "A barking dog, for example, will stimulate a different pattern from that of a ringing telephone" (p. 3). Somehow, it is difficult to believe that the deaf person fears being bitten by a telephone.

Yet not until the final column does the reader learn that this technology cannot deliver what it first appears to promise and that its uses are not those initially suggested. First, the warning: "But, like other systems for the hearing impaired, a tactile device is far from perfect" (p. 3). So far from perfect, one discovers, that the device is not useful for what had appeared the primary purpose of its development—speech: "The tactile system wasn't really designed for speech [the head reads]. So any code you impose on speech that puts it on the tactile system is by nature arbitrary. People are learning arbitrary patterns and learning to associate those patterns with particular speech sounds. It takes a long time to learn to integrate the information you're getting from the tactile device with the visual information you might be getting from lip-reading. It's not automatic" (p. 3).

Again, it must be observed that the referent of particular speech sounds is still unavailable to the subjects of this technology—those who are deaf. They don't hear them. More to the point, once again the promise extended is suddenly withdrawn. Though the lab exists to measure the results of this training, the researchers are honest enough to admit that they have no training method, as yet, although their optimism about the promises of the future (of their grants) is high: "It's not clear that the way you would train a person to use a hearing aid would be the same way you would train a person to use a tactile aid, she explains. It might be, but it might not be. . . . There seems to be a lot of individual variation. So maybe there are some characteristics of the person that also affect how good they are at using the tactile aid" (p. 3).

Perhaps how much they hear might have something to do with it. But we digress—though not as much as the article does. After basically admitting their device to be useless for the teaching of speech, observing they've not a clue on how to train users to best employ it, and, finally, putting the responsibility back onto the individual deaf person for learning how to hear, these researchers would seem to have completed the cycle. But the last item is not yet in place. The ironies are not quite over. After it has been made clear that the device is, at best, a clumsy joy-buzzer relating to frequencies of environmental noise, the final paragraph adds, as if only in passing: "Currently . . . tactile aids are used primarily in schools for the deaf. As they become more practical and as more practitioners come to understand how they work, perhaps they will be used more widely in the general population of the hearing-impaired" (p. 3).

There is no need to worry about the lack of results, as the devices are only being used on the deaf in institutions. They can't hear anyway, so any technical device translating noise, no matter how crude, must be an improvement for them. That those higher on the scale of normality, glossed in that seemingly innocent phrase "the general population of the hearing-impaired," might not be served by this device seems to justify its limitation to those who have the least practical use for such a device. Its designers admit it is of little use in the area of speech and hearing. It is, however, yet another useful appropriation of deaf bodies for the sake of knowledge, progress, and commerce.

6

Differences That Matter

For it is the nature of humanity to press onward to agreement with others;
human nature only really exists in an achieved community of minds.
—Hegel, *Phenomenology of Spirit*

When Language Belongs to Talk

Deafness is part of the biopolitics of nature; it involves the politics of being "normal," the politics of difference and deviance, the politics of identity. The politics of difference centers on issues of inclusion and cohesion. Mainstreaming, as a technique of inclusion, is only one of the programmatic responses in the ever-evolving attempt to abolish difference and reach the goal of a totalizing unity. But the tools of these politics emerge from specific linguistic economies.

The particular differences of deafness have been tightly policed, so tightly as to have made those who are Deaf essentially invisible [1] to the broader social polity, with only modest recent exceptions. While a direct and active policing has occurred within the institutions specifically designed to administrate "the deaf," a more powerful policing has occurred indirectly, through the naturalization of the accepted criteria of "normal" in the practices of "social norms."

1. We should note that deafness is often called the "invisible disability." Deafness cannot itself be seen as can, say, blindness, without other clues such as large hearing aids or an active use of sign language. Even these do not confirm deafness. Nor, would I hazard, has the recent "visibility" of deafness and some of the related concerns of Deaf people contributed much to meaningful changes for the lives of most Deaf people. The accommodations have been minor, leaving the policing of difference strongly in place.

Exploring the politics of identity requires questioning the normal, questioning the requirements for passing as normal.

There are consistent and recurring difficulties in the theoretical literature that are highlighted by questions raised by Deaf people about explicit and implicit language policy. The obvious problematics of language policy for deaf people occur on a terrain of language theory fraught with its own contradictory attempts to contain difference. Like the conflation of language with speech from which these difficulties emerge, the exclusion of the differences of deafness is deeply naturalized in dominant theories of language. A work on the politics of identity is primarily a work about cracks and breaks in the facades of accepted identities. It is also about tactics of resistance and the evasion of control by those who either choose to enter or are thrust into and through such breaks and fissures. The ways in which we collectively talk about resistance and accommodation both produce and are products of our notions of language.

For example, in beginning a carefully textured analysis of post-Marxist conceptions of economy and a post-Freudian understanding of the unconscious to discuss values, valence, and meaning, Jean-Joseph Goux poses the following question: "Why and how are 'facial expressions, gestures, the whole of the body and the mundane register, in a word, the whole of the visible and spatial as such,' why are all these 'excluded from meaning (*bedeuten*)' in favor of the signs of language alone?"[2] The general equivalence that Goux here assumes between "phonic signification" (speech) and "language" *slams shut* the very door the question is meant to open. While the terrain referred to was semiotically rich, it was strictly a spoken one.

While this chapter primarily is a closer consideration of the contested terrain of Deaf language rights and the discursive language of rights talk, a brief prefatory summary of the difficulties within the modern traditional theories of language gives useful context.[3] The twentieth-century English analytical philosophers focus on the context for speech acts, usually attending too much or too narrowly to

2. Goux 1990, p. 10.
3. For a more detailed overview, readers are referred to Shapiro 1981b.

the circumstances of the specific speech act and the conventions pertaining in that context. The arguments that emerged to counter
their linguistic theory[4] turned to an examination of language systems in which a play of differences occurs, producing theories in
which the relationship between the signifier and the signified is recognized as purely conventional. A conscious subject is not essential
for the production of meaning—a notion not unacceptable to the
earlier Anglo-American linguistic view but more clearly framed in
the later approach. The object/referent is not required, either. Thus
both the traditional empirical and phenomenological approaches are
displaced.

Jacques Derrida and Ludwig Wittgenstein each reacted against
traditional accounts of language, with Derrida criticizing a theory of
expression and Wittgenstein a theory of representation.[5] Both removed from consideration not only the object's (referent's) meaning but also the subject's aim or intention. They focused instead on
the linguistic structure in which the subjects are situated.[6] This is an
expressivist view of language.[7] That is, while it is problematic to "assign" or locate meaning, one can analyze the availability of meaning
to be expressed within a given linguistic structure.[8]

This would raise a further question. If focus on the context of
speech acts does in fact obscure the prior context of possibilities
from which speech acts are developed, why does the written sign,
which "breaks with its context and is more clearly weaned from ref-

4. As represented particularly by Austin 1962.
5. See especially Derrida 1973 and Wittgenstein 1953.
6. See also Shapiro 1984.
7. Taylor 1987, pp. 101–32.
8. The divergence between these sets of theories, one emphasizing speech practices and the other emphasizing writing practices, parallels a like divergence in
the study of order in aesthetics between music as practice (the aural) and art as
representation-practice (the visual; see Jay 1986, p. 177 n. 15). Jay (1986) has commented that it seems mandatory for French intellectual writers to focus on painting
and art representation, in contrast to the Germans, who are concerned with music,
but he fails to suggest that both forms represent norms of social order. As I would
further point out, both presume and require hearing and the spoken word for their
hermeneutical referent.

erent and initiating subject,"[9] not also obscure its prior context of spoken language? Meaning is cut loose from its moorings, but language is still tied—yet only by convention—to a linear and sequentially acoustical way of linguistic being. If meaning and its expression are related, as in the expressivist view, then our concern with either spoken or written signs obscures this prior choice, a concealment that even the expressivists overlook. Sign languages pose troubling questions to most of the dominant schools of language theory.

The postmodern analyses that question the conventions constituting the linguistic systems and underlying all contexts for speech acts can be used to interrogate the more fundamental convention that assumes an aural/oral modality as the cognitive locus for linguistic structure. More than one postmodern writer supply words adequate to frame the question, but each anchors his or her statements firmly in the terra cognita of the sole privileged modality. Fredric Jameson critiques Anglo-American philosophy as caught up in the problem of the referent and "deflected by [Saussure's] terminology from the whole question of the ultimate referent of the linguistic sign."[10] Yet he does not question the linguistic sign with which that question is concerned, or the modality to which it is tied. Derrida's inquiry stops at a similar point: "Austin . . . appears to consider solely the conventionality constituting the circumstance of the utterance (énoncé), its conventional surroundings, and not a certain conventionality intrinsic to what constitutes the speech act (locution) itself."[11] The next question would seem to be, what constitutes the circumstances for locution? *There are indeed circumstances in which language does not belong to talk.* Thus, both Derrida and Jameson provide openings to that field of politics in which theoretical presumptions determine institutional speech and language policy, and they make such policy instruments available for question. But neither questions his own presumptions of speech and language.

This brief map is of a politics of language, a map that locates

9. Derrida 1976, p. 182.
10. Jameson 1984, p. 181.
11. Derrida 1976, p. 189.

boundaries beyond which a certain group of "refugees" have been pushed. I use the term *refugee* with care, as much of our usual understanding of the word does not apply. Here, neither "return" nor "recovery" is necessarily sought, both of which tie refugee identity to place or location. Indeed, we have seen that the Deaf have never possessed an originary place but are merely citizens of a neighboring (ontological) "nation" that has been under attack for generations.

At least to the Hearing, the hermeneutical privileging of hearing and speech over sight seems related to traditions of the Reformation and its literal focus on "the Word of God." This bias remains embedded within the notions of textualization. Even texts that examine the visual, such as Martin Heidegger's famous discussion of Van Gogh's peasant shoes, or texts that are visually constituted through semiotic representation apply the metaphor of hearing and speech (and the perceptual mechanics of written representation of hearing and speech) to interpretation. To this extent, visual semiotics is still very much not simply about language but specifically about the spoken word.

This brief diversion into the arcane world of language theorists undertakes to disturb the usual understanding of the historical processes that have given rise not only to the social circumstances of the Deaf but also to our notions of distinction between—and conflation of—locution and articulation. We often valorize one phenomenological view, such as experiential roots of authenticity, over others, in a privileging that could be referred to as a romantic hermeneutic. Such a strategic application of hermeneutical frames may be accurate as well as often politically effective.[12] Yet we now also see that the prior conditions for such practices are problematic. The strategic claim to an "authentic voice" is compromised.

A similar notion was expressed by Deleuze when he observed Foucault pointing to "the indignity of speaking for others. . . . [T]he fact [is] that only those directly concerned can speak in a practical way on their own behalf."[13] The questions of "voice" and of speak-

---

12. See also Edelman 1977.
13. Deleuze in Foucault 1977, p. 209.

ing on behalf of others are thus vexed at nearly every level, but they continue to be engaged. It is through rights talk that the attempts to reclaim difference are most often waged. We shall examine these efforts and the ambivalent results they seem to produce.

Assimilation and Elimination

The terrain of deafness, like many other fields, produces its own vocabulary. It must be noted, however, that in this debate there is now no equal time, nor has there ever been. The terms of the discussions, as well as the discussions themselves, are located in spoken languages, even when the topic is sign language. Part of the policing process has been to exclude perspectives rooted in sign language terms—and of course those presented in sign language itself. Rather than claim an authentic rendering of a signed "voice," I will here discuss those terms that structure that part of the terrain in which such differences are addressed.

In chapter 2, the historical production of a deaf identity convenient for hearing administration was shown to emerge from a set of core practices that changed only in the interpretations of their intent. These practices were framed as follows:

Production and Administration of Deaf Identity

Traditional	Modern/mainstream
Separation (from society)	Separation (from their peers)
Isolation (as a type and group)	Isolation (from each other)
Denial by exclusion	Denial by dispersal
Objects of Christian salvation	Objects of scientific inquiry

This formulation of the techniques used to produce and police such an identity makes it clear that separation, isolation, denial, and objectification have survived shifts into their seemingly opposite forms. These themes may be better understood as outgrowths of a larger social project to achieve Hegel's highest goal, a totalizing human community of minds. Hegel's "natural" search for agreement with others builds from an interiorized telos or purpose to pursue each such moment of agreement. Contradictions, as they become visible, will further compel us to new and higher forms of agreement.

As William Connolly points out, there is a cost to this agreement:

> It is part of the essence of humanity to seek truth by pressing onward to agreement, and the highest form of politics . . . is one where the sphere of fundamental agreement is all-inclusive, virtue is highly developed, rationality flourishes and freedom reigns. *Put another way, the implicit purpose of human history is to eliminate otherness*—all that escapes knowledge, reason and normality—by pressing onward to agreements which assimilate it to higher forms of knowledge, reason and normality. *The politics of inclusivity engenders the assimilation of otherness.*[14]

It is "the essence of humanity" to search for the all-inclusive, for agreements that compel the achievement of further agreements, for a "normality" that is contained within the progress of human knowledge. Otherness, difference, and deviance are ultimately to be assimilated through an encompassing reasoning, a comprehensive community of intelligibility that establishes truth.

The oralists' frame of reference may be seen to be ultimately a religious one: in this view, conversion of the Deaf is not only desirable but, as speech was God-given, that which separated man from beast, also necessary—it is a sin to permit the deaf to remain silent.[15] Indeed, this religious justification shares the same "source code" as the project endorsed by Hegel. Hegel's comprehensive intelligibility is equally teleological, dependent on an attempt to save God—and politics—through a conversion of faith into knowledge. "The politics of inclusivity and the ontology of comprehensive intelligibility are bound together. For the ontology of comprehensive intelligibility postulates a time when the world as a totality is available to knowledge and where the highest purpose of humanity is incorporated into its frame. . . . Hegelian politics thus depends upon the view that the Christian God, understood properly and philosophically, is the subject whose truth is revealed both to itself and the world in history."[16]

14. Connolly 1988, p. 87 (emphasis added).
15. See chapter 1; see also Neisser 1983.
16. Connolly 1988, p. 87.

To understand the extent of the meanings available to "the politics of inclusivity," it is useful to explore various forms of otherness. Madness and the body have provided Connolly and others with a popular paradigm for discussion of philosophical and political exclusions. The immediate view, which draws on Foucault's work, is of the medical model's reinvention of madness. Connolly presents four of the basic shifts by which exclusions of various degrees and extent are exacted and maintained, arguing that otherness presents itself

1. As a sign from God. "Because it at once stands outside divinely sanctioned standards of life and inside the community of God's creations, it reveals darkly truths which transcend the human capacity for understanding. . . . [I]t may be excluded or it may be tolerated. . . . There is no call, though, to try to reform it so that it can be drawn fully into the life of the community."

2. As "the price of extreme sinfulness as the consequence of excessive pride, or resentment or desire. Hobbes tended to construe it in this way. . . . Though the mad may be enemies of the state, they are not signs of its failure or of its need to develop better cures."

3. As merely unreason. We need not be concerned about its origins, for it is only that which "lowers its victims below the level of reason. We can learn nothing from it, and it contains no value for us. It must simply be confined, or excluded or eliminated."

Whether through exclusion and isolation, through denial or extermination, each of these first three frames can be seen fitting snugly within what I have marked as the traditional approaches to the management of the Deaf. Connolly finds an opening, however, in a fourth viewpoint.

4. From a Nietzschean point of view. "Its cause is neither simply in the self who bears it nor simply in the world which recognizes it to be at odds with its standards of normality. . . . [B]ut since it does not define madness as a fault residing simply within its bearer, the space it establishes for ethical debate does not revolve simply around alternative strategies for controlling or curing the mad."[17]

17. Ibid., pp. 88–89.

This final shift allows for a rather wide range of responses. An ethic of revaluation of differences, an accommodation in which the social space for such difference is widened, is reached as easily as a view that would construct these others as villains or enemies to be vanquished. It is, as Connolly observes, an ontology that creates its own room for ethical debate, but at least it is free from the demand to control or cure. Within this frame there may be a way of allowing differences on their own terms.

Hegel, however, does see madness as a defect in its bearer. His ontology is one of historical progress and individual development. Any such defect must be overcome through a superior rationality, one that incorporates, assimilates, or eliminates difference. Hegel's own strategies for curative treatment aim at "pointing out the contradictions in the delusions of the insane. One famous example of such a "cure" is of a "lunatic" who thought he was dead, and refused to eat as this was incompatible with death: "The lunatic was put in a coffin and laid in a vault in which was another coffin occupied by a man who at first pretended to be dead but who, soon after he was left alone with the lunatic, sat up, told the latter how pleased he was to have company in death, and finally got up, ate the food that was by him and told the astonished lunatic that he had already been dead a long time and therefore knew how the dead go about things. The lunatic was pacified by the assurance, likewise ate and drank and was cured." [18] In this endearing theoretical kitsch, difference is no more than a "rationality gone awry." Hegel's ontology "demands a politics of inclusivity, and the politics of inclusive community cannot be at peace with itself unless it can sustain an ontology of Spirit," [19] an ontology that realizes itself through the formation of progressively more inclusive systems of intersubjectivity and through historical progress and individual development over time.

So the question is not whether I "agree" with Hegel's project of meaning, but rather to what extent the broader apparatus of disci-

18. Hegel, *Encyclopedia of the Philosophical Science,* part 3, quoted in Connolly 1988, p. 90.
19. Connolly 1988, p. 90.

pline and surveillance are manifest in "our" (the dominant Hearing) management of the Deaf, and to what extent the distinctive aspects of Hearing suppression of Deafness make visible the Hegelian shift suppressing other differences. Moreover, it is not the specific, explicit "goals" of the various and opposing factions within the subtexts of Deaf education that are of interest here, but instead the epistemological presumptions that have gone to make up the social "forest" the Scarecrow of Oz warned about in the opening epigraph of this work.

It is extremely difficult to fully evade Hegel in any project addressing otherness and difference. Almost by definition, reentrapment is assured. Deaf education and the education industry in general are part of a Hegelian-rooted apparatus for producing the inclusive state. Through disciplines of knowledge, the politics of citation, and the self-referential surveillance tactics of identity formation, differences are codified and cited for further processing into their demarcated place on the social food chain of the Scarecrow's forest. Yet my goal has been to compromise the certainty of the Hegelian hold by disrupting its claim on a particular and peculiar domain within modernity's project of determining acceptable identities. Such tactics clarify not only our understanding of those who are Deaf, the identities available to them, or the educational machinery dedicated to ceaselessly producing more new and acceptable identities, but also how such mechanisms, tactics, and practices circumscribe options for all.

Commodification and Erasure

To the previous historical framework must now be added the next configuration, the "commodification" of Deaf identity in the postmodern economy of images. In this arena of shifting commercial icons and marketing events, methods once again change yet reaffirm the now familiar functions. Here, the same carceral themes are played out through sophisticated new tactics. In a conflation of what was previously contrasted, the new frame, below labeled as "Postmodern" for lack of a better term, both deploys and subsumes tactics of the "Traditional" and the "Modern/mainstream" in an ever more sophisticated structure of surveillance:

Production and Administration of Deaf Identity

Traditional	Modern/mainstream
Separation (from society)	Separation (from their peers)
Isolation (as a type and group)	Isolation (from each other)
Denial by exclusion	Denial by dispersal
Objects of Christian salvation	Objects of scientific inquiry

Postmodern

Separation (by division)
Isolation (by differentiation)
Denial by absorption (by dissipation)
Objects of commerce

Each of these themes has already shown a remarkable adaptability, co-opting seemingly opposed viewpoints and tactics in the service of generalized goals. Separation pertains to the internal/external as well as the collective/specific distinction. The "traditional" separation of a group was a collective roundup to protect the whole against social contamination. The specific separation of individuals via mainstreaming controlled a potential social collective through dispersal and dilution. These collective/specific tactics are now conjoined with internal/external divisions, fostered by the internal colonialism of a social group's elites, as well as through multiplying, yet always restricted and conflicted, possibilities for personal self-identification. The terrain becomes increasingly local and personal, but the agenda has never changed: the containment of difference by erasing its possible significations.

The dissipative movement continues, however, as the growing number of options leads to authenticity claims that are more narrowly distinguished and further refined. In the mediascape of popular commercial images—currency in the hypereconomy of style and distinction—Deafness, as an identity, is simply lost amid the sea of possible choices for identity on display. Style itself becomes the most pervasive criterion. As Arthur Kroker notes, "There are no longer any necessary connections between culture and politics; it is now possible to be culturally hip, yet politically reactionary. Lifestyle has fled its basis in the domain of personal ethics, becoming an empty floating sign-object—a cynical commodity—in the mediascape. Consequently, the persistent question asked by the newly subscribed members of what Michael Boyce has named the vague generation: 'How did you get your lifestyle?' " [20]

In an economy of mass-produced lifestyle options, identity requires no referent, and referents float without place. Separation of the deaf, both as a group and from each other, is achieved through diffusion: the vast replication of multiple differences available to any constructed lifestyle simply erases the claims that any one difference has significance. Market surveillance data, including consumer histories and credit records, are guides to these highly commodified "identities." What were first termed "populations" in the late nineteenth century are called "markets" in the late twentieth, and they are mapped by market profiles. Each targeted profile is already identifiable or is seeking to be more readily identified. Capital formation in an economy of images relies on total recognition in a context of absolute differentiation.

Yet this capital is devalued or discounted with amazing speed by the absorptive gesture of "acknowledgment." By a simple act of refocusing recognition, that which was valued as unique becomes suddenly passé, last week's news. The unique is simply absorbed as commonplace. What was in is now out, what was wired is now tired.[21] The difference, or rather the potential of a difference, is acknowledged—then its "value" dismissed as insignificant. Value exists strictly as sign-object, the commodity image of value, to be retailed on this week's hip t-shirt. Lifestyle options are a huge business, however, and vast industries, including the t-shirts, have been marshaled in the support of sales, any sales. All that matters is that something is currently in, no matter how briefly, and currently on sale.

20. Kroker 1993, p. 6.
21. This borrows from *Wired* magazine, a journal on digital culture, which every month prints a faddish list comparing what's "wired" and what's "tired."

On a recent Channel V broadcast,[22] an Asian MTV announcer was backed by an animated ASL finger-spelling chart, each individual chart cell looping at different speeds. Another channel was playing yet another made-for-TV movie with a young deaf girl as a family member, in the role meant to pull the audience's heartstrings.[23] Signing here has only a cultural display function, commodified as a plus in the diversity supermarket. Yet it is a commodity valued as the new virtual poster child/object—the virtuality of a new technology of interactive images being of greater interest than the signing child those images depict. The display has value, the content/object does not. The display, too, is disposable, as the retail shelf life of all images is fleeting.

That such content may be a live person is of little concern to the economy that both selects and rejects the image of the moment. Once off the pages of *People* and out of the TV weekly human-interest clip, the deaf girl seeking court clearance to attend a deaf rather than hearing school is sent back to be mainstreamed, and none of her hearing classmates bother going to the beginning sign language class anymore. The result is mediocrity bound—or gagged; assimilation is declared a success. Deafness is made ever more visible, yet simultaneously made ever less significant.

Major shifts have occurred in the techniques deployed in the historical production and administration of deaf identity. Nevertheless, the guiding principles of separation, isolation, denial, and objectification remain unchanged. Moreover, it becomes clear that the major opponents in the battle over tactics share the desired goal of a form of deafness acceptable—or bearing commodity/use value—to hearing society. Hegel's general observation applies here: "when opponents love to oppose each other, they are likely to share some fundamental premises and demands neither is ready to thematize. The very sharpness of the debate expresses and obscures the fundamental

22. Star TV, a cable television provider based in Hong Kong, broadcast of 2 November 1994.

23. IBC, a cable provider based in Thailand, broadcast of *Guitarman*, 2 November 1994.

character of that which remains unthought within it."[24] This is no-where more apparent than in the field of children's rights when the object of attention is the deaf child.

The Signs of Rights Talk

The terrain of the "rights" of deaf children is as contentious as any other in the social arena. Claimants stand on either side of an imaginary divide, each claiming to speak for those rights. The "voice" of the deaf child is almost always absent, as is that of the former deaf child: the deaf adult. Like poster children who have grown up, their thoughts and concerns are somehow considered irrelevant—or impertinent. As the deaf adult literally embodies the failed hopes of hearing parents that their child will somehow be transformed into a hearing adult, the deaf adult is a particularly unwelcome participant in seeking a "solution." Before we turn to consider some of the mechanisms that effect this particular exclusion, it might be useful to look at where the various combatants have drawn their respective lines in the dust.

The terminology of rights—whether human, legal, or civil—is particularly attractive to those who would speak on behalf of others. No text that accepts the naming of an other based on any particular trait can fully escape the risk of this ventriloquism, including my own. This work both adopts and evades the unity of such a thing as "the deaf," but it attempts to remain attentive to the abuses the code may disguise. Because this code seems universal, it in effect homogenizes any representative group, even one whose base of experiences is very heterogeneous. As we saw in chapter 4, the process allows for endogenous colonialisms, as well. Rarely does this result from conscious effort, but such universal truth claims are sufficiently naturalized to accomplish the end quite effectively. A brief view of how rights talk is applied daily in the range of practices surrounding deaf children will be instructive.

When couching their claims in terms of rights, oralists (as that

24. A paraphrase of Hegel by Connolly 1988, p. 103.

label clearly would suggest) insist that "every child has a right to speech." Often, this is phrased as "every child has a right to language." As is by now obvious, this demand is based on the conflation of speech and language, a confusion that dominates the modern popular conception of language. This conflation does not rule out using "language" in other areas, such as machine language for computers, the language of dance, or other such applications of the term, but it does presume a special, primary meaning in human experience: speech is the only "real" language.

Oralists often assert that they are realists: "This is a 'hearing world,' and the deaf child cannot and should not be protected from the hearing world forever." In fact, from this viewpoint, any delay only puts the deaf child further "at risk" of not achieving the speaking skills necessary to participate in this "hearing world." The oralists maintain that because signing is easier for deaf children to learn, it inhibits the acquisition of speech. Thus, children who learn sign language will lose the will to speak. (They do not consider the possibility that deaf youths find signing so much more satisfactory that the frustrations of dealing with hearing people just don't seem worth the effort.) Deafness, or rather the denial and banishment of deafness, is but a matter of willpower. Integration, or rather assimilation, can only be achieved by applying indefatigable will and effort. Truth, in this case, is for the making.

In this positivist vein, assimilation is not simply a "right" but is usually cast as a "duty" that the deaf child cannot be allowed to shirk. This rests in part on the belief noted above that to face the hearing world, deaf people are required to avoid living in a deaf world. The task of instilling this "duty," and ensuring that deaf children fulfill that "requirement," of course, falls to the parents. This is cast as a form of "tough love." Any action that suggests an accommodation to deafness, most particularly the dreaded use of sign language, is portrayed as a form of "backsliding."

The association of this term with religion is not out of place. The task of inducing the thingly silent ones to speak requires a crucial faith and conviction. Any other course of action is cast not just as another possible approach to a child's needs; instead, it "must be constituted as heresy to protect the integrity of the self-identity it threatens through its existence. The indispensability of one conception [as 'hearing' in the 'real' world] . . . is established by defining what deviates from it as a heresy that must not be entertained as a counter-possibility."[25] It must not be an option. For the oralist, the rights of the deaf are those of assimilation and "participation" in the world of their parents. The children have the right to be the same, and any evidence that suggests they are different can and should be surmounted. The child may have been born with or may have acquired this difference, but, with sufficient effort and faith, it can be made to go away. Even to consider any other approach is tantamount to a heresy of faith; oralists are uncompromising dualists in the tradition of Manichaeanism.

To the oralist, mainstreaming is not merely an accommodation within the educational institutions. The broader goal, the "right," is to "pass" as hearing, to "become" or to be "acceptable" as a hearinglike person. However, *separate schools may still be required to achieve this goal.* These schools for oral education of deaf children focus exclusively on the production of speech sounds and zealously expunge any use of gesticulation. They focus on the production of speech almost to the total exclusion of any other subject or indeed curricular content of any kind. With the avowed goal of creating hearinglike subjects who will be "prepared to enter into the hearing world," these separate schools are thus part of the broader mainstreaming effort, even if the deaf children are educated separately from the public system for hearing children. As we saw in chapter 2, the irony is not innocent: Separation for the purpose of creating sameness is mainstreaming; separation in recognition of unique difference is not.

An important factor in the admission policies of traditional oral schools is the commitment of the parents to an oral-only approach to educating their deaf child. Children who have been exposed to

25. Connolly 1991, pp. 7–8.

sign language, particularly those from families with a history of deafness and of using sign language, are often not admitted, in order to protect the school environment from "contamination."

But these presumptions are not restricted to the education industries that have organized around the desire to produce hearinglike deaf children. They are also widely found in popular and commercial culture. Consider, for example, a high-profile public relations campaign cast as a consumer products company's "salute" to the hardworking, self-sacrificing, charity-minded workers of America. The feature story focuses on a speech therapist working with deaf children, and the sidebar, in bold type, says it all: "We teach children to speak because it is a hearing world out there." In an open letter to Amway Distributors, M. J. Bienvenu, a leading Deafeminist,[26] responds:

> Contrary to what Ms. Kantor may believe, it is not a "hearing world out there" any more than it is a white world or a man's world. I—and other Deaf people—have as much right to full and active participation in the world as she does. And we do not have to become quasi-hearing people to do it.
>
> It seems that in spite of her 22-year career, Ms. Kantor has not yet learned the difference between speech and language. Language is indeed the birthright of every child. Speech is simply a mode for expressing spoken language. Since we do not hear ourselves or others, speech has little value to Deaf people. . . . Deaf children cannot *acquire* English naturally because it is a sound-based language. Even the tiny percentage of Deaf children who manage to survive an oral education and develop some speech and written English skills are limited to functional *learned* language.[27]

It is a curious economy of duty and requirement, insistent that the deaf child must be "helped" in the process of accommodation, in adaptations that the child, particularly the body of the child, must undergo and accept. The workings of rights talk, when applied to children who diverge from the "normal," have consistently located the problem *in* the child. While a social environment may occasion

26. *Deafeminist,* or *Defeminist,* is a conjunction of *Deaf* and *feminist.*
27. M. J. Bienvenu, *TBC News* 22 (The Bicultural Center), February 1990; emphasis in original.

the need for either adaptation or accommodation, the meaning of this "need" is located in the body of the different child.

Federal legislation, intent on overcoming the past horrors of institutions and inspired by the partial successes of racial desegregation, requires that a "least restrictive environment" be made available to the disabled child. There is a particular irony in the choice of this terminology, which first appeared in rulings justifying the broad deinstitutionalization of mental patients from the asylums. Since deaf people were initially rounded up for imprisonment in the asylums along with the mad,[28] it seems somewhat fitting that the language deployed to "return" the insane to the community would reappear in legislation seeking a similar return of the disabled. Sadly, the interpretation of this vaguely phrased ideal has been left to partisan bureaucrats motivated as much by their concerns about financing these institutions as by any interest in the viewpoints of those involved.

Because strategies earlier used for civil right claims by women and racial minorities have been applied to disabled children, regardless of their "disability" or disabilities, a preoccupation with "integrated" settings in schooling now seems legitimate. This has directly threatened the unplanned "benefit" institutionalization has often provided deaf children, a locus or "place" of cultural and linguistic (re)generation in the residential schools, and has injected them into isolation within regular classrooms. Though not true for all disabled children, in the particular instance of deaf children there has been an excessive concern with *where* children are. While integration into a generalized setting seems a reasonably fair solution to achieve the goals of gender and racial assimilation, the reasoning seems less compelling for children whose difference from others helps constitute their linguistic being. Nor is it an accident that the school place, the former asylum, remains the terrain on which rights and identity battles must be waged.

The mainstreaming obsession seems a mocking compensation for

28. See Foucault 1965.

the deaf child's lack of place in which to locate a sense of identity. The institutional imperative has an obsession with "place," but in an opposing sense—the physical proximity or action that ensures a disambiguation of difference. As the shift in the techniques of separation outlined above would suggest, proponents of mainstreaming claim that deaf children benefit in full from their civil rights when they enjoy the privilege of being among the "normal" children. Yet for what they receive, they pay an unreasonably high cost in direct access to learning.

Early linguistic deprivation significantly marks the lives of a majority of deaf children. Once we recognize the need for a rich linguistic environment for both cognitive and emotional growth, we find several options emerging across the range of social practices explored in this work. The demands of achieving cognitive and emotional development require language. If we accept the value of a primary role given to sign languages for deaf children and the value of a learning environment of signing peers and instructors, while not excluding the usual exercises of "speech therapies" to teach rules of spoken languages, then the proponents of rights seem off target in their choice of schooling and their vocabulary. There can be little argument that, for a deaf student, the mainstream school environment is impoverished when compared to a residential environment of signing peers. But this set of arguments has not yet been foregrounded in the educational administration of deafness. It is rather the traditional fears of contamination by signing and the false promises hidden within the "either/or" choice of "speech first" that still dominate the production of deaf education, not only in Thailand but throughout most of the world.

The difficulty is compounded by the practice of mainstreaming itself. The criteria for placement and reform rarely seem concerned with the support needed to advance deaf children to their full intellectual and academic potential or to assist them to become well-adjusted people. As a result, in a crucial administrative move, the mainstreamed setting is conflated with the notion of a "least restrictive environment": "They have the idea that they're going to move everybody up one notch. The autistic are worse off than the re-tarded. The retarded are worse off than the deaf. Solution: move the autistic into the less restrictive environment of the retarded, and up-grade the retarded by putting them in those nice schools for the deaf. Then, what happens to the deaf? They have the thrill of getting to go to school with hearing kids. The problem is solved. Every-body's been promoted."[29]

What was the major administrative impetus to interpret "least restrictive environment" as mainstreaming? Was it the disturbing memories of the past horrors of institutions? Certainly the stark im-ages that emerged from Romanian state asylums for unwanted chil-dren following the breakup of the Soviet bloc evoked emotions not so long dormant or distant. But such feelings have only peripheral influence. There are also those whose support of mainstreaming is ideological—mainly educators, medical equipment and hearing aid manufacturers, and parents. However, the institutional backing has been inspired less by their concerns than by the desire to find pro-grammatic strategies to evade the financial burdens associated with state accommodations of difference. Cost remains one of the real driving forces behind mainstreaming. By pushing disabled children into local schools, the localities bear a heavier burden and those do-ing the pushing, the state and the federal governments, bear less.

The original promise of Public Law 94-142, used as a lure to gain public support and to ensure its adoption, was that the federal gov-ernment would provide substantial funding for the education of handicapped children. In 1975, P.L. 94-142 stated that the federally paid percentage of average per pupil expenditure would grow from the initial level of 5 percent to 40 percent within six years (by 1981). In fact, the federal government has paid no more than 12.5 percent over the sixteen years since the legislation passed into law. Today, the figure has fallen under 10 percent. Indeed, inflation-adjusted figures show a decline in appropriations. Writes C. Fraas of the Con-gressional Research Service, "After P.L. 94-142 appropriations are

29. Neisser 1983, p. 273.

adjusted to constant 1984 dollars there was an 11.1 percent real decrease in program funding between FY 1979 and FY 1984." [30]

The situation remains basically unchanged into the nineties, says Lonnie Floury, a congressional staff member and expert on special education legislation. [31] She notes that it is important to understand that people who were involved at the federal level in enacting the law knew that the promise of ever-increasing funding to the states was at bottom false. Says Floury, "Everybody involved in Washington knew that it would never happen, that funding levels would not rise to the promised level." However, these hollow commitments persuaded the states to cooperate.

In fact, the states did stand to benefit from shifting disabled children to mainstreamed placements. Of course, the increase in enrollments of the underserved group meant increased costs, but these costs were largely borne by the localities, not the states. The states, not the localities, had paid for the residential schooling of the disabled that previously had been the norm. The diminished enrollments in these institutions, as mainstreaming increased, reduced the direct burden of the states. For them, the promise of substantial federal funding was a potential windfall, in tandem with reduced cost and lessened responsibility for implementation. Even though the federal government reneged upon its original promise, the states still receive generous administrative overheads from federal contributions. And while there are obligations attached, the states have considerable latitude. Federal oversight authority is virtually never wielded in the area of special education. [32]

Whether inspired by religion, ideology, business, or bureaucratic self-interest, each of these strategies locates the problem on the body of the different child. As in other Hegelian exercises, the dialectic

30. C. Fraas, "P.L. 94–142, The Education for All Handicapped Children Act: Its Development, Implementation, and Current Issues," presented to hearing before the US Senate Subcommittee on the Handicapped of the Committee on Labor and Human Resources (S. Hrg. 99–392), 29 October 1985, p. CRS–49.

31. Letter to Charles Reilly, 28 April 1992; I am grateful to him for this information.

32. For details concerning P.L. 94–142, as well as other aspects of U.S. legislation on education for the deaf, I am particularly indebted to Charles Reilly.

binds the opponents to the particular framing. The dilemma of rights talk, pitting child rights against child rights, is yet another manifestation of the paradox of entitlement and resentment. This framing is rooted in established practices long naturalized into habits—and, as always, such naturalized practices are worth further consideration.

The Talk of Sign Rights

While tactics deploying the notion of rights, generally known as "rights talk," are a staple of modern life, questions continue to be raised about the extent to which their claims to universality can be sustained. That rights are a highly problematic weapon in the field of politics should be plain to nearly anyone who reads a newspaper. The most obvious examples are those contested terrains where proponents of conflicting rights claims seek to displace one another in the supposed hierarchy of "fundamental human rights." For example, in the battle over reproductive control opposing camps both justify their positions through strategic deployment of rights talk.[33] This competition for the moral high ground recurs in similar interpretive conflicts over individual "rights to language"—and what that might mean to the deaf child.

These appeals to the "rights" of "the individual" founder on what—and how—the "individual" is recognized. "Recognized" in this sense means valorized into an economy of recognitions. Both "mother" and "fetus" signify much more than the bodies to which they might at any particular time be connected. While it is fashionable to claim neutrality—one that does not exist—on such competing claims, I have no qualms about declaring my view here; there are very basic principles at stake. I argue strongly that practices of state control over the body are intimately connected with those applied

33. Whether such attacks mask real political issues depends very much on what one considers "real politics." In my neorealist mode, this use of rights talk to confound, disorient, undermine, or otherwise displace one's opponent or to compromise their claims to legitimacy is precisely what real politics is about. And this is just one tool in the arsenal of hardball politics.

to the deaf. *State control over seed of the body makes no more sense than state control over seed of the mind.* Consider language as the seed of the mind, where "language" means more than the speech with which it might be arbitrarily connected. Control over the deaf begins with regulating access to language in this larger sense. Freedom of first language choice for those who are deaf is simply that basic. Yet excluding this option remains the "normal" procedure.

The Deaf, taken very loosely as a collective group, represent a "dispersed" society, a diaspora from a sensory place, which is now attempting to reassert (reclaim) itself through several representative bodies and individual spokespersons. Both individually and collectively, Deaf people claim that they do form a "natural" society on the basis of a modality of language that, by the definition of "natural" identity, fulfills a basic human need. As the domination [34] of deaf people by hearing people has been based on the essentialist denial of this modality, refusing to accept either its very existence or its status as "language," such affirmations have had no effect externally— although widely acclaimed at large international gatherings and conferences on Deaf cultures. Moreover, as Deafness originates from neither a sense of geographical place, nor from a preexisting "society" with its own concretely organized institutions (which may be a distinct advantage in certain perverse ways), this "reassertion" looks back to no earlier assertion. These claims thus evoke even more than the usual complications that attend arguments over rights and identity.

Many of those complications are found in this book, which contains a multiplicity of voices and several distinct projects. The strategic use of rights talk to achieve specific program-related objectives

34. "This relationship of domination is no more a 'relationship' than the place where it occurs is a place; and precisely for this reason, it is fixed, throughout its history, in ritual, in meticulous procedures that impose rights and obligations. It makes itself accountable for debts and gives rise to the universe of rules, which is by no means designed to temper violence, but rather to satisfy it. The desire for peace, the serenity of compromise, and the tacit acceptance of the law, far from representing a major moral conversion or a utilitarian calculation that gave rise to the law, are but its result and, in point of fact, its perversion" (Foucault, "Nietzsche, Genealogy, History," in Foucault 1977, pp. 150–51).

is, from a theoretical standpoint, highly compromised. Accepting the institutions and landmarks as understood, those who deploy rights attempt to disguise the irony of their goals and intentions within the given vocabulary of fact, truth, and reason. The basic strategy is to accept the playing field but to explore unexploited loopholes and manipulate rules that can be used against the referees as well as against one's primary opponents. While this sounds fairly simple, questions of "voice" and of speaking on behalf of others are problematic at nearly every level. It is at the level of rights talk that the battles to reclaim difference are most often waged, and some of these efforts seem to produce mixed returns.

Deaf Thai leaders have used rights talk sparingly to support their arguments, preferring "fairness talk" as more culturally appropriate and more likely to resonate in their context. That context needs further elaboration. While most critics of rights talk rely on Foucault's account of the carceral/juridical arena that is implicitly valorized by its use, my street side wants to deploy rights talk to set the legitimacy of one juridical notion against another. That is, while rights talk depends on juridical notions and thus might suggest a particular juridical notion within a specific framework of meaning, rights talk in practice can both rely on that notion and, at least for that moment, evade particular juridical practices. Thus, in a cultural context in which Buddhism, and a distinctly Thai version of Buddhism, represents the epistemological base, rights talk may be used judiciously, so to speak, if placed in relief against that episteme.

In the Thai setting, fairness talk, as opposed to rights talk, explicitly recognizes a juridical authority and, in fact, seeks to specify clearly where the authority is vested in order to call upon that authority to act in a beneficent manner. Using a certain form of moral jujitsu, the obligations of the patron are invoked as the most likely avenue of receiving the nominal privileges sought. One noting the distinction between a right and a privilege might suggest that this discourse is less a substitute for rights talk than a simple maneuvering for the least disadvantaged position. Furthermore, this "least disadvantage" is still far from adequate. The existing structural relationships of inequality are reinforced, and the elite engaged in "charity" further mine a vein of merit as they repeat the usual pieties about helping the less fortunate.

We should note that Thais are not alone in "merit mining"; in the Western form, international corporations seek tax write-offs for minuscule donations reluctantly given to charitable projects. Though their gifts may be very modest, these businesses seek vast brand-name recognition through extensive public relations advertising campaigns (requiring expenditures exponentially greater than the amount donated) to tell the public about their generous corporate giving. This is functionally the same as the actions of the Thai elite, but it is justified/glorified through differing interpretive frameworks.

There are parallels here to the techniques of claiming moral reciprocity whose use by peasants James Scott (1985) describes, although a uniquely Thai application of such fairness talk is found at all levels, including that of national politics, to justify acts by all sides. For example, in 1990, the Thai supreme commander of the armed forces, under pressure to resign for political reasons, justified his eventual resignation as being fair to his subordinates, who otherwise could not be promoted.[35] This explanation, which appears to us to be hypocritical face-saving, was widely accepted by Thais, and the political stock of the then-eligible-for-politics army man rose to an all-time high.

Rights talk does not resonate too deeply in the Thai body politic; Amnesty International allegations of various rights abuses often spark defensive reactions from common Thais. To be sure, issues of pride and nationalism are also involved here. Still, unless some abuse has been truly egregious, Thais do not respond in the way, say, American citizens would. In those cases in which serious abuse has taken place, the focus is on how responsible authorities have failed in their duty or how principles of fairness have not been followed. Thus compensation is owed the injured parties less because of their rights than because of a just and due fairness. While Americans easily

35. *Bangkok Post,* 3 April 1990.

equate fairness with rights in everyday speech, for Thais the notions are not so closely related.

This is not to say that rights talk is unheard of. As a state, Thailand is very sensitive about its reputation and image. Amnesty International, which in the past has infrequently called the Thai military to task, particularly for its handling and mishandling of refugees, is roundly criticized in all the major Thai papers and by politicians on the stump. Amnesty representatives, however, note that after all the rhetoric has died down, the abuses they called into question subside or cease, even if only temporarily. Still, attempts to marshal concern at a more significant scale, such as the efforts of George Kent, among others, to make the "rights of the child" a matter for policy consideration, have made little headway. While the press is quick to home in on the horror (and the attendant excitement) of the abuse of children, the public response is limited to charity, if that. As described in chapter 4, while Thais hide certain selfless actions under claims of mere reciprocity, many basic relationships are very much conceived of in these material terms. The child's relationship to his or her parents is basically one of filial duty, and the sale of children for their "labor" is considered well within both the prerogatives of the parents and the duty of the children. If abuses occur, it is because those to whom they are sold lack fairness.[36] Thus foreign criticisms of the circumstances of poor children in Thailand are never understood on the structural or social level at which they are posed but rather are narrowly framed as issues of individual fortune.[37]

36. The Thai popular press routinely carry interviews with young prostitutes in which the discussions focus mainly on the working conditions, hours off, pay, etc. Little is said about the circumstances by which they came to the little tea houses (although they often justify their work—e.g., "I'm sending money to support my family upcountry") or about what might be better options (e.g., being in school).

37. This suggests the extent to which Thai culture generally buys into the symbolic deployments of language, as described by Murray Edelman (1977), which naturalize the placement of poor children in such circumstances. The discussion here focuses on particular Thai practices, without, however, implying that Thai perspectives should be solely privileged and unavailable for additional critique.

But Deaf Thais have not hesitated either to borrow the rights talk of others in formulating their own fairness claims or to use rights talk directly in areas outside the specifically Thai context. The important point, however, is that rights talk employed by foreigners, whether inside or outside Thailand, is used to help normalize what might first appear to local sensibilities as an unusual claim for fairness. In the case of the disabled, the distinction between fairness and rights, as well as the use value of that distinction, has been particularly clear. The difference was played out in efforts to institute interpreting of TV news for the Deaf, on the one hand, and to pass a Disabled Rights Act, on the other hand. The contrast is plain: one worked, the other didn't.

Requests for sign language interpreting of news broadcasts had been ignored for some years. The primary objection, odd as it may seem, came from the military, who felt they would be unable to monitor the interpreters for security purposes. While some sporadic protests demanding the service did occur, all such efforts were without success. The breakthrough occurred at one of the many charitable events at which the wealthy and famous show each other their compassion for the less fortunate. One of the more cheeky Deaf Thais approached the then supreme commander directly. With communication failing but public eyes on him, an interpreter was rustled up. Pointing out his failure to understand her, she said she had similar problems each night in watching the news about his (gush) accomplishments.[38] Wouldn't it be fair, she continued, to make sure that she, too, could understand the news? The program to provide sign interpreting for national broadcast news began within the month. The force of public embarrassment is obviously part of this story, yet the technique of requesting fairness succeeded when a demand for a "right" would have surely failed—call the move compromise or strategy.

38. Thai news broadcasts always begin with fifteen to twenty minutes of coverage of official activities during the day. They are presented in strict rank order of the persons involved, beginning with members of the royal family, the prime minister, the army, etc. The order of coverage itself often signals subtle shifts in rank, status, and favor.

In contrast are the efforts to pass a Disabled Persons' Rights Act, which spanned more than ten years. Although a legislative package was eventually passed in late 1991, it had been gutted in legislative committee sessions. There is little even of symbolic value in the final package. Much of the resistance, and perhaps some of the vindictive cutting of the package in legislative committee, was apparently provoked by some rather heavy-handed tactics and demands framed in rights talk by several local activists. In addition, the issues of "greater" concern to Thai politicians, particularly those being showcased in the popular press, may have pressured them to strip the bill quickly to the simple and cheap, pass it, and get back to where the money is. When the United Nations declared the International Year of the Disabled Person in 1981, the Thai Government had publicly pledged to pass legislation concerning disabled people. The general willingness was there. The tactics employed, however, required a decade to achieve very little.

It is clear from such examples that a more critical questioning of the power relationships is not taking place within the episteme. Such reluctance to question is also deeply tied to notions of Thai identity, which the elite ruling structure continues to exploit quite nicely. M.R. Kukrit Pramoj, former prime minister (among many other accomplishments), once noted in an interview that, as a young man, he had returned from abroad in 1933 in great excitement at the news of the revolution that overthrew the absolute monarchy. "I came to join the new democracy that would take its place, but all I saw were lots of new little kings." [39] In essence, the blood nobility, of which M.R. Kukrit is a lesser member, were displaced in favor of a military and economic nobility. While no political analysis of Thailand I have read follows this line very far, I find it more useful than the depiction of a "loosely structured" society favored by the more traditional anthropologists. [40] The point is that highly complicated forms of shifting patron-client relationships mark Thai social interactions. The Thai language is rich with formal discursive mark-

39. Gray, Everingham, and Wrigley 1988, p. 98. "M.R." stands for "Mom Rajavongse," a royal title.
40. See Embree 1969.

ers of status and relative position. Such relative positions may be valid only for the duration of a specific interaction and may be quite different for the same individuals at another time. These variations take place within a more rigid structuring that may be temporarily displaced but is known by all concerned to remain in force beyond the circumstances of any given exchange.

That said, both I and the Deaf Thais with whom I have worked have frequently used rights talk in conversations about "sign language rights" and other Deaf-related issues. The reasons are primarily strategic and were developed together with my research partner, Manfa Suwanarat, a Deaf Thai woman.[41] The following account illustrates the tactics at work.

In 1987, I served as a voting delegate to an Asia-Pacific Regional UN meeting prior to the Mid-Term Assessment of the UN Decade of Disabled Persons; there, my motion for a UN resolution in recognition of sign language as a basic right for indigenous deaf populations was blocked by a delegate from the World Blind Union. The reason given was the lack of "sufficient proof" of unqualified support from the "international deaf community." I will leave aside larger questions of conflict between deaf and blind activists in the disability rights movement. Two months later, the Thai delegation to the Tenth World Congress of the World Federation of the Deaf in Helsinki rammed the same resolution past the Italian oralists and through Executive Session to reach the floor of the congress, where formal approval was achieved to wide acclaim. The congress was historic, as the old school of Italian oralists, who had controlled the WFD for decades, was swept aside during this process.[42]

One month after that, the United Nations and the government of Sweden cohosted the UN Global Meeting of Experts (GME) for the Mid-Term Assessment of the UN Decade of Disabled Persons in Stockholm. I served as interpreter for Manfa Suwanarat, who further maneuvered to be elected to the report-writing committee. The re-

41. I view her Award Testimonial from the UN Secretary-General as evidence that we were more than modestly successful in that ploy.

42. The WFD headquarters were also moved out of Italy, where they had been for forty years, and are now located in Helsinki, Finland.

port of the GME included the statement that had been defeated at the UN regional meeting three months earlier but had become in the interim a formal WFD resolution.

The objective of Manfa and myself was to use the UN imprimatur to legitimate the resolution, which could then be presented to the Royal Thai Government as part of a broader set of discussions about educational policy. The document, which was carefully never identified in the Thai context as having originated in Thailand, at this point would no longer be used as an instrument of rights talk; instead, it was evidence of what foreigners at the global level were doing in this area. The presentation to the Thai officials would stress issues of the image of Thailand and the significant favorable attention that Thailand would gain if similar steps were taken, with the rights talk in the document itself merely serving as a persuasive backdrop. The approach is crafted to emphasize fairness and economy.[43]

Six months later in the United States came the student uprising at Gallaudet University, which led to the first Deaf president of Gallaudet University in its 125-year history. Nevertheless, neither Gallaudet University nor any unit of the U.S. government has yet to formally accept American Sign Language (ASL) as a distinct language, full stop. The official language policy of Gallaudet University remains today what is known as SimCom or SSS (Simultaneous Communications or Sign-Supported-Speech): that is, spoken English, with an artificial sign code used at the same time that matches English syntax. In an interview shortly after the GME, Gil Eastman, a highly acclaimed Deaf American, noted the pressure the WFD resolution put on Gallaudet University to formally recognize ASL. This pressure has been resisted to date, but increasing demands for higher status for ASL do continue to plague the Gallaudet University administration.

This was a further subplot of our project. Rights talk resonates quite strongly in the United States and in the UN system (albeit with sharp ironies). As noted, ASL is still not formally recognized as a

43. It is more cost-effective to have Deaf teachers, because they can more easily teach a regular-sized class. There are other reasons for favoring Deaf teachers, but we know what bureaucrats like to hear.

distinct linguistic entity for use in U.S. school systems. This is not to say that it should become part of the battle for an "official U.S. language." However, many U.S. states still maintain educational policies for the deaf that exclude sign language on the grounds that ASL is not formally recognized as a "language." Even in 1995, most states in America pursue oral-only or manually coded English language policies for deaf education.[44] In this arena, regardless of the problematic status of the resource, rights talk is still an effective cudgel to wield in war. While war metaphors are rarely appreciated in academe, the Deaf on the streets don't necessarily consider them inappropriate—or metaphorical. Deaf children remain the innocents caught in the path of such cudgels and such wars.

The Politics of Reclaiming Difference

Neither separation nor integration can eradicate the meaning of difference as long as the majority locates difference in a minority group that does not fit the world designed for the majority.
—Martha Minow, *Making All the Difference*

Martha Minow is a professor of law at Harvard University. In *Making All the Difference* (1990), she examines the treatment of difference in legal theory, and much of her analysis is directly applicable here. Nevertheless, while marshaling a powerful argument for recasting differences, she clearly fails in one of her own core case studies to understand the distinct linguistic battleground that is the terrain of difference for people who are deaf.

In her nuanced study, Minow explores the dilemma of difference, with a particular emphasis on the dynamics of educational policy. She focuses on the deep similarity between programs that partially segregate students with language barriers and those that attempt to

44. Although significant exceptions do exist and may be increasing in the United States. A number of schools are adopting "bi-bi policies," meaning bicultural and bilingual policies that, in theory, grant full recognition to sign language and Deaf cultural issues. An increasing number of schools are also appointing Deaf professionals into senior administrative positions. This may well suggest a certain degree of success has resulted from the use of rights talk in this domain.

integrate children with other differences, generically known as "special education" students, as educators attempt to deal with students who are "different"—without reinforcing stigma. Both kinds of program were part of educational reform efforts in the 1960s and 1970s: students were removed, at least part-time, from the mainstream classroom for bilingual instruction, and simultaneously disabled and handicapped children were pushed into mainstream schools. Thus, particularly in the American context, both bilingual and special education represent contested terrain on which the dilemma of difference is most easily visible. Unfortunately, while Minow's analysis of the problem is carefully explained, her conclusions do little to address that dilemma and, in fact, reinforce misconceptions about the meanings of certain differences.

In her treatment of bilingual education, Minow correctly asserts that "There is no neutral history of bilingual education."[45] She outlines the moves taken by communities at the turn of the century in the United States to legally forbid the teaching of any foreign language to children below the eighth grade. The famous 1923 Supreme Court decision in *Meyer v. Nebraska*[46] concluded that such laws violated the Constitution. While the ruling did not entitle children to bilingual education, it forbade laws proscribing such education. While it did nothing to assist, it did remove the overt oppression. Regrettably, it did not signal a return to benign neglect.

In describing the tortured history of minority language groups' efforts, Minow calls it "the story of a political struggle over cultural dominance and tolerance perhaps even more than a struggle over educational policy."[47] This statement is richer than her own analysis makes clear. Because she implies that the struggles involve only ethnicity, nationality, and spoken language, the Deaf and the visual-gestural sign languages are excluded—as either "too" natural, as in the Rousseau-rooted educational literature, or, in the medical model already discussed, subnatural.

---

45. Minow 1990, p. 26. That this includes any "objective" or "empirical" view is a point rarely acknowledged by partisans.
46. 262 U.S. 390, 402 (1923).
47. Minow 1990, p. 27.

There is a politics of reclaiming difference amid such presumptions. Minow frames the opening such questioning creates:

If we identify the unstated points of comparison necessary to the idea of difference, we will then examine the relationships between people who have and people who lack the power to assign the label of difference. If we explore the environmental context that makes some trait stand out and some people seem not to fit in, we will have the opportunity to reconsider how and for what ends we construct and manage the environment. Then difference will no longer seem empirically discoverable, consisting of traits inherent in the "different person." Instead, perceptions of difference can become clues to broader problems of social policy and human responsibility.[48]

This implicit clarion call for a society in which the majority willingly accepts minorities as equal participants through a restructured environment that succeeds in relocating the meaning of difference, dislocating it from the body, sounds throughout Minow's text. There is, of course, a long tradition of claims that various rearrangements of the physical environment will solve social inequities and questions of access, many of which might be better characterized as "deck chairs on the Titanic" theories. Anthropologist Mary Douglas redirects the discussion away from the physical by pointing to the role of institutions in shaping what are usually naturalized as individually derived assumptions: "Nothing else but institutions can define sameness. Similarity is an institution. . . . Our social interaction consists very much in telling one another what right thinking is and passing blame on wrong thinking. This is indeed how we build the institutions, squeezing each other's ideas into a common shape so that we can prove the rightness by sheer numbers of independent assent. . . . The high triumph of institutional thinking is to make the institutions completely invisible."[49] Nevertheless, noble as it seems, the notion that a redesigned institutional environment will either

48. Ibid., p. 23.
49. Douglas 1986, pp. 55, 91, and personal communication with Mary Douglas at the University of Hawaii's Summer Institute for Semiotic and Structural Studies, June 1991. See also Minow 1990, pp. 79–80.

alter fundamental assumptions or solve inequities is also flawed, as will be seen in Minow's analysis of the case of Amy Rowley.[50]

Amy Rowley was a deaf girl mainstreamed in a hearing school system. Minow describes her as having "developed this condition"—her profound hearing impairment—"before she learned language." Both halves of this phrase make clear Minow's distinct perspective and presumptions. First, this "condition" is one that Amy "developed." The implication, of course, is that a "condition" that can develop can also be developmentally surmounted. It is part of the ethos of will needed to overcome, if not outgrow, deafness. Second, she was deaf "before she learned language." This way of referring to children either born deaf or becoming so in early infancy, sometimes phrased as "prelingually deaf," reflects and reproduces the naturalizing of speech alone as constituting language. While frequently criticized by Deaf activists at conferences and in other public forums, this distinction of "prelingual" and "postlingual" deafness remains common in both educational and medical literature.

The "case" of Amy Rowley revolved around efforts by her parents to move her into an ASL learning environment, or, alternatively, to obtain a qualified ASL interpreter in the mainstream school environment. Minow characterizes the parents as "committed to a method called 'total communication,' which involves *not only* lip-reading and speech development but also sign language, finger-spelling, touching, and visual cues."[51] The "not only" phrasing strongly reemphasizes speech production as the central rehabilitative goal, which might also be augmented by the other techniques of "total communication." As noted in chapter 1, the implementation of "total communication" often falls far short of the basic ideal of the approach. Because Amy's performance was "above average" without the additional support sought by her parents, the case, which eventually reached the Supreme Court, was denied. The modest supplemental tutoring and three hours of speech therapy was ruled

50. Minow 1990, p. 81.
51. Ibid., p. 81 n. 5 (emphasis added).

"appropriate." The Court concurred that "the individualized educational program developed through the Act's procedures [was] reasonably calculated to enable the child to receive education benefits."[52]

Minow provides an enlightened discussion of the agonistic relation between the concerns of Amy's parents for her educational needs and the school's concern for the general needs of the school as a whole, noting in particular that each side located the difference—and thus the problem—in Amy. Both focused on Amy in searching for a solution. As Minow briefly contrasts the choice of an "integrated" school or specialized schooling in a "segregated" school, her argument is rooted in the same naturalized presumption we have seen so often: the crucial duty facing a deaf child is "fitting into" a hearing world.[53] Legislatures tend to react against the previous excesses of isolation and exclusion into drab institutions; moreover, the option of "integration" has the additional cultural resonance of the civil rights programs for racial equality. "Separate" schools likewise simply sound wrong.

Still working from within that frame, Minow tries to relocate the perceived difference onto the social organization of the classroom, focusing particularly on the relationships among all the students and the cultural experience of the difference. While she intends to create a setting in which the cultural meaning of deafness loses its significance, her solution fails utterly because of several misperceptions of the difference at stake. "What if the teacher instructed all the students in sign language and ran the class in both spoken and sign language simultaneously?"[54] Ever try to speak, let alone teach a class, in two distinct languages—at the same time? To state the obvious: this is simply not possible.

The idea of simultaneous bilingual instruction is slipped quietly

52. *Rowley v. Board of Education,* 483 F. Supp. 528, 532 (S.D. N.Y. 1980); aff'd, 632 F2d 945 (2d Cir. 1980); rev'd, 458 U.S. 176 (1982). Quoted in Minow 1990, p. 82 n. 7. The "Act" is the federal Education for All Handicapped Children Act, adopted 1975, 20 U.S.C. sec. 1400–61 (1982).

53. A favorite old Deaf joke: Q: "What is the biggest problem facing Deaf people today?" A: "Hearing people."

54. Minow 1990, p. 84.

into the discussion, which centers on the less onerous solution of teaching sign language to all of Amy's classmates. Minow concludes that this is the best way to overcome the isolation of the single deaf child. She does not specify whether this is to be ASL, one of the hybrid creoles, or one of the artificial codes of manually encoded spoken language. Yet this suggestion, too, falls far short of remedying the distinct dilemma of difference she seeks to address. By merely proposing that Amy's hearing school classmates be taught a system of sign language, which will open up improved avenues for communication with her and among each other, Minow still leaves Amy to engage the full curriculum in a linguistic modality other than what she is able to directly experience. Under this plan, at best one hour a day might be allowed for teaching "baby talk" signing skills to hearing children; and Amy would spend the rest of the day guessing about curricular topics alone or through an underpaid and poorly trained interpreter. The child might do better socially, and as well academically, without "interpreters"[55] of this type. Furthermore, just who will teach the sign language? Who are the linguistic models, the fluent users of the language from whom the beginning students can learn? It would almost appear to be assumed that Amy, simply through having "developed" deafness, must know sign language without the need herself to have learned it from fluent linguistic models.

There is a more important difference that Minow overlooks. Although numerous social and economic conditions may limit opportunities to develop or excel, a child in America speaking, say, Spanish can directly experience English, even while his or her chances to actually do so may be significantly limited. A deaf child, however, does not directly experience or acquire any spoken language. The arduous processes of mediation that attempt to deny this blunt observation only confirm it. There are many distinct national sign languages that a deaf child can experience, but the meaning of deafness, expressed here as a negative, is that the auditory channel is missing.

---

55. The ironicizing quotation marks here are intended to make very clear my respect for hardworking, underpaid interpreters, many of whom are both skilled and motivated, working in less than ideal circumstances.

Sound-based exchange systems must be permanently mediated through a visual-spatial-gestural modality. Spoken languages are based on written forms of sound-rooted grammars; each is taught through a metalanguage "about" its construction that assumes a full acquaintance with the auditory modality of the language—that is, the direct experience of listening to others possessed by the average hearing child. The importance attached to learning only through this modality is, in large part, its meaning.

Minow is right that the hearing children could gain new insights into communication, as well as learn to appreciate their lone deaf classmate (usually teased, taunted, pitied, or, mostly, ignored), under her program. But it does not deliver the "grade-level" curriculum in a linguistic modality immediately accessible to Amy. The accommodation made shows compassion, but a clear-eyed critic must still insist that it denies direct "accessibility"—in a Deaf (visual-spatial) sense of the word. This access was at issue in the legal case, and it was the very issue that was ignored in the decision so carefully criticized by Minow, as well as by her own suggested "solution."

The challenge "What would you do?" often follows such brash statements. I offer a partial response. The most ideal arrangement might include large residential Deaf schools near or within university communities and closely linked to Hearing schools at the same grade level. All Deaf children could be educated by Deaf teachers, with other school management staff providing adult Deaf role models. Interpreters would sign for guest instructors from the other school systems. Hearing instructors whose signing skills were fluent would also be welcomed. Middle-grade Deaf children would also attend classes, in pairs or in small groups, at adjacent Hearing schools either for core or elective classes. Interpreting would be arranged for any Deaf student on request. Middle and high school Hearing students would also be able to attend classes in the Deaf academic setting—with a clear understanding that no loss in quality, depth, or range of academic coverage or curriculum would occur, assuming that their signing skills are on par with fellow students who are Deaf. Interpreters to reverse interpret (sign to voice) could also be made available.

In both settings, English (or the prevailing national spoken language) should be available as a foreign language and tailored to specific needs. Foreign language credits should also include foreign sign languages. For example, British Sign Language, or BSL, is very different from ASL. They are mutually unintelligible, and BSL fully constitutes a foreign language for those whose native language is ASL. Neither ASL nor BSL is based on spoken or written English.

This program also assumes and would require that serious attention has been given to promoting Deaf university education to the extent that Deaf teachers are not only qualified but are also legally certified to teach the full academic curriculum—and in the native sign language. This expansion in Deaf higher education is essential for the remainder of the academic program to succeed.

None of these goals can be achieved by adding a single class in basic sign language skills for Amy Rowley's classmates. These children might become more sympathetically inclined toward individual deaf people, but they have certainly made no more than the mildest accommodation. As the next section makes clear, "accommodation" actually makes no change at all. In practice, these classmates are likely to feel that they can't be bothered by this new class requirement to which they thus devote minimal attention. Indeed, Minow's "solution" emphasizes more surely that nothing more than simple toleration is needed. The difference itself is of passing interest, part of the popular smorgasbord of objects and images on display in modern life, but nothing of any particular importance. Thus assured, we can return to ignoring that difference in an other's life. It is not a difference that matters.

Talking to Belong: Accommodation and Resentment

"Difference, after all, is a comparative term. It implies a reference: different from whom?" And, perhaps even more interesting, how much does it matter, and to whom?

Minow's question[56] and mine, like many others posed in this work, have no simple answers, but instead highlight ongoing negotiations

56. Minow 1990, p. 22.

of political paradox. No final, overarching resolutions are available. The contingencies of each choice are as likely to encode the possibility of misfortune as to contribute to success. To some extent, of course, the paradox is inherent in the meaning frame, in which any outcome might be weighted as a "success"—or its opposite.

As I move toward my conclusion, issues of otherness and difference, both how we talk about it and how social space is made available for those "meant" to fit such descriptions, return to the foreground. Deafness has, by now, been examined from a range of divergent perspectives. Each of these perspectives illustrates distinct ways in which differences are routinely managed, whether appropriated for the use of the dominant or excluded through discursive economies. While I have certain sympathies for the consensual movements to reconstitute new forms of communities, such as those represented in the globally resurgent Deaf Culture movement, I resist the attempts to dissolve the dilemmas of late modernity into any pragmatic conception of community. Like the "more slippery terrain" charted by Nietzsche, Heidegger, Freud, and Foucault, otherness is better seen "as a mysterious or intractable feature of existence, reacting back upon forms of knowledge, individuality, community and freedom which compete for hegemony in modern life."[57] The stable consensus on which "community" depends is achieved only at the price of suppressing certain differences. Deafness is best understood as an exemplar of such differences and of the techniques of their suppression.

The late-modern pursuit of identity formation is most often cast in the discourse of discovery. Whether the identity seeker is Columbus, a recent boat person, a rural migrant to an urban center, an urbanite seeking roots in a small rural community, or an individual expressing an unsanctioned sexual orientation, he or she is an explorer on a voyage. Their voyages are intimately connected with the paradox of inclusivity, a recurring topic in recent political theory. Many of the previous discussions have focused on lapses within the Hegel-influenced search for unity in identity and on the evasions of

57. Connolly 1988, p. 115.

exclusionary practices meant to enforce this ideal of "unity." However, the other side of that same coin is the genre that codes the search for escape. Many, if not all, of the voyages previously noted have been as coded by resistance to, evasion of, or escape from the demands of what was known as coded by a search to discover new unities. Difference, either as something desired or something to be survived, has been on board each vessel that set sail. Whether the voyage was one of discovery or escape depends primarily on the viewpoint of those who subsequently tell its story. It has been suggested that much of the American project is expressed in a mix between this search for autonomy and separation,[58] and that the search for a new unity has led to the attempt to secularize the moral source of authority.[59] The American faith in the notions of rights and equal justice is founded on this latter search; the voyages of discovery emanate from the former.

As long as community is conceived according [to] the romantic American folk vision of a warm, intimate, and supportive social group, it is hard to understand why anyone would give it up. But the very intimacy and totality of such a social world make it miserable for the person who cannot or will not go along. . . . Indeed, historian Robert Wiebe argues that it is a fundamental cultural logic in America to deal with difference by living apart. "What held Americans together," he says, "was their ability to live apart. Society depended on segmentation."[60]

That segmentation, however, has increasingly relied on a troubling development in the second attempt: locating the moral source of authority again in the state, which was the primary source of abuse in centuries past. The paradox of this shift has been observed by Sally Merry as she examines the legal consciousness of rights and justice in working-class America.

Merry discusses how, during the twentieth century, the legal system became increasingly accessible to citizens and came to be seen

58. Wiebe 1975.
59. Jacobs 1991.
60. Merry 1990, pp. 173–74.

as the guardian of the average citizen. She identifies four distinct periods of change: (1) the Progressive Era in the early decades of the century, (2) the New Deal programs in the 1930s, (3) the legal rights activism of the 1960s, and (4) the extension of therapeutic services attached to the courts in the 1970s and 1980s. These were all periods of liberal reform "in which the state expanded its role in order to provide improved benefits and services, new rights and protections, and a more accessible and efficient legal system."[61] These changes, broadly considered, by which the law became understood as being on the side of "the little guy," formed "a new ideology of the state as friendly and supportive, as the protector of the poor and weak and as the regulator of the strong. In the era of liberal legal reformism, old concerns about the tyranny of the state disappeared. Americans in the eighteenth century feared state domination; twentieth-century Americans look to the state for protection against the giant corporations."[62]

But in gaining that "protection" of perceived personal autonomy, the modern individuals divest themselves of what had been such a major part of the original journey: the secularizing of moral authority, particularly insofar as it had been vested in themselves. Wrested first from the priests and then from the monarchy, this authority is now in the process of being returned, unchallenged, to the state. Thus the price exacted has been an increasing accommodation to the needs of state, whose apparatuses of surveillance are presented as necessary, even crucial, to produce the missing unity and to contain the escalating threat of difference.

William Connolly probes the paradox of accommodation and difference by posing a question: "What, though, are the compulsions that drive a church, a state, a culture, an identity to close itself up by defining a range of differences as heretical, evil, irrational, perverse, or destructive, even when the bearers of difference pose no direct threat of conquest? What is it in the terms of interaction between competing identities that fosters the probability of this response by

61. Ibid., p. 177.
62. Ibid., p. 178.

one or both of the contending parties?"[63] Social accommodation to those perceived as different may be generally understood as toleration. But tolerance is a tactic of denial, not of affirmation. It is a management technique to contain the threat that difference might pose to existing privilege. Accommodation is most often a change that is no change, a shuffling aside on a park bench to give another person the room that was already there. Minor modifications are made to entrances and workplaces to allow people of different physical abilities access and use. A class of beginning sign language is offered to hearing classmates of a mainstreamed deaf student. Audible crosswalk signals demarcate street corners for those who are blind, but equally serve to bracket socially ordered space for all pedestrians.[64] These are all changes that seek to limit and contain possible demands for further changes.

Sweden offers a clear example of this state strategy in dealing with difference. Swedish social programs in support of those who are Deaf are among the best in the world. Nevertheless, the Swedish tactics are those of social accommodation. The perfect Deaf Swede is now just like any other Swede, except he or she comes with an interpreter, or is (sufficiently) socialized to "appear" only in those social spaces where the state provides interpreters. Such official largess has less to do with encouraging the creative functioning of cultural difference than it does with state-supported reformism to contain the threat of difference.

63. Connolly 1991, p. 3.

64. Adding audible cross walk signals, ramps, and other official signals of order to the "human" terrain actively contributes to structural measures of surveillance and self-identification. For example, on the streets of Tokyo, where the semiotics of social order abound, jaywalkers seem nonexistent. The average (hearing, sighted, physically able) Tokyo resident, facing a red cross-light on an otherwise barren street, readily waits for the light to change before ever venturing to cross. There are many small streets with little or no traffic, but no jaywalkers. On a quiet Sunday afternoon with no cars to be seen, the behavior is the same. On such afternoons, as well as on busy working days, the audible crosswalk signal is a further disembodied aid or agent of this self-regulation. It is hard to accurately measure out the exact impact of this little detail in the hyper-group-conscious and tightly surveilled world of urban Japan, but it seems an added formal and self-consciously observed marker of acceptable ways of Japanese social being.

While such accommodations are important methods of rehumanizing and relocalizing—"rerooting"ourselves in—our daily worlds, they often represent no greater changes than a modest expansion of tolerance within the existing framework of privileges. The limits of such tolerance are equally defined by those existing frames of privilege. Indeed, the larger accommodations or adjustments are required of those who are marked as different. For those who seek to escape the constraints of an imposed identity, who claim the right to be free from family and neighborhood demands that they be the same, that they assimilate and accept their integration, must turn to the state for assistance in gaining their "freedom." The result is an increasing dependency on the power and supervisions of the state in defining the terms and terrain of their lives. It is no escape.

As Merry observes, the cloistered totality so often romanticized in American folk vision as an intimate and supportive community can also be miserable for the person who cannot or will not go along. The deaf child is a crucial example of those who can not "go along," yet have no "place" to escape to—except, that is, into a consensual place, the linguistic community of Deaf signers. Still, the existence and availability of this new place rely on stringent preconditions. A minimum body count—call it a cultural critical mass—must be randomly regenerated in each new cohort generation, collected and warehoused simply in order for the community to exist; this has most often taken place in the residential schools for the deaf. Furthermore, that cultural existence is not a product legitimated or even tolerated by the state or its institutions, but is achieved only through resistance and evasion of the stated intent and function of the warehousing authorities. This cultural "place" must be constantly regenerated, as members of each cohort can only hope to create, almost from scratch, what they later come to understand and perhaps contribute to as a cultural "tradition." It is a tradition both unaided and unfettered by prior generations, as contact with older members of the culture is usually limited. The regenerative task that awaits them is not easy. Hearing people don't seem to help much, either.

The response by families of deaf children, more than 90 percent of whom are hearing, is rarely in support of this task of the deaf child. As discussed in chapter 1, most family responses are coded in resentment. After they discover their child's deafness, hearing parents usually intensely resent the contingency that has visited this difference upon their own child. The politics of resentment—the demand to determine culpable agency for each of life's misfortunes, the litigious search for compensation for the injustices of life—fuels the demand that otherness be banished so that the search for a responsible agent may be less impeded. The paradoxical cycle is completed through the denial of resentment. The parents believe their desire for sameness in their different child is motivated by a need for their child to "belong." This positivist coding first denies difference and then forgets not only the denial but also the resentment of that which required banishment—the experience of contingency itself.

Otherness is often presented as an experience of contingency. Yet, if this is true, then there is all the more reason to follow Connolly's suggestion that otherness "be treated as one sign of human finitude. . . . [A]nd perhaps the quest to assimilate otherness into higher forms of community should be understood as the demand to imprison difference within the frame of a unity shaken by any sign of its own limit and uncertainty."[65] But there is considerable resistance to any sign of human finitude: as a blunt sign of human finitude, disability is thus often vigorously denied. Perhaps, as some disabled activists have said, we should consider ourselves as all involved in the process of disablement, that we are each, personally and individually, situated somewhere along that spectrum that shifts throughout life and ends in the unavoidable disability of death. The only distinction is that some begin at different points along that spectrum.

Yet within that constructed category of "disabled," those who are Deaf—and their demand for linguistic equality—have represented a particularly potent threat. They have apparently been dealt with accordingly. The institutions of deafness, as well as the proponents on either side of what is described as the great oral-manual divide, manifest a neorealism that reflects the Western will to truth, interpreting the world and then insisting that the interpretation reflects

65. Connolly 1988, p. 114.

the world as it is in itself. This neorealism, bound to its positivist claim of empirical data, is a major force in the policing of diversity and difference.

Diversity has more than one face. Diversity is a fact, when placed in the context of the vast extent of biological life on this planet. Diversity is a goal, when placed into the context of human societies. Neither is faring very well as we move into the twenty-first century. Diversity of the biosphere of this fragile planet is decreasing as an ever-increasing percentage of biological life forms are lost to extinction, while diversity in the human terrain is rapidly falling prey to increasing discipline, surveillance, and marketing practices of late modernity. But in the context of difference, diversity, like accommodation, is about difference contained.

Homi K. Bhabha (1994) critiques the notion of cultural diversity as a limiting factor in critical theory, a limitation to be overcome through a careful reconsideration of cultural difference. To Bhabha, cultural diversity is another form of essentialism, recognizing only pregiven cultural contents and customs and justifying the relativistic smorgasbord of liberal multiculturalism. This late-modern deployment of cultural diversity is crucially distinct from the process by which subjugated peoples may seek to assert indigenous cultural traditions and retrieve repressed histories. However, Bhabha recalls Franz Fanon's warnings of "the dangers of the fixity and fetishism of identities" within calcified colonial and colonized cultures, as well as his command that roots be not constructed by "the celebratory romance of the past or by homogenizing the history of the present."[66] These monitory words resonate powerfully within the struggles to inscribe Deaf history. Expanding on Fanon's observations, Bhabha distinguishes between liberal notions of cultural diversity and the productions by which cultural difference is known: "Cultural diversity is an epistemological object—culture as an object of empirical knowledge—whereas cultural difference is the process of the enunciation of culture as 'knowledgeable,' authoritative, adequate to the construction of systems of cultural identification. If

66. Fanon 1986, p. 231.

cultural diversity is a category of comparative ethics, aesthetics or ethnology, cultural difference is a process of signification through which statements of culture or on culture differentiate, discriminate and authorize the production of fields of force, reference, applicability and capacity."[67]

The issue here is a place from which or in which a distinct difference can itself exist, rather than be defined only in terms of its relationship with—"difference from"—something else. Diversity is about where one fits on a spectrum, how this artifact varies from that artifact. Interest and value are determined by the terms of the dominant framing that circumscribes both ends of the spectrum. Yet performative markers, expressivist constructions by which difference might be articulated and known as distinct from the dominant, allow a cultural understanding of difference as measured by its own terms of reference, as an ongoing process. The authority of the constables of culture is thus compromised. As Bhabha explains:

> The concept of cultural difference focuses on the problem of the ambivalence of cultural authority: the attempt to dominate in the name of a cultural supremacy which is itself produced only in the moment of differentiation. And it is the very authority of culture as a knowledge of referential truth which is at issue in the concept of moment of enunciation. The enunciative process introduces a split in the performative present of cultural identification; a split between the traditional culturalist demand for a model, a tradition, a community, a stable system of reference, and the necessary negation of the certitude in the articulation of new cultural demands, meanings, strategies in the political present, as a practice of domination, or resistance.[68]

The split Bhabha refers to is manifest at various levels, including that troubled terrain of "passing," clearly a performative realm in which an active and ongoing (re)negotiation of negations and identifications is enacted. Passing, like diversity and difference, has multiple faces. Each is also heavily compromised. The question of passing, a strategy of "safe passage" through which codes of assimilation with a dominant culture or other are deployed, is fraught with tense

67. Bhabha 1994, p. 34.
68. Ibid., pp. 34–35.

ambivalence. Yet those who condemn coping strategies such as passing as being merely bad faith and false consciousness are closing off a crucial performative arena in which cultural authority is left in flux.

Branding certain coping strategies as unacceptable not only restricts the tactics available to negotiate cultural distance but also reinscribes the problem of difference on the body of the individual rather than on the social body of dominating relationships. Thus, these "purists" themselves reproduce the tactics of domination, which locate difference in the body of the deviant.

As was noted in chapter 2, the question of belonging, whether to the dominant culture or to the self-identified "community" of an excluded group, is under constant (re)negotiation. Passing includes both evasion and accommodation. More important, it involves negotiating claims by which an articulation of cultural difference might authorize a culturally hybrid creativity. As Bhabha confirms, "The 'right' to signify from the periphery of authorized power and privilege does not depend on the persistence of tradition; it is resourced by the power of tradition to be reinscribed through the conditions of contingency and contradictoriness that attend upon the lives of those who are 'in the minority.'"[69] Clearly echoing bell hooks' (1990) demand to reclaim the boundaries as the place from which to speak, from which to reclaim difference, Bhabha notes that "the boundary becomes the place from which something begins its presencing."[70]

That one must be "talking to belong" holds an especially heavy irony for those who are Deaf. Not only does such a phrase resonate with the discursive economies of allowable identities, but it also evokes the very mechanics by which their "belonging" through passing is to be made material—"oral rehabilitation." Regaining the "lost word" to become a hearinglike person is the overt goal of mainstream deaf education. The mechanics, as in Alexander Graham Bell's age, remain those of speech "therapy." The goal of speech

69. Ibid., p. 2.
70. Ibid., p. 5.

therapy, like most other forms of what Murray Edelman (1977) has called therapeutic discourse, is passing. Yet even speech therapy is a ground on which authority can be ambiguated.

For example, if speech therapy is *all* a child is offered, it is a site and tactic of oppression. If, however, a child is fully fluent in a "mother" sign language and is being taught the dominant spoken language as a second language, then speech therapy can become a terrain of acquiring strategic skills for coping/countering/confronting the dominant culture on terms it cannot deny. This is not to say that deaf people "have" to learn speech, per se; but as a strategic weapon/tool in the arsenal of personal/personnel techniques, speech can be used selectively to individual taste and advantage when so desired. If use of this learned skill is repeatedly demanded, then the resistance value of the strategy may be recaptured into a space of oppression. As with any such identity resource, there are no guarantees, but the act of reclaiming the margin as a site of strength remains the necessary first step.

The tactics of passing raise serious questions about how high a price those who are different must pay if they are to acquiesce or accommodate to the demands of the larger community. Even more than rights talk, these tactics are problematic in negotiating for political participation. In general, passing may provide opportunities to gain useful knowledge from dominating groups through participation in dominant ways of knowing and being; yet that very participation poses the risk of estrangement, alienation, and co-optation. The distinction is between a strategic view of passing and the actual practices of passing that might limit other strategic options. Moreover, for those who are Deaf, the possible "benefits" of passing are critically compromised, as such direct participation that is held out as one of the "rewards" is simply not available. Because it rests on the direct experience of a sound-based language, it is merely an illusion—like the option of "speech first" for the deaf child, cherished by the dominant. For the Deaf, passing generally offers only risks, without viable opportunities to gain the supposedly useful knowledge.

Sound Knowledge

It is useful to again recall the words of a staff member of the Alexander Graham Bell Association for the Deaf: "They can't hear, but they catch on. Some say there's no such thing as a deaf child. Not if it's done right."[71] The false promises of passing, contained within the oralist and mainstreamed illusions of "doing it right," underscore the role of marginality as site and place of both repression and of resistance. Participation is itself a false promise never fulfilled. This promise is either the most vicious lie or most taxing paradox of oralist/auralist presumptions of sound-bound knowledge.

The cultural difference made manifest by deafness, together with the aggressive history of the suppression of that difference, illuminates the extent to which those hidden presumptions pervade our dominant ways of knowing. This bastion of accepted truth, which I ironically call "sound knowledge," is seen as a historical construction not entirely innocent. It is also one now open to challenge.

The debate on difference has been opened in new ways, but still it has proven difficult not to succumb to the Hegelian shift, the desire that yet a new and higher level of unity be achieved. While not reducing people to one trait, this hope for deliverance nevertheless remains a refusal to see the significance of traits that do "matter." Deafness is more than a color in the pastiche of social differences. It is also a marker of oppression and marginalization in very real lives. It is a difference that does matter. I have explored numerous perspectives from which consideration of things deaf and the difference of deafness offer new vantage points for framing critical political questions.

My appropriation of both the "voice" and "signs" of Deaf cultures was deliberate, but I have remained attentive to what I have been led to understand of Deaf perspectives across more traditional ethnic and national borders. I have particularly tried to convey my respect for the many Deaf people who continue to feel that overt oppression severely affects their daily lives. The most obvious sites of

71. Neisser 1983, p. 32. See also chapter 5.

this oppression are education and sign language rights, as have been highlighted throughout this work.

The mechanisms by which the separation, isolation, denial, and objectification of Deaf people have been achieved have been both widely varied and curiously effective. Yet certain spaces have been opened, often indirectly, that continue to produce pockets of creative resistance and cultural regeneration. Making space for difference certainly reduces the semblance of control and order, yet it greatly enlivens prospects for possible social exchanges. To the extent that this work is part of a larger endeavor, it attempts to create additional openings for differences, openings that require us to reconsider what are thought to be normal relationships, as well as make major changes in how "normal" is constructed. In the process, I hope I have also helped illuminate further the peculiar manner in which lives are hopelessly restricted by current policies and practices whose foundations ceased to exist long ago. *Peculiar* is the least pejorative term I can muster.

> Every culture seems to contain some themes that are both indispensable to it and inherently problematic within it. The pressure of their indispensability works to conceal their problematic character. This sometimes becomes clear retrospectively after the indispensability of a theme has been lost or compromised; then aporias within it flood into the open, making contemporaries wonder how their forerunners could ever have entertained such superstitious or absurd ideas. But this very portrayal of superstitions of the past increases the probability that the problematic character of indispensable themes in the present will not be probed vigorously.[72]

Certainly the theme of sound knowledge is one that, in the present, remains deeply buried. Such a realization need not spell defeat, but rather might invigorate a struggle to create, to enunciate, boundary spaces in which further differences and a growing number of critical questions might thrive. Questions are indeed increasing, both those raised by members of that long-excluded linguistic minority and those being forced by the rapid shift in technological protocols for

72. Connolly 1991, p. 3.

advanced communications. As suggested in chapter 5, Deaf identity and the money in your ATM are connected. Neither is secure.

It has been my purpose to leave a lingering memory of questions: questions of how those who are deaf, and those who are Deaf, "matter" in our postmodern claims of knowledge. How these claims are dealt with—what is allowed to matter—is not simply determined by the defining characteristics of democracy. It is intimately connected with presumptions—behind the rules and procedures, be they epistemic or ontological—about those "eligible" to participate.

Bibliography

Ackerman, Diane. 1991. *A Natural History of the Senses*. New York: Vintage Books.

Alloula, Malek. 1986. *The Colonial Harem*. Minneapolis: University of Minnesota Press.

Anderson, Benedict. 1983. *Imagined Communities: Reflections on the Origin and Spread of Nationalism*. New York: Verso.

Aramburo, Anthony. 1989. "The Sociolinguistic Aspects of the Black Deaf Community." In *The Sociolinguistics of the Deaf Community*, edited by Ceil Lucas, pp. 103–19.

Ashcroft, Bill, et al., eds. 1989. *The Empire Writes Back*. New York: Routledge.

Attali, Jacques. 1985. *Noise: The Political Economy of Music*. Minneapolis: University of Minnesota Press.

Austin, John. 1962. *How to Do Things with Words*. Cambridge: Harvard University Press.

Babbage, Charles. 1989. *The Works of Charles Babbage*, edited by Martin Campbell-Kelly. New York: New York University Press.

Baker, Charlotte, and Robbin Battison, eds. 1980. *Sign Language and the Deaf Community: Essays in Honor of William C. Stokoe*. Washington, D.C.: National Association of the Deaf.

Baker-Shenk, C., and D. Cokely. 1980. *American Sign Language: A Teacher's Resource Text on Grammar and Culture*. Silver Spring, Md.: T. J. Publishers.

Barthes, Roland. 1981. *Camera Lucida*. New York: Hill and Wang.

———. 1982. *Empire of Signs*. New York: Hill and Wang.

Bateson, B. A. 1984. *The End of Absolute Monarchy in Siam*. Singapore: Oxford University Press.

Battelle, John. 1991. "Filesavers: The DataClub Difference." *MacUser*, September, pp. 231–32+.

Baudrillard, Jean. 1987. *Forget Foucault*. New York: Semiotext(e).

Baum, L. Frank. 1986. *The Wonderful Wizard of Oz*. 1900. Reprint, Berkeley: University of California Press.

Becker, Gaylene. 1980. *Growing Old in Silence*. Berkeley: University of California Press.

Bell, Alexander Graham. 1884. *On the Formation of a Deaf Variety of the Human Race*. Washington, D.C.: U.S. Government Printing Office.

271

———. 1898. *Marriage: An Address to the Deaf.* Washington, D.C.: Sanders Printing Office.

———. 1908. "A Few Thoughts Concerning Eugenics." *National Geographic* 19: 119–23.

———. 1914. "How to Improve the Race." *Journal of Heredity* 5: 1–7.

———. 1919. "Who Shall Inherit Long Life?" *National Geographic* 35: 505–14.

———. 1920. "Is Race Suicide Possible?" *Journal of Heredity* 11: 339–41.

Benedict, Michael, ed. 1991. *Cyberspace: First Steps.* Cambridge: MIT Press.

Bernauer, James, and D. Rasmussen, D., eds. 1988. *The Final Foucault.* Cambridge: MIT Press.

Bey, Hakim. 1985. *T.A.Z.: The Temporary Autonomous Zone, Ontological Anarchy, Poetic Terrorism.* Brooklyn, N.Y.: Autonomedia.

Bhabha, Homi. 1984. *Of Mimicry and Man: The Ambivalence of Colonial Discourse.* Cambridge: MIT Press.

———. 1994. *The Location of Culture.* New York: Routledge Press.

Blonsky, Marshall, ed. 1985. *On Signs.* Baltimore: Johns Hopkins University Press.

Boothroyd, Arthur. 1990. "Impact of Technology on the Management of Deafness." *Volta Review* 92.4: 73–82.

Bornstein, Harry, ed. 1990a. *Manual Communication: Implications for Education.* Washington, D.C.: Gallaudet University Press.

———. 1990b. "A Manual Communication Overview." In *Manual Communication: Implications for Education,* edited by Harry Bornstein, pp. 21–44. Washington, D.C.: Gallaudet University Press.

Bourdieu, Pierre. 1984. *Distinction: A Social Critique of the Judgement of Taste,* translated by Richard Nice. Cambridge: Harvard University Press.

Branwyn, Gareth. 1991. "The World's Oldest Secret Conspiracy—Fronted by Steve Jackson Games, Inc.: An Interview with Steve Jackson." *Mondo 2000,* no. 3 (Winter): 64–68.

Brennan, M., M. Colville, and L. Lawson. 1980. *Words in Hand.* Edinburgh: Moray House College.

Breunig, H. Latham. 1990. "The Legacy of Dr. Bell." *Volta Review* 92.4: 83–96.

Bruce, Robert. 1973. *Bell: Alexander Graham Bell and the Conquest of Solitude.* New York: Little, Brown.

Brunn, Stanley D., and Thomas R. Leinbach, eds. 1991. *Collapsing Space and Time: Geographic Aspects of Communications and Information.* London and Cambridge: HarperCollins.

Bulwer, John. 1648. *Philocophus: Or the deaf and Dumbe Mans Friend.* London: Humphrey Moseley.

Burchell, Graham, Colin Gordon, and Peter Miller. 1991. *The Foucault Effect: Studies in Governmentality.* Chicago: University of Chicago Press.

Butler, Judith. 1987. *Subjects of Desire: Hegelian Reflections in Twentieth-Century France.* New York: Columbia University Press.

———. 1990. *Gender Trouble: Feminism and the Subversion of Identity.* New York: Routledge.

Carmel, Simon. 1976. "Ethnic Identity and Solidarity in the Deaf Community in the United States." National Technical Institute for the Deaf, Rochester, N.Y. Photocopy.

Chai-anan Samudavanija. 1982. *The Thai Young Turks*. Singapore: Institute of Southeast Asian Studies.

Chaiwat Satha-anand. 1989. "Hijab and Moments of Legitimation: Islamic Resurgence in Thai Society." Paper presented to the Conference on Communities in Question, hosted by the Social Science Research Council and the U.S. American Council on Learned Studies, Hua Hin, Thailand, 4–8 May.

Chattip Nartsupha. 1984. "The Ideology of 'Holy Men' Revolts in Northeast Thailand." In *Historical and Peasant Consciousness in Southeast Asia*, edited by Andrew Turton and Shigeharu Tanabe. Osaka: National Museum of Ethnology.

Chula Chakrabongse, H.R.H. 1960. *Lords of Life: A History of the Kings in Thailand*. London: Alvin Redman.

Clawson, Mary Ann. 1989. *Constructing Brotherhood*. Princeton: Princeton University Press.

Clifford, James. 1983. "On Ethnographic Authority." *Representations* 1.2: 118–46.

Clifford, James, and George Marcus, eds. 1986. *Writing Culture: The Poetics and Politics of Ethnography*. Berkeley: University of California Press.

Cocks, Joan. 1989. *The Oppositional Imagination*. New York: Routledge.

Connolly, William E. 1987. *Politics and Ambiguity*. Madison: University of Wisconsin Press.

———. 1988. *Political Theory and Modernity*. Oxford: Basil Blackwell.

———. 1991. *Identity/Difference: Democratic Negotiations of Political Paradox*. Ithaca: Cornell University Press.

Costa Lima, Luiz. 1988. *Control of the Imaginary: Reason and Imagination in Modern Times*. Minneapolis: University of Minnesota Press.

Crary, Jonathan. 1990. *Techniques of the Observer: On Vision and Modernity in the Nineteenth Century*. Cambridge: MIT Press.

Croneberg, Carl. 1976. "The Linguistic Community." In *A Dictionary of American Sign Language on Linguistic Principles*, edited by W. C. Stokoe, D. Casterline, and C. Croneberg, pp. 297–311. Silver Spring, Md.: Linstok Press.

Darby, Phillip. 1972. *Three Faces of Imperialism: British and American Approaches to Asia and Africa, 1870–1970*. New Haven: Yale University Press.

de Certeau, Michel. 1986. *Heterologies: Discourse on the Other*. Minneapolis: University of Minnesota Press.

Deleuze, Gilles, and Félix Guattari. 1986. *Nomadology: The War Machine*, translated by Brian Massumi. New York: Semiotext(e).

DeLillo, Don. 1978. *Running Dog*. New York: Knopf.

———. 1982. *The Names*. New York: Knopf.

———. 1986. *White Noise*. New York: Penguin.

Demaine, Harvey. 1986. "*Kānpatthanā*: Thai Views of Development." In *Context, Meaning, and Power in Southeast Asia*, edited by Mark Hobart and Robert Taylor, pp. 93–114. Ithaca: Southeast Asia Program, Cornell University.

de Nerval, Gérard. 1972. *Journey to the Orient* (1851), selections translated by Norman Glass. New York: New York University Press.

Dennett, Daniel C. 1991. *Consciousness Explained*. Boston: Little, Brown.

der Derian, James, and Michael Shapiro, eds. 1989. *International/Intertextual Relations*. Lexington, Mass.: Lexington Books.

Derrida, Jacques. 1973. *Speech and Phenomena, and Other Essays on Husserl's Theory of Signs*, translated by David B. Allison. Evanston, Ill.: Northwestern University Press.

———. 1977. "Signature Event Context," translated by Samuel Weber and Jeffrey Mehlman. *Glyph* 1: 172–97.

———. 1980. *The Archeology of the Frivolous: Reading Condillac*, translated by John P. Leavey Jr. Pittsburgh: Duquesne University Press.

———. 1985. *The Ear of the Other: Otiobiography, Transference, Translation*, translated by Peggy Kamuf. New York: Schocken Books.

Doerner, Klaus. 1981. *Madmen and the Bourgeoisie*. Oxford: Basil Blackwell.

Douglas, Mary. 1986. *How Institutions Think*. Syracuse, N.Y.: Syracuse University Press.

Dreyfus, H. L., and P. Rabinow. 1983. *Michel Foucault: Beyond Structuralism and Hermeneutics*. Chicago: University of Chicago Press.

Edelman, Jacob Murray. 1977. *Political Language: Words That Succeed and Policies That Fail*. New York: Academic Press.

Eichengreen, Barry. 1992. *Golden Fetters: The Gold Standard and the Great Depression, 1919–1939*. Oxford: Oxford University Press.

Elias, Norbert. 1978. *The History of Manners*. New York: Pantheon Books.

Embree, John F. 1969. "Thailand—A Loosely Structured Social System." In *Loosely Structured Social Systems*, edited by Hans-Dieter Evers, pp. 3–15. New Haven: Yale University, Southeast Asia Studies.

Erting, Carol. 1978. "Language Policy and Deaf Ethnicity in the United States." *Sign Language Studies* 19: 139–52.

———. 1982. *Deafness, Communication and Social Identity: An Anthropological Analysis of Interaction among Parents, Teachers, and Deaf Children in a Preschool*. Ann Arbor, Mich.: University Microfilms.

Erting, Carol, and James C. Woodward. 1974. "Sign Language and the Deaf Community: A Sociolinguistic Profile." Paper presented at the American Anthropological Association meeting, Mexico City. A revised version is found in *Discourse Processes* 2 (1979): 283–300.

Evans, A. Donald, and William W. Falk. 1986. *Learning to Be Deaf*. New York: Mouton de Gruyter.

Ewen, Stuart. 1988. *All Consuming Images: The Politics of Style in Contemporary Culture*. New York: Basic Books.

Fabian, Johannes. 1983. *Time and the Other*. New York: Columbia University Press.

Fanon, Frantz. 1986. *Black Skins, White Masks* (1952), translated by Charles Lam Markman. London: Pluto Books.

Fawcett, Brian. 1991. *Unusual Circumstances, Interesting Times*. Vancouver, B.C.: New Star Books.

Ferguson, Kathy E. 1984. *The Feminist Case against Bureaucracy*. Philadelphia: Temple University Press.

———. 1993. *The Man Question: Visions of Subjectivity in Feminist Theory*. Berkeley: University of California Press.

Fiedler, Leslie. 1978. *Freaks: Myths and Images of the Secret Self*. New York: Simon and Schuster.

Fishman, Joshua. 1977. "Language and Ethnicity." In *Language, Ethnicity, and Intergroup Relations*, edited by Howard Giles, pp. 15–59. New York: Academic Press.

Foster, Hal, ed. 1983. *The Anti-aesthetic: Essays on Postmodern Culture*. Port Townsend, Wash.: Bay Press.

———, ed. 1987. *Discussions in Contemporary Culture*. Vol. 1. Seattle: Bay Press.

Foucault, Michel. 1965. *Madness and Civilization: A History of Insanity in the Age of Reason*, translated by Richard Howard. New York: Pantheon Books.

———. 1973. *The Birth of the Clinic: An Archaeology of Medical Perception*, translated by A. M. Sheridan Smith. New York: Pantheon Books.

———. 1977. *Language, Counter-memory, Practice*, translated by Donald F. Bouchard and Sherry Simon. New York: Cornell University Press.

———. 1979. *Discipline and Punish*, translated by Alan Sheridan. New York: Vintage Books.

———. 1980a. *History of Sexuality*, translated by Robert Hurley. Vol. 1. New York: Vintage Books.

———. 1980b. *Power/Knowledge*, edited and translated by Colin Gordon. New York: Pantheon Books.

———. 1988. *Politics, Philosophy, Culture: 1977–1984*, translated by Alan Sheridan et al. New York: Routledge.

———. 1989. *Foucault Live: Interviews, 1966–84*, translated by John Johnston, edited by Sylvere Lotringer. New York: Semiotext(e).

Fraser, Nancy. 1989. *Unruly Practices: Power, Discourse and Gender in Contemporary Social Theory*. Minneapolis: University of Minnesota Press.

Flournoy, J. J. 1856. "A Deaf Mute Commonwealth." *American Annals of the Deaf* 8: 120–25.

Freire, Paulo. 1986. *Pedagogy of the Oppressed*, translated by Myra Bergman Ramos. New York: Continuum.

Gallagher, Catherine, and Thomas Laqueur, eds. 1987. *The Making of the Modern Body: Sexuality and Society in the Nineteenth Century*. Berkeley: University of California Press.

Galtung, Johan. 1971. "A Structural Theory of Imperialism." *Journal of Peace Research* 8: 82–117.

Gans, David, and R. U. Sirius. 1991. "Civilizing the Electronic Frontier: An Interview with Mitch Kapor and John Barlow of the Electronic Frontier Foundation." *Mondo 2000*, no. 1 (Winter): 45–49.

Gates, Henry Louis Jr., ed. 1986. *"Race," Writing, and Difference*. Chicago: University of Chicago Press.

Geertz, Clifford. 1980. *Negara: The Theatre State in Nineteenth-Century Bali*. Princeton: Princeton University Press.

———. 1983. *Local Knowledge*. New York: Basic Books.

Genovese, Eugene D. 1974. *Roll, Jordon, Roll: The World the Slaves Made*. New York: Random House.

Gibbons, Michael T., ed. 1987. *Interpreting Politics*. New York: New York University Press.

Gibson, William. 1983. *Burning Chrome*. New York: Ace Books.

———. 1984. *Neuromancer*. New York: Ace Books.

———. 1987. *Count Zero*. New York: Ace Books.

———. 1988. *Mona Lisa Overdrive*. New York: Bantam Books.

Gibson, William, and Bruce Sterling. 1991. *The Difference Engine*. New York: Bantam Books.

Gleick, James. 1987. *Chaos: Making a New Science*. New York: Viking.

Golding, William. 1954. *Lord of the Flies*. London: Faber and Faber.

Goux, Jean-Joseph. 1990. *Symbolic Economies: After Freud and Marx*, translated by J. C. Gage. Ithaca: Cornell University Press.

Gray, D., J. Everingham, and O. Wrigley, eds. 1988. *The King of Thailand in World Focus*. Bangkok: Siriwattana Press.

Hafner, Katie, and John Markoff. 1991. *Cyberpunk: Outlaws and Hackers on the Computer Frontier*. New York: Simon and Schuster.

Hall, Edward T. 1992. *An Anthropology of Everyday Life: An Autobiography*. New York: Doubleday.

Hanks, Lucien M. 1962. "Merit and Power in Thai Social Order." *American Anthropologist* 64: 1247–61.

Haraway, Donna. 1989. *Primate Visions: Gender, Race, and Nature in the World of Modern Science*. New York: Routledge.

Hardison, O. B., Jr. 1989. *Disappearing through the Skylight: Culture and Technology in the Twentieth Century*. New York: Penguin Books.

Hart, Mickey. 1990. *Drumming on the Edge of Magic*. New York: HarperCollins.

Harvey, David. 1989. *The Condition of Postmodernity: An Enquiry into the Origins of Cultural Change*. Oxford: Basil Blackwell.

Hegel, G. W. F. 1967. *Philosophy of Right*, translated by T. M. Knox. Oxford: Oxford University Press.

———. 1977. *Phenomenology of Spirit*, translated by T. M. Knox. Oxford: Clarendon Press.

Heidegger, Martin. 1976. *The Piety of Thinking*, translated by James G. Hart and John C. Maraldo. Bloomington: Indiana University Press.

———. 1979. *Nietzsche*. Vol. 2, *The Eternal Recurrence of the Same*, translated by David Farrell Krell. San Francisco: Random House.

———. 1982. *Basic Problems of Phenomenology*, translated by A. Hofstadter. Bloomington: Indiana University Press.

Herder, Johann Gottfried von. 1969. *J. G. Herder on Social and Political Culture*, translated by F. M. Barnard. London: Cambridge University Press.

Higgins, Paul C. 1980. *Outsiders in a Hearing World*. London: Sage Publications.

———. 1990. *The Challenge of Educating Together Deaf and Hearing Youth: Making Mainstreaming Work*. Springfield, Ill.: Thomas Books.

Hirsch, E. D., Jr. 1989. *A First Dictionary of Cultural Literacy*. Boston: Houghton Mifflin.

Hirsch, Ira J., and Carl E. Scherrick, Jr. 1961. "Perceived Order in Difference Sense Modalities." *Journal of Experimental Psychology* 62: 423–32.

hooks, bell. 1984. *Feminist Theory: From Margin to Center*. Boston: South End Press.

————. 1990. *Yearning: Race, Gender, and Cultural Politics*. Boston: South End Press.

Hoy, David Couzens, ed. 1986. *Foucault: A Critical Reader*. Oxford: Basil Blackwell.

Ishii, Yoneo. 1975. *Sangha, State, and Society: Thai Buddhism in History*, translated by Peter Hawkes. Honolulu: University of Hawaii Press.

Jacobs, Margaret C. 1991. *Living the Enlightenment: Freemasonry and Politics in Eighteenth-Century Europe*. New York: Oxford University Press.

Jakobson, Roman. 1971. *Selected Writings*. Vol. 2, *Word and Language*. The Hague: Mouton.

Jameson, Fredric. 1984. "The Linguistic Model." In *Language and Politics*, edited by Michael J. Shapiro, pp. 168–94. New York: New York University Press.

————. 1987. *The Origins of a Style*. Chicago: University of Chicago Press.

Jay, Martin. 1986. "In the Empire of the Gaze." In *Foucault: A Critical Reader*, edited by David C. Hoy, pp. 175–204. Oxford, Basil Blackwell.

Johnson, Robert E., Scott K. Liddell, and Carol J. Erting. 1989. "Unlocking the Curriculum: Principles for Achieving Access in Deaf Education." Working paper 89–3, Gallaudet Research Institute, Gallaudet University, Washington, D.C.

Kafka, Franz. 1971. "The Burrow," translated by Willa and Edwin Muir. In *The Complete Stories*, edited by Nahum Glatzer, pp. 325–59. New York: Schocken.

Keller, Helen. 1905. *The Story of My Life*. New York: Grosset and Dunlap.

Kessel, Frank, ed. 1988. *The Development of Language and Language Researchers: Essays in Honor of Roger Brown*. Hillsdale, N.J.: Lawrence Erlbaum.

Keyes, Charles. 1978. "Political Crisis and Militant Buddhism in Contemporary Thailand." In *Religion and Legitimation of Power in Thailand, Laos, and Burma*, edited by Bardwell L. Smith, pp. 147–64. Chambersburg, Pa.: Anima Books.

————. 1987. *Thailand: Buddhist Kingdom as Modern Nation-State*. Boulder, Colo.: Westview Press.

————. 1989. "Buddhist Politics and Their Revolutionary Origins in Thailand." *International Political Science Review* 10.2: 121–42.

Kittler, Friedrich A. 1990. *Discourse Networks 1800/1900*, translated by Michael Metteer, with Chris Cullens. Stanford: Stanford University Press.

Klima, Edward. 1974. *The Role of Speech in Language*. Cambridge: MIT Press.

Klima, Edward S., and Ursula Bellugi. 1970. *The Signs of Language*. Cambridge: Harvard University Press.

Krishna, Sankaran. 1992. "Inscribing the Nation: The Politics of Identity in India." Department of Political Science, University of Hawaii at Manoa.

Kristeva, Julia. 1980. *Desire in Language,* edited by Leon S. Roudiez, translated by Thomas Gora, Alice Jardine, and Leon S. Roudiez. New York: Columbia University Press.

———. 1982. *Powers of Horror,* translated by Leon S. Roudiez. New York: Columbia University Press.

———. 1986. *The Kristeva Reader,* edited by Toril Moi. New York: Columbia University Press.

Kroker, Arthur. 1993. *Spasm: Virtual Reality, Androic Music, and Electric Flesh.* New York: St. Martin's Press.

Kroker, Arthur, and Michael A. Weinstein. 1994. *Data Trash: The Theory of the Virtual Class.* Montreal: New World Perspectives.

"Lab Voices That 'Feel' Sound." *Inside* (Oho State University College of Social and Behavioral Science), Spring, p. 3.

Lacan, Jacques. 1968. *The Language of the Self,* translated by Anthony Wilden. Baltimore: Johns Hopkins University Press.

Landau, Barbara, and Lila R. Gleitman. 1985. *Language and Experience: Evidence from the Blind Child.* Cambridge: Harvard University Press.

Landon, Brooks. 1989. "Bet on It: Cyber Punk Video Performance." *Mondo 2000,* no. 1: 143–45. Rpt. from *Mississippi Review,* nos. 47/48 (1988).

Lane, Harlan. 1976. *The Wild Boy of Aveyron.* Cambridge: Harvard University Press.

———. 1984. *When the Mind Hears: A History of the Deaf.* New York: Random House.

———. 1992. *The Mask of Benevolence: Disabling the Deaf Community.* New York: Knopf.

Lorde, Audre. 1984. *Sister Outsider.* Trumansburg, N.Y.: Crossing Press.

Lucas, Ceil, ed. 1989. *The Sociolinguistics of the Deaf Community.* New York: Academic Press.

Lyotard, Jean-François. 1984. *The Postmodern Condition: A Report on Knowledge,* translated by Geoff Bennington and Brian Massumi. Minneapolis: University of Minnesota Press.

———. 1990. *Heidegger and "the Jews,"* translated by Andreas Michel and Mark S. Roberts. Minneapolis: University of Minnesota Press.

Mackenzie, Catherine F. 1928. *Alexander Graham Bell: The Man Who Contracted Space.* Boston: Houghton Mifflin.

MacKinnon, Catharine A. 1987. *Feminism.Unmodified: Discourses on Life and Law.* Cambridge: Harvard University Press.

Mandelbrot, Benoit B. 1982. *The Fractal Geometry of Nature.* San Francisco: W. H. Freeman.

Mannix, Daniel P. 1990. *Freaks: We Who Are Not As Others.* San Francisco: Re/Search Publications.

Markowicz, Harry, and James C. Woodward. 1978. "Language and the Maintenance of Ethnic Boundaries in the Deaf Community." *Communication and Cognition* 11: 29–38.

Masdit, Supatra (Khunying). 1991. *Politics in Thailand.* Singapore: Times Academic Press for the Institute of Policy Studies.

Masters, Patricia. 1992. "The Politics of Memory: Creating Self-Understandings in Postwar Japan." Ph.D. diss., University of Hawaii.

McBeth, Sally J. 1983. *Ethnic Identity and the Boarding School Experience of West-central Oklahoma American Indians*. Washington, D.C.: University Press of America.

McCaffery, Larry, ed. 1991. *Storming the Reality Studio: A Casebook of Cyberpunk and Postmodern Fiction*. Durham, N.C.: Duke University Press.

Meadow, Kathryn P. 1972. "Sociolinguistics, Sign Language, and the Deaf Sub-Culture." In *Psycholinguistics and Total Communication: The State of the Art*, edited by T. J. O'Rourke, pp. 19–33. Washington, D.C.: American Annals of the Deaf.

Merry, Sally Engle. 1990. *Getting Justice and Getting Even: Legal Consciousness among Working-Class Americans*. Chicago: University of Chicago Press.

———. 1991. "Law and Colonialism." *Law and Society Review* 25: 889–922.

Melville, Stephen. 1986. *Philosophy Beside Itself: On Deconstruction and Modernism*. Minneapolis: University of Minnesota Press.

Milhon, Judith. 1989. "Call It . . . Revolutionary Parasitism: An Interview of John Shirley." *Mondo 2000*, no. 1: 88–92.

Minow, Martha. 1990. *Making All the Difference: Inclusion, Exclusion, and American Law*. Ithaca: Cornell University Press.

Moore, Christopher. 1990. *A Killing Smile*. Bangkok: White Lotus Press.

———. 1991. *A Haunting Smile*. Bangkok: White Lotus Press.

———. 1992a. *Asia Hand*. Bangkok: White Lotus Press.

———. 1992b. *Heart Talk*. Bangkok: White Lotus Press.

Moraga, Cherríe, and Gloria Anzaldúa, eds. 1983. *This Bridge Called My Back: Writings by Radical Women of Color*. New York: Kitchen Table Press.

Morse, Richard, A. Rahman, and K. L. Johnson, eds. 1995. *Grassroots Horizons: Connecting Participatory Development Initiatives East and West*. New Delhi: Mohan Primlani for Oxford and IBH Publishing; London: Intermediate Technology Publications.

Musashi, Miyamoto. 1982. *A Book of Five Rings*, translated by Bradford J. Brown et al. New York: Bantam Books.

National Identity Promotion Office. 1984. *National Ideology*. Bangkok: Office of the Prime Minister.

Neisser, Arden. 1990. *The Other Side of Silence: Sign Language and the Deaf Community in America*. Washington, D.C.: Gallaudet University Press.

Nietzsche, Friedrich W. 1967. *On the Genealogy of Morals*, translated by Walter Kaufmann and R. J. Hollingdale. New York: Vintage Books.

———. 1968. *The Will To Power*, translated by Walter Kaufmann and R. J. Hollingdale. New York: Vintage Books.

———. 1974. *The Gay Science*, translated by Walter Kaufmann. New York: Vintage Books.

Office of the National Culture Commission. 1986. *National Culture Policy*. Bangkok: Ministry of Education.

Ong, Aihwa. 1987. *Spirits of Resistance and Capitalist Discipline: Factory Women in Malaysia*. Albany: SUNY Press.

Orpen, Charles. 1836. *Anecdotes and Annals of the Deaf and Dumb*. London: Robert H. C. Tims.

Osberger, Mary Joe. 1990. "Audition." *Volta Review* 92.4: 33–53.

Padden, Carol. 1980. "The Deaf Community and the Culture of Deaf People." In *Sign Language and the Deaf Community: Essays in Honor of William C. Stokoe*, edited by Charlotte Baker and Robbin Battison, pp. 89–103. Washington, D.C.: National Association of the Deaf.

Padden, Carol, and Harry Markowicz. 1975. "Cultural Conflicts Between Hearing and Deaf Communities." In *Proceedings of the Seventh World Congress of the World Federation of the Deaf*, pp. 407–11. Silver Spring, Md.: National Association of the Deaf.

Padden, Carol, and Tom Humphries. 1989. *Deaf in America: Voices from a Culture*. Cambridge: Harvard University Press.

Paglia, Camille. 1992. *Sex, Art, and American Culture*. New York: Vintage Books.

Penley, Constance, and Andrew Ross, eds. 1991. *Technoculture*. Minneapolis: University of Minnesota Press.

Pfohl, Stephen. 1992. *Death at the Parasite Cafe: Social Science (Fictions) and the Postmodern*. New York: St. Martin's Press.

Poizner, Howard, Edward S. Klima, and Ursula Bellugi. 1987. *What the Hands Reveal about the Brain*. Cambridge: MIT Press.

Pollock, Griselda. 1988. *Vision and Difference*. New York: Routledge.

Postman, Neil. 1985. *Amusing Ourselves to Death*. New York: Penguin Books.

Quintanales, Mirtha. 1983. "I Paid Very Hard for My Immigrant Ignorance." In *This Bridge Called My Back: Writings by Radical Women of Color*, edited by Cherríe Moraga and Gloria Anzuldúa, pp. 150–56. New York: Kitchen Table Press.

Rabinow, Paul, ed. 1984. *The Foucault Reader*. New York: Pantheon Books.

Rafael, Vicente. 1990. "Nationalism, Imagery, and the Filipino Intelligentsia in the Nineteenth Century." *Critical Inquiry* 16: 591–611.

Reilly, Charles B. 1995. "A Deaf Way of Education—Interaction among Children in a Thai Boarding School." Ph.D. diss., University of Maryland.

Reilly, Charles B., and Sathaporn Suvannus. In press. "Education of Deaf People in the Kingdom of Thailand." In *Global Perspectives on Education of the Deaf*, edited by H. W. Brelje.

Rich, Adrienne. 1978. *The Dream of a Common Language*. New York: W. W. Norton.

Rodda, Michael, and Carl Grove. 1987. *Language, Cognition, and Deafness*. Hillsdale, N.J.: Lawrence Erlbaum.

Ronell, Avital. 1989. *The Telephone Book: Technology, Schizophrenia, Electric Speech*. Lincoln: University of Nebraska Press.

Rucker, Rudy von Bitter. 1981. *Spacetime Donuts*. New York: Ace Books.

———. 1982. *Software*. New York: Ace Books.

———. 1984. *The Fourth Dimension: Toward a Geometry of Higher Reality*. Boston: Houghton Mifflin.

———. 1985. *The Secret of Life*. New York: Bluejay Books.

————. 1987. *Mind Tools: The Five Levels of Mathematical Reality*. Boston: Houghton Mifflin.

————. 1988. *Wetware*. New York: Avon Books.

————. 1989. "Rudy Rucker on 'What Is Cyberpunk?'" *Mondo 2000*, no. 1: 79.

Sacks, Oliver. 1988. "The Revolution of the Deaf." *New York Review of Books* 35.9: 23–28.

————. 1989. *Seeing Voices: A Journey into the Land of the Deaf*. Berkeley: University of California Press.

Said, Edward W. 1989. *Orientalism*. New York: Random House.

Sapir, Edward. 1966. *Culture, Language, and Personality*. Berkeley: University of California Press.

Schwartz, John. 1991. "Inside the Head of the Hacker." *Nation* (Bangkok), 5 August, International Business section.

Scott, James C. 1985. *Weapons of the Weak: Everyday Forms of Peasant Resistance*. New Haven: Yale University Press.

Scott, Robert. 1981. *The Making of Blind Men*. New Brunswick, N.J.: Transaction Books.

Scull, Andrew. 1989. *Social Order, Mental Disorder*. Berkeley: University of California Press.

Shapiro, Michael. 1981a. "Disability and the Politics of Constitutive Rules." In *Cross National Rehabilitation Policies: A Sociological Perspective*, edited by Gary Albrecht, pp. 83–96. London: Sage Publications.

————. 1981b. *Language and Political Understanding*. New Haven: Yale University Press.

————, ed. 1984. *Language and Politics*. New York: New York University Press.

————. 1988. *The Politics of Representation*. Madison: University of Wisconsin Press.

————. 1992. *Reading the Postmodern Polity: Political Theory as Textual Practice*. Minneapolis: University of Minnesota Press.

Shattuck, Roger. 1980. *The Forbidden Experiment: The Story of the Wild Boy of Aveyron*. New York: Farrar, Straus, Giroux.

Shirley, John. 1985. *Eclipse*. New York: Warner Books.

————. 1988. *Eclipse Penumbra*. New York: Warner Books.

————. 1990. *Eclipse Corona*. New York: Warner Books.

Sombat Chantornvong. 1978. "Cosmological Basis of Thai Bureaucratic Behavior: The Missing Link." *Social Science Review*, no. 5: 117–30.

Sontag, Susan. 1990. *Illness as Metaphor; and, AIDS and Its Metaphors* (combined edition). New York: Anchor Books.

Spivak, Gayatri Chakravorty. 1987. *In Other Worlds*. New York: Methuen.

————. 1990. *The Post-Colonial Critic*. New York: Routledge.

Stephenson, Neal. 1994. "Hack the Spew." *Wired*, October, pp. 91–95, 142–47.

Sterling, Bruce. 1985. *Schismatrix*. New York: Arbor House.

————, ed. 1986. *Mirrorshades: The Cyperpunk Anthology*. New York: Arbor House.

————. 1989. *Islands in the Net*. New York: Ace Books.

Stokoe, William C. 1960. *Sign Language Structure: An Outline of the Visual Communication Systems of the American Deaf.* Studies in Linguistics: Occasional Papers 8. Buffalo: Department of Anthropology and Linguistics, University of Buffalo.

————, ed. 1980. *Sign and Culture.* Silver Spring, Md.: Linstok Press.

Stokoe, William C., H. Russell Bernard, and Carol Padden. 1980. "An Elite Group in Deaf Society." In *Sign and Culture,* edited by William C. Stokoe, pp. 295–317. Silver Spring, Md.: Linstok Press.

Suvannus, Sathaporn. "Education of the Deaf in Thailand." In *Gallaudet Encyclopedia of Deaf People and Deafness,* edited by J. V. Van Cleve, 3:282–84. New York: McGraw-Hill.

————. 1990. "The National Association of the Deaf." In *The Thai Sign Language Dictionary,* revised and expanded, edited by Manfa Suwanarat, Owen Wrigley, et al., pp. xxxv-xliv. Bangkok: Thai Wattana Panich.

Suwanarat, Manfa, Charles B. Reilly, and Owen Wrigley, et al. 1986. *The Thai Sign Language Dictionary, Book One.* Bangkok: Thai Wattana Panich Press.

Suwanarat, Manfa, Owen Wrigley, et al. 1990. *The Thai Sign Language Dictionary,* revised and expanded. Bangkok: Thai Wattana Panich.

Swaine, Michael. 1991. "Beating the System: Lighting the Way." *MacUser,* April, pp. 229–32.

Synergy, Michael. 1991. Interview in *Mondo 2000,* no. 3 (Winter): 51–54.

"Talking to the Brain." 1991. *Discover,* December, p. 74.

Tambiah, S. J. 1978. "Sangha and Polity in Modern Thailand: An Overview." In *Religion and Legitimation of Power in Thailand, Laos, and Burma,* edited by Bardwell L. Smith, pp. 111–33. Chambersburg, Pa.: Anima Books.

Taylor, Charles. 1987. "Language and Human Nature." In *Interpreting Politics,* edited by Michael T. Gibbons, pp. 101–32. New York: New York University Press.

Todorov, Tzvetan. 1984. *The Conquest of America: The Question of the Other,* translated by Richard Howard. New York: Harper and Row.

————. 1989. *The Deflection of the Enlightenment.* Palo Alto: Stanford Humanities Center.

Trinh, T. Minh-ha. 1987. "Of Other Peoples: Beyond the 'Salvage' Paradigm." In *The Anti-aesthetic: Essays on Postmodern Culture,* edited by Hal Foster, pp. 138–41. Port Townsend, Wash.: Bay Press.

————. 1989. *Woman, Native, Other.* Bloomington: Indiana University Press.

————. 1991. *When the Moon Waxes Red: Representation, Gender, and Cultural Politics.* New York: Routledge.

Tufte, Edward R. 1990. *Envisioning Information.* Cheshire, Conn.: Graphics Press.

Turner, William W. 1856. "To J. J. Flournoy, December 6, 1855: Scheme for a Commonwealth." *American Annals of the Deaf* 8 (January): 118.

UNESCO. 1984. *Consultation on Alternative Approaches for the Education of the Deaf: Final Report.* Paris.

United Nations. 1987. *Global Meeting of Experts to Review the Implementation of the World Program of Action Concerning Disabled Persons at the Mid-Point of the U.N. Decade of Disabled Persons: Final Report.* Stockholm.

Van Cleve, John V., and Barry A. Crouch. 1989. *A Place of Their Own: Creating the Deaf Community in America*. Washington, D.C.: Gallaudet University Press.

Van Uden, A. 1968. *A World of Language for Deaf Children*. Saint Michielsgestel, Netherlands: Institute for the Deaf.

Varley, John. 1978. *The Persistence of Vision*. New York: Dial Press/James Wade.

Veditz, G. W. 1913. *The Preservation of the Sign Language*. Silver Spring, Md.: National Association of the Deaf. Film.

Vella, Walter F. 1978. *Thai Yo! King Vajiravudh and the Development of Thai Nationalism*. Honolulu: University Press of Hawaii.

Virilio, Paul. 1989. *War and Cinema: The Logistics of Perception,* translated by Patrick Camiller. London: Verso.

Volterra, Virginia, and Carol Erting, eds. 1988. *From Gesture to Language in Hearing and Deaf Children*. New York: Springer-Verlag.

Wallace, Michele. 1979. *Black Macho and the Myth of the Superwoman*. New York: Dial Press.

Wang, W. S.-Y. 1974. "How and Why Do We Study the Sounds of Speech." In *Proceedings of the International Conference on Computers and the Humanities,* edited by L. Mitchell. Edinburgh, Scotland: Edinburgh University Press.

Webb, R., et al. 1991. "Surgical Complications with the Cochlear Multiple-Channel Intracochlear Implant: Experience at Hannover and Melbourne." *Annals of Otology, Rhinology, and Laryngology* 100: 131–36.

Weber, Samuel. 1987. *Institution and Interpretation*. Minneapolis: University of Minnesota Press.

White, Hayden. 1987. *The Content of the Form*. Baltimore: Johns Hopkins University Press.

Wiebe, Robert H. 1975. *The Segmented Society: An Introduction to the Meaning of America*. New York: Oxford University Press.

Wilcox, Sherman, ed. 1989. *American Deaf Culture*. Silver Spring, Md.: Linstok Press.

Williams, Robert A., Jr. 1990. *The American Indian in Legal Thought*. Oxford: Oxford University Press.

Winefield, Richard. 1987. *Never the Twain Shall Meet: Bell, Gallaudet, and the Communications Debate*. Washington, D.C.: Gallaudet University Press.

Wittgenstein, Ludwig. 1953. *Philosophical Investigations,* translated by G. E. M. Anscombe. New York: Macmillan.

Wixtrom, Christine. 1988. "Alone in the Crowd . . . "*The Deaf American* 38.2: 12, 14–15.

Wolf, Eric R. 1982. *Europe and the People without History.* Berkeley: University of California Press.

Woodward, James C. 1972. "Implications for Sociolinguistic Research among the Deaf." *Sign Language Studies* 1: 1–7.

———. 1973. "Some Observations on Sociolinguistic Variation and American Sign Language." *Kansas Journal of Sociology* 9: 191–200.

———. 1982. *How You Gonna Get to Heaven If You Can't Talk With Jesus: On Depathologizing Deafness*. Silver Spring, Md.: T. J. Publishers.

Woodward, James C., and Harry Markowicz. 1975. "Some Handy New Ideas on Pidgins and Creoles: Pidgin Sign Languages." Paper presented at the International Conference on Pidgin and Creole Language, The East-West Center, Honolulu, Hawaii, June.

World Federation of the Deaf. 1987a. "Recommendations of the Scientific and Cross-Scientific Commissions." In *Proceedings of the Tenth World Congress of the World Federation of the Deaf,* July.

————. 1987b. "Resolution on Sign Language Recognition." In *Proceedings of the Tenth World Congress of the World Federation of the Deaf,* July.

————. 1991. *Survey of Deaf People in the Developing World.* Helsinki: World Federation of the Deaf.

Wrigley, Owen. 1992. "Hearing Deaf History: The Politics of Reclaiming Difference." In *Proceedings of the Eleventh World Congress of the World Federation of the Deaf,* July.

————. 1993. "Kulturimperialismus unter Gehörlosen: Aus– und Einschluß in Deaf Identity." *Das Zeichen* 23 7:14–19.

————. 1994. "Die 'Deaf History' der Hörenden; oder: Strategien zur Rettung der Andersartigkeit." *Das Zeichen* 27 8:38–43.

————. 1995. "Signs of Community." In *Grassroots Horizons: Connecting Participatory Development Initiatives East and West,* edited by Richard Morse, A. Rahman, and K. L. Johnson, pp. 123–50. New Delhi: Mohan Primlani for Oxford and IBH Publishing; London: Intermediate Technology Publications.

Wyatt, David. 1984. *Thailand: A Short History.* New Haven: Yale University Press; Bangkok: Thai Wattana Panich Press.

Young, Iris Marion. 1991. *Justice and the Politics of Difference.* Princeton: Princeton University Press.

Index

Acknowledgments

As is usual in such circumstances, it is not possible to fully thank all who have helped me in this effort. I can, however, completely exonerate them from any responsibility for positions I take.

The friends and colleagues in Thailand to whom I owe thanks are legion. In particular, I will forever remember my Deaf research colleague, Manfa Suwanarat, who died tragically in 1989 at the age of thirty-six. *The Thai Sign Language Dictionary,* the production of which partly inspired this work, is dedicated to Manfa. Originally, I had planned a very different document to have been jointly written with her.

This work contains repeated references to the work of my close friend and colleague, Charles B. Reilly. His wife, Nipapon Wonnuwin Reilly, was my first serious sign teacher. The nearly five years that we all lived and worked together in Thailand rank as some of the happiest years of my life. I am the very proud godfather to their son, Chawin.

None of my work in Thailand, including this research, would have been possible without the close support of Khun Patra Daroj Vanij-Vongse, Khun Phongchan Na Bangchang, and Khun Prapa Pandon. They ran my office and, in the better sense, my life and made it possible to accomplish as much as we did.

Additional friends in Thailand I must acknowledge include Mia Lewis; her brother and my great pal, Jamie Lewis Zellerbach, and his wife, Bonnie; the Wonnuwin sisters, Supannee, Porntip, and Rochana; Christopher Moore; Lynn Klapecki and Geoffrey Blake; and Tom Seale.

In Hawaii, I would like to thank my great friends and intellectual partners Patricia Masters, Jan Crocker-Fukino and Rod Fukino, Arthur Getz, and, now ex-Hawaii, Steven Shelendich, Zoe Wolfe, and their daughter, Shanan Mango Wolfe.

Support for writing, primarily in 1991–92, came from an East-West Center grant and the collaborative community of the EWC and the University of Hawaii. From the EWC, I thank Richard Morse, Bruce Koppel, and Mendl Djunaidy, each of whom has been a friend for more than twenty years. In particular, Dick Morse offered me a home within the dynamic group of passionate scholars constituting the center's Participatory Development Group. I am very grateful for the extended support of the East-West Center, first from 1976 through 1979 and then from 1989 through 1992.

The University of Hawaii provided the other half of my happy Hawaiian home. For their crucial intellectual guidance and supportive friendships over many years, I particularly thank Neal Milner, Kathy Ferguson, Michael Shapiro, Carolyn Stephenson, Kem Lowry, Jim Dator, and Manfred Henningson, as well as our super secretaries, Carol Moon and Evelyn Ho.

I am extremely pleased to publish this manuscript through Gallaudet University Press. I am grateful to Ivey Pittle Wallace and Alice Falk for their gentle hands during the process. Given my own cultural and spatial dis-location, I am specifically grateful to the Internet, and our access to it, for conducting our many conversations.

Both first and last, the inspiration for this work was provided by the many Deaf Thai and other friends who opened a door into a very different place and have made me a welcome guest and sojourner among them.

To all who have helped and guided me, I offer my grateful thanks.

Owen Wrigley
Yangon, Myanmar
January 1996